TAXATION

Taxation is a subject of enquiry that cuts across a range of disciplines, including law, economics, politics, psychology, history and accountancy, to name a few. However, research into taxation as a social and institutional phenomenon – rather than as abstraction from the real world – is largely neglected.

Taxation: A Fieldwork Research Handbook opens up new avenues of enquiry in the research of taxation by offering suggestions on how research might be conducted into taxation as a social and institutional practice. This book:

- Introduces tax as a field of potential research for all social scientists
- Explains the methodological issues relating to tax research
- Provides inspiration for tax researchers to widen the scope of their enquiries
- Encourages researchers to think differently about this subject

Given the importance of taxation to modern society, not only as a revenue-raising mechanism, but also as a tool of governance used to influence social actors, this unique text is a vital read for any social science researcher interested in this subject.

Lynne Oats is Professor of Taxation and Accounting at the University of Exeter, UK. Her research interest is taxation policy and practice in social and institutional contexts, in both historical and contemporary settings. She has published extensively in the field and is co-author of three books, *Taxation Policy and Practice* (Fiscal Publications, 2011), *Principles of International Taxation* (Bloomsbury Professional, 3rd edn 2012) and *Accounting Principles for Tax Purposes* (Bloomsbury Professional, 2010). She is Assistant Editor of *British Tax Review* and Vice Chair of the UK Tax Reasearch Network.

TABLE OF CONTENTS

ILLUSTRATIONS

Tables

Figures

CONTRIBUTORS

Editor

Lynne Oats Professor of Taxation and Accounting, University of Exeter, UK. Co-author of *Taxation Policy and Practice* (Fiscal Publications, 18th edn 2011), *Principles of International Taxation* (Bloomsbury 3rd edn, 2011) and *Accounting Principles for Tax Purposes* (Bloomsbury, 2010). She is Vice Chair, UK Tax Research Network and Assistant Editor of *British Tax Review*. Lynne's research interest is taxation policy and practice, in both contemporary and historical settings, and she has published numerous journal articles and book chapters in the field.

Contributors

Rebecca Boden Professor of Critical Management at the University of Roehampton Business School in London, where she directs the Centre for Organisational Research. Previously a tax inspector with the UK's HMRC, she now researches the role of accounting and management in the shaping of power relationships between citizens and the state, including through tax systems and welfare benefits/tax credits. She publishes extensively and has won a number of funded projects, including for the UK government on self-employed people and welfare benefits/tax credits. With Debbie Epstein and Jane Kenway she co-authored the *Academic's Support Kit* (Sage, 2005).

Karen Boll Postdoc., Copenhagen Business School. PhD (IT University, Denmark) awarded in 2011 for *Taxing Assemblages. Laborious and Meticulous Achievements of Tax Compliance*. Karen's PhD examines the construction of tax compliance with particular focus on how tax inspectors interact with taxpayers to enhance compliance.

The PhD study is based on ten months on-and-off fieldwork in Danish Tax and Customs Administration. Karen's research interests include ethnography, tax compliance, governance, actor-network theory and organisational theory.

Kate Collier Senior Lecturer and Program Director of the Graduate Diploma and Certificate courses in Adult Education, University of Technology, Sydney, Australia. She began her career as a drama and theatre arts specialist but has subsequently been involved for many years in adult education in the tertiary sector both in Australia and the UK. She has been a learning and development and training consultant to many organisations, including Australian and overseas tax authorities.

Elaine Doyle teaches a range of accounting- and taxation-related subjects to both full-time and part-time students at undergraduate and postgraduate level. Her research interests include inter alia, professional ethics and risk management in tax practice, the tax aggression of tax practitioners, procedural justice and ethical reasoning. She has a PhD in taxation from the University of Sheffield, UK. Elaine is an associate member of the Irish Taxation Institute, a member of the governing council of the Irish Accounting and Finance Association and is the Chairperson of the KBS Research Ethics Committee.

Chris Evans Professor of Taxation, ATAX, University of New South Wales, Australia. He has undertaken research projects in many countries including Australia, Canada, New Zealand, the UK, Ireland, Indonesia, Nigeria and South Africa. He has written many articles and papers published in Australian and international journals, and authored and edited several texts and chapters. He is joint author of *Australian Taxation Law* (now in its 21st edn) and of *Cooper and Evans on CGT* (3rd edn), and General Editor of *Australian Tax Review.*

Jane Frecknall Hughes Professor of Law and Head, Open Univesity Law School, The Open University, UK. her current research focuses on taxation from an interdisciplinary perspective, including the linkages with strategic management (with particular reference to multinational enterprises and tax planning), also taxation history, the tax profession and ethics. She is the former Chair, UK Tax Research Network.

Judith Freedman Professor of Taxation at the University of Oxford and Director of Legal Research, Oxford Centre for Business Taxation. She is joint Editor of the *British Tax Review* and an Editorial Board member of the *Modern Law Review*, the *eJournal of Tax Research*, the *Canadian Tax Journal* and the *Australian Tax Review*. She is a member of the Council of the Institute for Fiscal Studies and of the Tax Law Review Committee and a contributor to the Mirrlees Review's *Dimensions of Tax Design* (Oxford University Press, 2010). She was a co-editor of *Taxation: An Interdisciplinary Approach to Research* (Oxford University Press, 2004). Her recent work has been on small business taxation, tax avoidance and tax risk management in relation to large corporations. She is a member of the Office of Tax Simplification,

Consultative Committee on Small Business Taxation and is one of the study group appointed to work with Graham Aaronson to advise the UK Exchequer Secretary on a General Anti-avoidance Rule.

Keith W. Glaister Professor of International Strategic Management and Dean, Sheffield University Management School, UK. As a leading researcher in the field of strategic management, he has published five books and over 50 articles and book chapters. He is an Editorial Board member of the *International Journal of Enterprise Network Management*, the *European Management Journal*, the *British Journal of Management* and the *International Journal of Applied Business and Economic Research*. He was recently elected to serve on the Council of the British Academy of Management.

Louise Gracia is Assistant Dean (UG) and Director of the BSc in Accounting and Finance at Warwick Business School, University of Warwick, UK. Her current research interests include the use of social theory to explore regulatory aspects of taxation practice and the development of critical accounting education through creative approaches. She also holds an Academic Fellowship from the Institute of Advanced Teaching and Learning at Warwick University.

John Hasseldine Associate Professor of Accounting at the Whittemore School of Business & Economics, University of New Hampshire, USA. He has published widely on tax compliance costs, tax compliance and tax administration and was a member of the HMRC Consultative Committee on Powers, Deterrents and Safeguards. Originally a tax inspector in New Zealand, he received his PhD in accounting in 1997 from the Kelley School of Business at Indiana University, USA.

Gitte Heij has a Masters degree in Tax Law from the University of Groningen, and a PhD in Law from the same university in The Netherlands. Gitte worked at the Asia Research Centre at Murdoch University from 1993 to 2001, where she completed a variety of publications on tax and investment topics in South-East Asia. In addition to her work as a researcher, she worked as an international/Asian tax adviser to Australian and European companies. Over the last 15 years she has been involved in various multi- and bilateral aid projects. She is a company director of several companies in Western Australia. She teaches an intensive course in Asian Comparative Tax Laws in the University of Melbourne's Tax Law programme and she is a senior Adjunct at Murdoch University where she teaches an intensive course in development studies.

Kevin Holland Professor of Accounting and Taxation, University of Southampton, UK. Chair, UK Tax Research Network. A chartered accountant previously employed as a tax manager with Pricewaterhouse Coopers, he is a Council Member of the Institute of Fiscal Studies. He has published papers examining corporate tax burdens, the relationship between taxation and earning management, tax capitalization in equity pricing, dividend taxation issues and tax knowledge management. Other published research interests involve audit pricing, perceived auditor independence and research methodological issues. External research funding has been obtained from the Institute of Chartered Accounts in England and Wales (ICAEW) Charitable Trusts, Association of Certified Chartered Accountants (ACCA) and the National Audit Office.

Geoffrey Loomer Assistant Professor, Schulich School of Law, Dalhousie University, Canada. International Research Fellow, Oxford University Centre for Business Taxation. He has Canadian degrees in both economics and law and obtained his DPhil from the University of Oxford in 2011. His research interests and publications involve the intersection of corporate law, tax law and public international law, including issues relating to corporate tax competition, tax avoidance and tax compliance.

Margaret McKerchar Professor of Taxation, ATAX, University of New South Wales, Australia. Has an international reputation as a leading researcher in taxpayer compliance and has published previously on the design and conduct of research in tax, law and accounting.

Lisa Marriott Senior Lecturer in Taxation and Accounting at Victoria University of Wellington, New Zealand. She is the author of several publications on the subject of taxation and retirement savings in Australia and New Zealand. Lisa's primary research interest is the behavioural impact of tax policy.

Emer Mulligan Head of School, J.E. Cairnes School of Business and Economics, National University of Ireland, Galway. She worked for a number of years as a Tax Manager at Price Waterhouse, Dublin, and had also been a part-time lecturer at Dublin City University. She is a member of the Irish Taxation Institute. Her PhD (University of Warwick) was awarded in 2009 for *Tax Planning in Practice: A Field Study of US Multinational Corporations*.

Helen Rogers Senior Lecturer in Accounting and Taxation, Oxford Brookes University, UK. Helen is a fellow of the Institute of Chartered Accountants in England and Wales. Her current research focuses on international corporation tax in practice, particularly transfer pricing.

Barbara Summers Senior Lecturer in Decision Making, University of Leeds, UK. Barbara's research interests are in the area of individual decision making with a focus on financial decisions. Recent work has focused on issues such as the role of emotions on financial decision making; how individuals evaluate investments in relation to time and risk; factors affecting consumers' financial choices; and the acquisition of expertise in credit risk management.

Penelope Tuck Associate Professor of Public Finance and Policy, University of Warwick, UK. PhD awarded in 2007 for *A Study of the Changing Relationship between Large Corporates* and *the Inland Revenue* (University of Warwick). Co-author of *The*

Relationship between HM Revenue & Customs and Large Corporate Taxpayers: The Changing Role of Accountants (Institute of Chartered Accountants in England and Wales Centre for Business Performance, London).

Pernill G.A. van der Rijt completed a PhD in 2007 (University of Amsterdam, the Netherlands) on the willingness to share knowledge in organisational teams. She has worked as a research fellow at the University of Nottingham, UK as a lecturer at the Radboud University Nijmegen, the Netherlands and as a research consultant in market research. She is experienced in conducting quantitative and qualitative research in the areas of knowledge management, organisational communication, and market research in the public and private sector.

John Vella Senior Research Fellow at the Oxford University Centre for Business Taxation and a member of the Faculty of Law at the University of Oxford. John first studied law at the University of Malta, obtaining a BA and an LLD. He was admitted to the Maltese bar and practised briefly. He then obtained an LLM and a PhD from the University of Cambridge. Following the completion of his PhD he joined the Faculty of Law at the University of Oxford as Norton Rose Career Development Fellow in Company Law. He has been a Program Affiliate Scholar at New York University and has acted as a co-arbitrator in a tax dispute before the ICC International Court of Arbitration. His main research interests are in Corporate Taxation, Company Law and Corporate Finance Law.

PREFACE

The motivation for this book came from several sources. In 2009 Emer Mulligan and I presented a paper at the Tax Research Network Conference in Galway, in which we bemoaned the lack of debate in tax scholarship around philosophical underpinnings. There we drew on philosophical discussions within accounting scholarship (we are both located within accounting departments in our respective universities). In particular, we drew on the debates within accounting, and also finance, calling for more critical and interpretive research and questioning the positivist mainstream. The largely positive reception of our paper, by an interdisciplinary audience, gave encouragement to this current endeavour. In addition, Christopher Humphrey and Bill H.K. Lee's (editors) *The Real Life Guide to Accounting Research* (Elsevier, 2004) demonstrated the value of open debate about the actual practices of research. The contributions to that volume are frank and insightful descriptions of the processes of actually doing research, mostly fieldwork. I was also shocked to read several articles by leading North American tax accounting academics that displayed an astonishingly narrow view of tax research within the discipline of accounting. These all led me to think that tax research, on the whole, lacks an element of reflexivity, to its detriment, because the absence of debates about issues such as unspoken assumptions and philosophical underpinnings lead to particular ways of thinking becoming embedded: the only way to do 'proper' tax research.

This book would not have been possible without the generosity of its contributors, who have not only provided thoughtful and insightful commentaries on their work and methods, but have also been extremely patient with the delays along the way in pulling this work together. I am extremely grateful to them, and hope that, in the same spirit as *Critical Tax Theory* (edited by Anthony C. Infanti and Bridget J. Crawford, Cambridge University Press, 2009) and *The New Fiscal Sociology* (edited by Isaac William Martin, Ajay K. Mehrotra and Monica Prasad, Cambridge University Press, 2009) amongst others, this work will serve to inspire creativity in tax research from whichever disciplinary background we come.

Lynne Oats

PART I
Researching tax

Tax research is not known for its reflexivity, and methodology is something we tend not to talk about much, even in work where it assumes central importance such as the capital markets based work within tax accounting scholarship. Tax researchers come from a variety of disciplinary backgrounds, and may have some research training acquired from that particular disciplinary perspective. What we often lack is an understanding of research approaches and methods from other disciplines, and so the purpose of Part I is to begin to think about some broad issues relating to actually doing tax research, from whatever disciplinary background we come, followed by some more specific discussions of particular methodological approaches.

Although some of the chapters contained in this part reflect positivist approaches (Chapters 5, 6 and 8 in particular), the overall leaning of the book is towards interpretive work, and this is reflected in the choice of contributions, not only here but in later parts also. This part is not intended to be a 'research methods' discussion, although some methods are discussed in some detail. Most of us have ready access to generic methods texts that help with specific research design. Rather, this part of the book is designed to introduce the reader to some broad issues in a tax specific context; in particular it will introduce some social research concepts to those whose previous training may have omitted this, for example legal scholars and those who have entered research from a background in tax practice.

1
TAX AS A SOCIAL AND INSTITUTIONAL PRACTICE

Lynne Oats

Introduction

It is without doubt currently an exciting time to be a tax researcher, notwithstanding the institutional pressures in terms of measurement of research output (which is particularly acute in the UK). The past decade has witnessed important advances in tax research across the various disciplines for which it is an area of interest. In addition to numerous journal articles across the spectrum of disciplines, a number of books and edited collections have appeared that indicate a burgeoning interest in tax scholarship. To canvass some recent contributions (with apologies for any missed):

In law, the publication in 2002 of Mumford's book *Taxing Culture* enhanced a growing acknowledgement of the need to step outside of traditional black letter, formalistic, modes of enquiry and draw on historical analyses and cultural theories in understanding how tax works in practice.

This was followed closely by Valery Braithwaite's *Taxing Democracy* in 2003, which showcased the work of the Centre for Tax System Integrity in Australia. Braithwaite's later (2008) work *Defiance in Taxation and Governance* highlights the interconnections between her research findings and those of her colleagues in a tax-specific context and the broader governance arena. In furthering the debates on tax regulation, the 2007 special issue of *Law and Society* also brought together a set of papers that contribute to raising the profile of tax regulation as an important avenue for enquiry.

In 2004, Lamb *et al.*'s *Taxation: An Interdisciplinary Approach to Research* illustrated how tax is analysed from a range of disciplinary perspectives and those perspectives can be usefully integrated, although often are not. Without underestimating the difficulties entailed, Lamb and her co-authors argue the case for complementing multidisciplinary perspectives: that is approaching tax as an object of inquiry from the viewpoint of single disciplines, with truly interdisciplinary work that adopts perspectives and approaches from at least two disciplines. John Braithwaite's 2005

Markets in Vice, Markets in Virtue is a good example of how we can draw on a variety of disciplinary lenses coupled with fieldwork to add to our understanding of, in this case, US and Australian tax-shelter activity in practice.

More recently, Infanti and Crawford's *Critical Tax Theory*, published in 2009, brings together abridged versions of some 50 previously published tax law articles, primarily from the US, which push the boundaries of analysis and open up tax as an important object of critical scrutiny. This work is particularly important in gathering together in one place work that would potentially be overlooked by scholars from outside the close circle of US tax law professors, having been published in sometimes difficult-to-find places. In accounting, the more modest 2010 special issue of *Critical Perspectives on Accounting* brought together a group of papers further illustrating the richness of tax as a field of inquiry for critical scholarship.

A resurgence of interest in fiscal sociology saw the publication of Martin *et al.*'s *The New Fiscal Sociology* in 2009, a collection of papers from authors across a variety of backgrounds exploring tax from a variety of sociological perspectives. This work serves to remind us of the importance of thinking about tax phenomena not only diachronically, but also contextually.

In history, the collections published by the Cambridge Centre for Tax Law under the title *Studies in Tax Law History*, demonstrate the breadth of interest in tax as an object of historical inquiry, as does Nehring and Schui's (2007) *Global Debates About Taxation*. Peter Harris' (2006) *Income Tax in Common Law Jurisdictions to 1820* meticulously traces the historical emergence of income tax and its spread across a variety of jurisdictions. Economic historian Martin Daunton's (2001, 2002) two works provide an authoritative history of British taxation from 1799.

In the behavioural sciences, work done by Kirchler (2007) *The Economic Psychology of Tax Behaviour*, and Valery Braithwaite's (2008) *Defiance in Taxation and Governance* exemplifies new understandings emerging from psychological analyses. Torgler (2007) has popularised the concept of tax morale, and Alm *et al.* bring together a set of essays dealing with tax compliance in their 2010 book *Developing Alternative Frameworks for Explaining Tax Compliance*, and demonstrate the current move to improve our understanding of compliance motivations beyond the traditional deterrence models.

In political science, Steinmo's (1996) *Taxation and Democracy* demonstrates the value of institutional theory (historical institutionalism) as well as comparative work. Rixen's (2008) *The Political Economy of International Tax Governance* showcases developments in rational choice institutionalism as applied to the international tax arena. Stephen Ganghoff (2006) *The Politics of Income Taxation* is another example of the value of comparative work, underscoring the similarities and differences between income tax systems in different jurisdictions.

Brautigam *et al.* (2008) *Taxation and State Building in Developing Countries* brings together a collection of papers that consider taxation as a key element of the state-citizen relationship. This collection shines a light on aspects of tax and development, a theme that is attracting increasing attention, not least through the work of non-governmental organisations (NGOs) and various polemicists such as those associated with the Tax Justice Network.

In economics, Slemrod and Bakija's (2008) *Taxing Ourselves* attempts to popularise, with considerable success, current economic debates and developments in tax policy. The substantial work of the Mirrlees Review[1] in the UK brings together a series of papers exploring prospective developments in tax policy, primarily from an economic viewpoint. The first volume is *Dimensions of Tax Design* and the second is *Tax by Design*, both available online.

The attention of feminist scholars to tax issues is reflected in McCaffery's (1997) *Taxing Women*, and more recently Mumford's (2010) *Tax Policy, Women and the Law: UK and Comparative Perspectives*, which, together with numerous individual articles, some of which are included in Infanti and Crawford (2009), demonstrates the power of feminist critique to undermine taken-for-granted assumptions about how tax policy affects us all.

Yet tax research remains paradoxical. Its inherent interdisciplinarity brings depth in terms of the variety of lenses through which it can be viewed (Lamb *et al.* 2004), but as the inevitable omissions from the previous discussion of recent scholarship show, it is very difficult to keep abreast of developments across a wide range of disciplines, and so interdisciplinarity is a double-edged sword: fragmentation arguably leads to dilution in terms of the wider impact of our scholarship.

There is also evidence of a systematic, if to some extent inadvertent, dismissal of tax from academic debate across a range of disciplines, which is cause for considerable concern, perhaps arising from a mistaken assumption that tax as a field of enquiry is being dealt with adequately in other disciplines. As Clemens (1999: 518) astutely observed in her review of McCaffery (1997) and Howard (1997), '[t]axation has been ignored for precisely the same reason that it turns out to be so fascinating: taxes are obscenely complex' and further '[c]loaked in an appearance of technical rationality, the politics of taxation are deeply structured by imperfect information, institutional embeddedness, and ideological commitments' (ibid.).

The neglect of tax is then compounded by dominance of positivist approaches in those areas where tax is accepted as a valid field of inquiry. The dead hand of positivism pervades tax research in a variety of ways that contribute to the perception of tax as a highly technical endeavour, dealt with by a cadre of specialised experts not to be scrutinised by lay concerns (Boden *et al.* 2010). Importantly, and partly because of our research training, often the implications of unstated positivist assumptions are not fully acknowledged, or even appreciated, and the limitations of work done under this banner are often overlooked. This is not to say that positivist enquiry does not add to the body of tax knowledge: indeed, it produces some significant and important insights. However, tax is very much a social and institutional practice and this needs to be recognised as such to a much greater extent. Despite the recent inclusion of 'the social' (for example, in the guise of social capital) in recent behavioural work, such as on tax compliance (see Alm *et al.* 2010), arguably there is still not enough attention paid to this important aspect of tax as an institution. The other important aspect of tax as a social and institutional practice is the word *practice*. Armchair theorising is an important endeavour and not to be discouraged; however, a neglected aspect of tax scholarship is what actually happens in the real world when tax rules and regulations are put into play.

The title of this chapter is adapted from an influential piece in accounting scholarship. In 1994 Hopwood and Miller produced a book entitled *Accounting as Social and Institutional Practice*, which was the first major collection of critical and socio-historical analyses of accounting, all of which challenged the conventional view of accounting as a mere technical practice. This, amongst other calls for diversity, led to a wide and growing range of accounting scholarship that calls into question the positivist mainstream. It is in the same spirit that this current volume is offered.

One of the purposes of this book is to showcase the potential for more *interpretive fieldwork* research in tax, as an extension of and complement to existing research approaches. Interpretivism is a broad church with a growing influence in the wider social sciences, although not without difficulties as a result of methodological and epistemological confusion (see Chapter 2). In part, this is attributable to the difficulties in establishing criteria for the adequacy of knowledge claims produced within an interpretive tradition, which links back to the two points made earlier. We need to become more reflexive and receptive to methodological and philosophical debates taking place in other disciplines. However, we also need to challenge the hegemony of positivist approaches.

This book is divided into three parts. The first of these deals with questions of methodology, in a selective review of particular forms of inquiry following an initial discussion of the questions we need to ask in order to begin to be more reflexive about our research efforts. Two of these chapters demonstrate more practical aspects of implementing methodology: Boll in her discussion of ethnography, and Doyle, Frecknall Hughes and Summers in their description of the development of a survey instrument. These two are, of course, poles apart in their respective philosophical approaches, but are nonetheless illustrative of the rich possibilities available to us to draw from other areas of the social sciences in studying tax phenomena.

Part II of this book introduces a variety of social theories that can be used fruitfully to help us to think differently about tax. Similarly to the previous part, it does not purport to give exhaustive coverage of possible theoretical frameworks, and is to some extent an eclectic mix. There are some notable omissions, for example feminism and legal philosophy: these are not covered as they are dealt with admirably in other works and here will only be referred to in passing.

Part III of the book is entitled 'Tales from the field', and is designed to present some recent fieldwork studies from different traditions. Some, but not all, draw on the social theories discussed in Part II. The aim is to provide some inspiration for future tax research and to foster a spirit of creativity in the way we approach the important task of improving our knowledge of tax in all its myriad guises.

Note

1 www.ifs.org.uk/mirrleesReview

References

Alm, J., Martinez-Vazquez, J. and Torgler, B. (2010) *Developing Alternative Frameworks for Explaining Tax Compliance*, Abingdon: Routledge.

Avery Jones, J., Harris, P. and Oliver, D. (eds) (2008) *Comparative Perspectives on Revenue Law: Essays in Honour of John Tiley*, Cambridge: Cambridge University Press.
Boden, R., Killian, S., Mulligan, E. and Oats, L. (2010) 'Critical perspectives on taxation', *Critical Perspectives on Accounting* 21(7): 541–44.
Braithwaite, J. (2005) *Markets in Vice, Markets in Virtue*, Oxford: Oxford University Press.
Braithwaite, V. (2003) *Taxing Democracy. Understanding Tax Avoidance and Evasion*, Aldershot: Ashgate.
——(2007) 'Responsive regulation and taxation: Introduction', *Law & Policy* 29(1), January: 3–10.
——(2008) *Defiance in Taxation and Governance*, Cheltenham: Edward Elgar.
Brautigam, D., Fjedlstad, O. and Moore, M. (2008) *Taxation and State Building in Developing Countries*, Cambridge: Cambridge University Press.
Clemens, E.S. (1999) 'Good reasons to stop avoiding taxes' (review), *Law & Social Inquiry* 517, 24(2): 517–31 (April).
Daunton, M. (2001) *Trusting Leviathan: The Politics of Taxation in Britain 1799–1914*, Cambridge: Cambridge University Press.
——(2002) *Just Taxes: The Politics of Taxation in Britain 1914–1979*, Cambridge: Cambridge University Press.
Ganghoff, S. (2006) *The Politics of Income Taxation: A Comparative Analysis of Advanced Industrial Countries*, Colchester: ECPR Press.
Harris, P. (2006) *Income Tax in Common Law Jurisdictions to 1820*, Cambridge: Cambridge University Press.
Hopwood, A. and Miller, P. (1994) *Accounting as Social and Institutional Practice*, Cambridge: Cambridge University Press.
Howard, C. (1997) *The Hidden Welfare State: Tax Expenditures and Social Policy in the United States*, Princeton, NJ: Princeton University Press.
Humphrey, C. and Lee, B. (2008) *The Real Life Guide to Accounting Research*, Oxford: Elsevier.
Infanti, A. and Crawford, B. (2009) *Critical Tax Theory*, Cambridge: Cambridge University Press.
Kirchler, E. (2007) *The Economic Psychology of Tax Behaviour*, Cambridge: Cambridge University Press.
Lamb, M., Lymer, A., Freedman, J. and James, S. (2004) *Taxation: An Interdisciplinary Approach to Research*, Oxford: Oxford University Press.
McCaffery, E.J. (1997) *Taxing Women*, Chicago, IL: University of Chicago Press.
Martin, I.W., Mehrotra, A.K. and Prasad, M. (eds) (2009) *The New Fiscal Sociology: Taxation in Comparative and Historical Perspective*, Cambridge: Cambridge University Press.
Mirrlees, J., Adam, S., Blundell, R., Besley, T., Bond, S., Chote, R., Gammie, M., Johnson, P., Myles, G. and Poterba, J. (2011a) *Mirrlees Review: Vol.1, Dimensions of Tax Design*, Institute for Fiscal Studies, available at: www.ifs.org.uk/mirrleesReview (accessed 14 November 2011).
——(2011b) *Mirrlees Review: Vol.2, Tax by Design*, Institute for Fiscal Studies, available at: www.ifs.org.uk/mirrleesReview (accessed 14 November 2011).
Mumford, A. (2002) *Taxing Culture: Towards a Theory of Tax Collection Law*, Dartmouth: Ashgate.
——(2010) *Tax Policy, Women and the Law: UK and Comparative Perspectives*, Cambridge: Cambridge University Press.
Nehring, H. and Schui, F. (eds) (2007) *Global Debates About Taxation*, London: Palgrave Macmillan.
Rixen, T. (2008) *The Political Economy of International Tax Governance*, London: Palgrave Macmillan.
Slemrod, J. and Bakija, J. (2008) *Taxing Ourselves: A Citizen's Guide to the Debate over Taxes*, 4th edn, Cambridge, MA: MIT Press.
Steinmo, S. (1996) *Taxation and Democracy: Swedish, British and American Approaches to Financing the Modern State*, New Haven, CT: Yale University Press.

Tiley, J. (ed.) (2004) *Studies in the History of Tax Law, Volume 1*, Oxford: Hart Publishing.
——(2007) *Studies in the History of Tax Law, Volume 2*, Oxford: Hart Publishing.
——(2009) *Studies in the History of Tax Law, Volume 3*, Oxford: Hart Publishing.
——(2010) *Studies in the History of Tax Law, Volume 4*, Oxford: Hart Publishing.
——(2011) *Studies in the History of Tax Law, Volume 5*, Oxford: Hart Publishing.
Torgler, B. (2007) *Tax Compliance and Tax Morale: A Theoretical and Empirical Analysis*, Cheltenham: Edward Elgar.

2

ON METHODS AND METHODOLOGY

Lynne Oats

Before moving on to consider a selection of specific research methodologies this chapter lays some preliminary groundwork, clarifying key issues that will help to orientate the reader in reading subsequent chapters. At the outset, it is important to clarify what is meant by three key terms – method, methodology and theory – all of which are intertwined in the research process.

Method refers to the specific techniques employed in the pursuit of research, including data collection and data analysis. Methodology, on the other hand, is concerned with the practices and assumptions of the researcher, with the ideas and presuppositions that they carry into and through a research project. Theory, for the purposes of this book, is to be thought of in broad terms, in contrast to the narrower view espoused in the natural sciences. As Czarniawska (1997: 71) observes, theories impose cohesion and stability; we all use theories in our everyday lives to make sense of the world in which we live, and theorising, in this view, refers to 'express [ing] the meaning and significance of social phenomena' (Llewellyn 2003: 667).

For researchers working in positivist traditions, in particular those using quantitative techniques, questioning of methodology does not usually occur. Universal research techniques can be deployed that make sense in different settings and transcend disciplinary boundaries. Game theory makes sense in economics as well as politics, regression analyses make sense in psychology as well as accounting, and even law as we are starting to see. Much of the output from this tradition does not acknowledge questions of ontology and epistemology. We return to these (daunting) terms later, but for now, generally speaking ontology refers to *what* it is possible for us to know, and epistemology asks the question *how* can we know what we know? Along the same lines, legal research traditionally does generally debate research paradigms (McKerchar 2009: 67) and here positivism manifests itself in doctrinal or black letter law. The position is not so clear, however, for research in the interpretivist tradition; there is a lack of clarity about what interpretivism means within different disciplines. As Sandberg (2005: 43) observes, 'the roots of interpretive research traditions are many and it is not a single unified approach'. Indeed, the increasing use of interpretivist approaches has led to considerable confusion in both epistemological and methodological terms (ibid.).

McKerchar (2010) suggests a close correlation between research approach, in particular positivism and interpretivism, and method, specifically quantitative methods and qualitative methods, respectively. It is important to underscore that this is only a correlation, not a hard and fast rule. It is possible for a positivist researcher to make use of qualitative data in the form of words; the positivism comes into the analytical approach. So we find forms, for example, of content analysis that entail careful counting of words to measure their frequency of use as a means of identifying trends and causal relationships – matters with which positivist researchers are concerned. It is also possible for researchers working within an interpretive paradigm to make use of quantitative data, in the form of statistical analyses for example. Margaret McKerchar reiterates this in Chapter 5, where she provides an overview of survey research. In keeping with the observed correlation, however, most, but not all, of the contributors to this volume would most likely be classified as interpretivists (but may not have thought of their own work in those terms).

In tax research, on the whole we tend not to enter into debates about philosophical underpinnings of our research. We take tax as our object of research, and build research questions from within our disciplinary base. The research approach we take is then largely dictated by more pragmatic concerns: How will my department view the research? What approaches do the leading figures (with whom I'm familiar) in my field adopt? Where can I get my work published and what approach will be more acceptable to that outlet? Arguably we need to be more reflective about the nature of our research, in particular be aware of the philosophical assumptions on which it is based.

Philosophical positions

The way we approach research will be deeply affected by certain philosophical positioning, not all of which is overtly acknowledged. There are five basic categories of belief that underpin any research endeavour, even if we are unaware of it, described here as assumptions with the caveat that there is an argument that we should not 'assume' anything when approaching our research:

1 Ontological assumptions – relate to what we can know, the philosophy of reality. Is reality external to consciousness, or is it a product of individual consciousness? Here we can distinguish between:
   - nominalism, where society is viewed as relative and the social world consists of the names, concepts, labels by which individuals structure reality; and
   - realism, which views the real world as having tangible structures and the social world exists independently of the individual's perception of it. There are a range of positions between these two extremes.

2 Epistemological assumptions – relate to how we can know, how knowledge can be acquired. Here we can distinguish:
   - positivism, which seeks to explain and predict by searching for causes, patterns and relationships that hold across space and time. Hypotheses are developed from theories and then tested; and
   - anti-positivism, or interpretivism, which is a belief that social science cannot create true objective knowledge of any kind. The social world is produced through human actions and interactions and we need to get inside the worlds of those involved in meaning construction, which is viewed as context dependent and also time dependent.

3 Assumptions about agency and structure – are we products of our environments or do we create our environments? Here we can distinguish:
   - determinism – individuals are determined by the situation and environment; and
   - voluntarism – individuals are completely autonomous and possess free will.

4 Methodological assumptions. Here we can distinguish:
   - objectivists searching for universal laws to explain reality; and
   - subjectivists focused on how individuals create, modify and interpret the world.

5 Axiological assumptions – specifically what is the role of values in research? Are researchers value free or value laden?

In relation to the question of realism, Law (2007: 597) says that 'research needs to be messy and heterogeneous ... because that is the way the largest part of the world is: messy, unknowable in a regular and routinized way'. He suggests that there are five forms of 'realism' in terms of what counts as 'out-thereness', as follows:

1 Primitive out-thereness – assumes that there is a 'reality out there and beyond ourselves'.
2 Independent – 'common sense realism assumes that whatever is out there is substantially independent of our actions and especially of our perceptions'.
3 Anteriority – 'whatever is real out there in general precedes any attempt to know it'.
4 Definiteness – 'we should be researching and writing about something definite ... if findings are vague, then it isn't reality that is vague, but those doing the research'.
5 Singularity – 'the world is a single reality that is more or less shared, held in common. There may be different perspectives, but there is a single reality' (quoted from Law 2007: 603).

Law goes on to argue that the problem with mainstream research methods (that is, from a positivist perspective) is that they are posited on the assumption that all of these conceptions of 'out-thereness' must be held, yet we need not subscribe to the whole package. So the challenge is to reflect on our ontological beliefs and their consequences in terms of how we approach research.

Social constructionism

Associated with interpretive approaches is the concept of social constructionism, although not all interpretivists would consider themselves to be social constructionists. Social constructionism rejects the notion that explanations of social phenomena can be found inside the person, as traditional psychology suggests, and also the traditional sociological view that social phenomena are the product of social structures. Instead, social constructionism suggests that we should focus on social practices and the interactions between people, the complex middle ground between individual cognition and social structure (Burr 2003: 8). 'Language is not transparent'; indeed 'we should guard against the (common sense) assumption that language is nothing more than a clear, pure medium through which our thoughts and feelings can be made available to others' (ibid.: 34).

Importantly, Burr (2003: 6) notes that 'our knowledge is not a direct perception of reality. We construct our own versions of reality (as a culture or society) between us. There are no objective facts. All knowledge is derived from looking at the world from some perspective or other; and is in the service of some interests rather than others.' It is this strand of social constructionism that informs many critical approaches.

The various assumptions lead to differing conceptual frameworks, or research paradigms. In the next section, several attempts to categorise research frameworks will be reviewed.

Research paradigms: some typologies

Open any book on social science research methods and you will almost certainly find an attempt to categorise different research approaches, conceptual frameworks or theories, often using a 2x2 matrix form. In UK scholarship, particularly in management and organisation behaviour, but also accounting, a particularly influential book is Burrell and Morgan (1979). They distinguish between theories of society, specifically order vs conflict. The former is an integrationist view; society is relatively stable and based on consensus. The latter is a coercion view that sees society as constantly changing and disintegrating. This distinction creates one axis that divides research paradigms – radical change at one end and regulation at the other. The second axis is subjective at one end and objective at the other.

These two dimensions lead to four typologies that Burrell and Morgan posit are incommensurable. In the box created by the radical change/subjective quadrant is radical humanism (e.g. critical theory). Here the researcher sees current dominant ideologies as separating people from their true selves. In the box created by radical change/objective is radical structuralism, which includes Marxism. Here inherent structural conflicts occur within society that generate constant change through political and economic crisis. In the box created by regulation/subjective we find interpretivism, including phenomenology and hermeneutics. Researchers here seek to explain stability of behaviour from the individual's point of view. In the box created by regulation/objective we find functionalism, which would include, for example, systems theory. Functionalism assumes rational human action and believes that we can understand behaviour through hypothesis testing.

The most important contribution of Burrell and Morgan was to 'sensitis[e] theorists to the notion of paradigms – the assumptions, practices, and agreements among a scholarly community – and legitimise less mainstream alternatives' (Lewis and Grimes 1999: 672). They were writing at a time when dominant functionalist orthodoxy was attracting increasing, but fragmented criticism. The Burrell and Morgan typology has not been without criticism. Willmott (1993), for example, is of the view that their important contribution to making other forms of research approach acceptable was undermined by their division of research paradigms into four mutually exclusive enclaves. Their uncompromising stance of paradigm incommensurability has certainly led to heated debates, but on the other hand, as a consciousness-raising exercise it was extraordinarily successful.

Chua (1986) makes another seminal contribution to delineating research paradigms; critical of Burrell and Morgan's uncompromising classification scheme, she restricts her discussion to three paradigm classifications, namely positivist, interpretivist and critical. Chua's paper has been influential in accounting research, particularly in the UK and Australia, appealing to those who are uncomfortable with dominant positivist approaches in accounting scholarship. It is a good starting point for researchers who are trying to understand the dominance of positivism within accounting research, which acts as a constraint on tax researchers who choose to work, or find themselves in, accounting departments in business schools.

More recently, and also in the discipline of accounting, Merkl-Davis and Brennan (2011) have developed a taxonomy of research approaches to help to explain the specific field of impression management in a corporate reporting context. They identify five perspectives which can be arranged diagrammatically on two axes – objective/subjective and agency/structure.

Unlike Burrell and Morgan, Merkl-Davis and Brennan are at pains to stress that each dimension represents a continuum and, further, that the boundaries between the four quadrants are fluid. Located in the top left quadrant is an orthodox economic perspective, which recognises agency (*homo economicus*) and adopts an objective ontological status of human action and behaviour. Here we find, for example, agency theory. Also located in this quadrant is mainstream social psychology, which similarly recognises agency and has an objective ontology. Here we find attribution theory, which considers how people explain their behaviour. Another form of social psychology, however, while retaining an objective ontology, is more concerned with structure. Here we find stakeholder theory, legitimacy theory and (some forms of) institutional theory (see Chapter 9). A social constructionist perspective will be located in the bottom left quadrant, where agency is the focus but a subjective ontological stance is adopted. In the bottom right quadrant are critical perspectives, which also adopt a subjective ontological stance, but focus more on structure. The top half of the diagram essentially captures functionalist perspectives that, by adopting an objective ontological status, tend to ignore the creative aspects of agency and are therefore deterministic. The bottom half of the diagram captures non-functionalist perspectives. While considerably improving the more rigid depiction of Burrell and Morgan's incommensurable paradigms, this model is also potentially misleading (as are all models) by suggesting alignment between disciplines and methodologies.

Postmodernism

One area that is often difficult to penetrate for new researchers, or those previously trained in more traditional and mainstream ways of approaching research, is postmodernism. It is difficult for several reasons. First, it is not a coherent theoretical approach, but rather a mixture of different approaches, although they share the same common theme of seeking to disrupt modernist ways of thinking, such as structuralism, functionalism and those based on rationalism. Jarvis (1998: 97), writing from a politics perspective, has produced a 'critical typology' that attempts to explain the various strands and streams of postmodern thought. He observes that '[p]ostmodernism is … best viewed not as a statement of principles, methodological formulae, or grand theory so much as a cathartic apostasy – a renunciation of faith in modernism, rationality, science, technology, and the philosophy of presence (representation)'.

The second reason postmodernism is difficult to come to grips with, is that postmodern writers often use cryptic and even impenetrable language. Though daunting for the novice researcher, postmodernism in all its various guises offers some interesting ways of approaching research topics for those who seek to question orthodoxy. To quote Jarvis again, '[p]ostmodernism can thus be understood as "political resistance" rather than theoretical innovation, a means of stepping outside the established practices of (Western) scholarship and infusing it with critical insight' (Jarvis 1998: 99).

In recognition of the diversity of interpretive and postmodern positions, Deetz (1996: 194) proposes an alternative typology to that of Burrell and Morgan, which he believes better captures the nuances of more contemporary research approaches. He argues that the 'most problematic legacy of Burrell and Morgan's analysis is the perpetuation of the subjective-objective controversy'. In this regard, he suggests that 'the control orientation of much "objective" research can be seen as domination of a particular group's desires over and against existing communities and the natural environment … [yet] in practice so-called interpretivists and others often labelled as "subjective" often have the better claim to objectivity through the way they allow alternative language games and the possibility of alternative constructions arising from existing communities'. Deetz believes that it is difficult to position critical theorists, postructuralists and postmodernists on a subjective-objective continuum because they dispute the dualism itself. He proposes an alternative characterisation based on the origins of concepts: whether they are local/emergent or elite/a priori. The first of these includes researchers who recognise the situated nature of their research, whereas the second privilege language systems and are largely theory driven. The second axis of Deetz's characterisation relates to the relationship between the research and existing social orders, in particular whether the research adopts a consensus view where the existing social order is accepted as natural and unproblematic, or a 'dissensus' view which sees struggle, conflict and tension as the natural state of affairs.

All of these are attempts to make sense of a vast array of research across different fields. Burrell and Morgan and Deetz are concerned with wider management and organisational behaviour research, whereas Chua and Merkl-Davies and Brennan are interested in accounting research. What we must be careful of, therefore, is how we interpret these categorisations in the context of tax research. This is particularly problematic in light of the way in which tax research spans a number of different disciplines, each of which has different ways of approaching (or not) these philosophical assumptions. So any endeavour to categorise tax research along these lines must bear this in mind.

One attempt, again from the management literature, to rise above the paradigm debates is Lewis and Grimes (1999: 672), who out of concern that the 'now pervasive paradigm mentality simultaneously proliferates and polarises perspectives, often inhibiting discourse across paradigms', propose a strategy of metatriangulation. Triangulation is a term that most commonly refers to the use of more than technique or method to validate findings from a research study, in recognition that every research method has limitations of some description, so as to reduce the impact of these limitations. Lewis and Grimes' conception of metatriangulation refers to a theory-building strategy whereby researchers explore 'complex phenomena from disparate theoretical and epistemological perspectives' (ibid.: 686). They suggest the strength of such an approach is greater recognition of alternative paradigms and also, importantly, recognition that 'theory building is not solely a methodological rule-based process but also an ideological, political and moral engagement' (ibid.). Lewis and Grimes caution against reifying paradigm boundaries, suggesting that we should always view them as 'fictitious heuristics for distinguishing disparate views' (ibid.). What is important is a constant questioning of the limits of chosen lenses.

One should not underestimate the challenges that this approach presents, however, nor its capacity to fall into the very trap it seeks to avoid, namely perpetuating arbitrary and fictitious divisions. The focus of Lewis and Grimes (1999) is multi-paradigm analyses within a single discipline, but an obvious extension, with which we as tax researchers are intimately familiar, is interdisciplinarity.

Interdisciplinary research

According to Klein, 'new divisions of intellectual labour, collaborative research, team teaching, hybrid fields, comparative studies, increased borrowing across disciplines and a variety of "unified", "holistic" perspectives have created pressure upon traditional divisions of knowledge' (Klein 1990: 11, quoted in Greckhamer *et al.* 2008: 309). At the outset it is important to acknowledge that disciplines as we currently experience them are completely artificial creations of the academic world. They have no intrinsic rationales, their boundaries are not clearly defined, and yet they are pervasive in many aspects of being an academic researcher. 'Disciplines are comprised of [sic] professional groupings who form discursive communities' (Greckhamer *et al.* 2008: 309), responsible for the creation and maintenance of boundaries, worldviews, criteria for knowledge production and validity, concepts and procedures. Disciplines have their own ways of speaking about research as well as doing research, but, importantly, also powerful actors (Deans, journal editors, mentors) who exert considerable control over knowledge production. Some tax researchers are happy to remain within the realms of orthodoxy for the discipline to which they are attached (whether through their own undergraduate studies or by accident of fate), acquiescing to the dominant view of what constitutes 'good research'. Others take more radical paths, either challenging the orthodoxy within the discipline, or crossing the boundaries into other disciplines to embark on interdisciplinary endeavours. A flavour of this in tax is found in Lamb *et al.* (2004), and the difficulties for accounting researchers in Lamb and Lymer (1999).

Despite increasing calls for interdisciplinarity, the institutional barriers are formidable, not least because of the way mainstream academic journals, contributions to which are one of our key performance indicators, remain firmly wedded (on the whole) not only to single disciplines (or geographic areas, but that's another story), but usually also to the dominant research approach within that discipline. '[T]he legitimacy of knowledge is determined by the rules of a certain group or discipline; thus, different disciplines may decide legitimacy according to very different, mutually irrelevant, or even mutually exclusive rules. These rules are reconstructed and negotiated through interactions within the research community' (Greckhamer *et al.* 2008: 315).

More thoughts on theorising

Why do we need theory anyway? What is wrong with just investigating an interesting question and describing what we find? At one level, there is nothing wrong with doing just that, and there are plenty of exemplary scholarly works in tax research that make no reference to theory at all. There is an argument, however, that by using existing theories to help to explain phenomena, and by contributing to the development of theories, we are able to contribute to social science more widely. Llewellyn (2003) describes theorisation as the 'value added of qualitative academic research' (ibid.: 662), and goes on to describe five levels of theorisation. Although presented as 'levels', Llewellyn concedes that these types of theorising may be more appropriately considered as a circle, or even spiral, rather than a ladder. At the lowest level (1), she positions metaphor: the use of familiar images to establish a correspondence between something we already know and a new phenomenon. Level two theorising under Llewellyn's schema is differentiation which entails 'cutting up experience [to] create meaning and significance through setting up contrasts and categories that order the world' (ibid.: 672). At the next 'highest' level is concepts: 'the fundamental tools used in social practice … both to observe and represent the world and to act and work in it' (ibid.). Level four is theorising settings, in which a range of lower-level approaches are brought together to construct a broad schema but which focuses on specific events or issues: 'context bound theories … create meaning and significance through explaining relationships between phenomena' (ibid.: 676). Finally, the highest level comprises grand theorising: far less, if at all, concerned with practices, this is the realm of ideas with a focus on 'large scale and enduring aspects' of the social world (see Table 2.1).

Conclusion

This introductory chapter has attempted to introduce some debates about the philosophical underpinnings of social science research. In tax, we certainly do not want

Table 2.1 Levels of theorising

Level of theorising	*Type of phenomena*	*What it does*	*What it seeks*
Metaphor	Micro reasons, actions, social production	Grounds experience	Understanding
Differentiation	Micro social processes	Cuts up experience	Understanding
Concepts	Meso agency, how individuals make things happen	Explicates practices	Understanding and explanation
Context-dependent theory	The social organisation of relationships between individuals, organisations and environments	Explains relationships between social phenomena in context	Contextualisation
Grand theory	Class, gender, power relations, and the distribution of resources	Explains universal, ahistorical, large-scale dimensions of social life	Explanation

(Adapted from Llewelyn 2003)

to go down the paradigm wars route that business and management research, including accounting, has taken. However, we do need to be aware that these debates exist so that we can relate to the work being done by colleagues. This brief overview has also highlighted the need for tax researchers to develop a sensitivity towards underlying assumptions (unstated) that lead to limitations to research findings that are frequently unacknowledged. This applies not only to those of us working in business school environments, but to tax researchers in all disciplinary 'boxes'. The danger is that by not being explicit about our philosophical beliefs, those relying on our 'truth claims' are not in a position to judge their validity. This includes not only academic audiences from other disciplines or other areas of research, but also policy-makers who draw on academic research to inform their decision-making.

References

Burr, V. (2003) *Social Constructivism*, 2nd edn, London: Routledge.

Burrell, G. and Morgan, G. (1979) *Sociological Paradigms and Organizational Analysis*, London: Heinemann.

Chua, W.F. (1986) 'Radical developments in accounting thought', *The Accounting Review* LXI (4): 601–32.

Czarniawska, B. (1997) *Narrating the Organization*, Chicago, IL: University of Chicago Press.

Deetz, S. (1996) 'Describing differences in approaches to organization science: Rethinking Burrell and Morgan and their legacy', *Organization Science* 7: 191–207.

Dutton, J.E. and Dukerich, J.M. (2006) 'The relational foundation of research: An under-appreciated dimension of interesting research', *Academy of Management Journal* 49: 21–6.

Greckhamer, T., Koro-Ljungberg, M., Cilesiz, S. and Hayes, S. (2008) 'Demystifying Inter-disciplinary qualitative research', *Qualitative Inquiry* 14(2): 307–31.

Jarvis, D.S.L. (1998) 'Postmodernism: A critical typology', *Politics and Society* 26(1): 95–142.

Lamb, M. and Lymer, A. (1999) 'Taxation research in an accounting context: Future prospects and interdisciplinary perspectives', *European Accounting Review* 8(4): 749–76.

Lamb, M., Lymer, A., Freedman, J. and James, S. (2004) *Taxation: An Interdisciplinary Approach to Research*, Oxford: Oxford University Press.

Law, J. (2007) 'Making a mess with method', in W. Outhwaite and S.P. Turner (eds) *The Sage Handbook of Social Science Methodology*, London: Sage, pp. 595–606.

Lewis, M.W. and Grimes, A.J. (1999) 'Metatriangulation: Building theory from multiple paradigms', *The Academy of Management Review* 24(4): 672–90.

Llewellyn, S. (2003) 'What counts as "theory" in qualitative management and accounting research?' *Accounting Auditing and Accountability* 16(4): 662–708.

McKerchar, M. (2010) *Design and Conduct of Research in Tax, Law and Accounting*, Sydney: Thomson Reuters.

Merkl-Davis, D. and Brennan, N. (2011) 'Homo economicus, homo psychologicus, homo socialis, homo fabulans and homo publicus: A theoretical framework of impression management', working paper (on file with the author).

Sandberg, J. (2005) 'How do we justify knowledge produced within interpretive approaches?' *Organizational Research Methods* 8(1): 41–68.

Willmott, H. (1993) 'Breaking the paradigm mentality', *Organization Studies* 14(5): 681–720.

3

GATHERING AND INTERPRETING QUALITATIVE DATA

Lynne Oats

Interviews are an important source of information for interpretivist researchers, but may also be used within positivist approaches, although the manner in which the interview is conducted and then subsequently analysed will vary considerably depending on the perspective of the researcher. The first part of this chapter will explore the nature of interviews, the forms they take and some hints and tips for conducting interviews. The second part will then turn to the question of interpreting the findings from interviews, and raise issues relevant to the interpretation of qualitative data more broadly.

Conducting interviews

There are many 'how to' references available to help researchers come to grips with research interviews as a method for obtaining data, and this section draws on one of these in particular, Kvale and Brinkmann (2009), for two reasons. First, it is one of the leading references in business and management research. Second, the tenor of the work fits particularly well with the aims of this book. They state that the 'qualitative interview has a unique potential for obtaining access to and describing the lived everyday world' (ibid.: 29), and further, that qualitative interviews are 'not merely a few entertaining curiosities added to some basic scientific quantitative facts obtained by experiments and questionnaires. The qualitative interview is a research method that gives privileged access to people's basic experience of the lived world' (ibid.). It is in this spirit that many (but not all) of the studies described in Part III of this book are undertaken. It is this interpretive approach, valuable in its own right and not as some 'add on' to more 'scientific' approaches, that is surprisingly absent from extant tax research across all of the disciplines within which it takes place, and which this book seeks to encourage.

For researchers approaching interviews from a traditional/mainstream research training background, usually underpinned by positivist approaches, the knowledge produced by qualitative interviews may appear to be of dubious value. Kvale and

Brinkmann (2009) propose two metaphors to depict two different ways of approaching qualitative interviewing as a knowledge-producing activity. The first is the researcher as 'miner', that is, digging for precious metal: 'The interviewer digs nuggets of information out of a subject's pure experiences unspoiled by any leading questions' (ibid.: 48). These nuggets of information subsequently retain their objective status either as 'real data' or the subject's 'authentic' meanings. The second metaphor is that of a 'traveller on a journey to a distant country' (ibid.), who interprets what he or she finds there and creates a narrative based on that interpretation that is then brought 'back to the home audience' (ibid.). The miner, then, will perceive a separation between the collection of data and its subsequent analysis. The traveller, on the other hand, will see both processes as being intertwined. For the miner the emphasis is on the way in which the data is collected; for the traveller it is the narrative created that is important.

Kvale and Brinkmann further suggest four conceptions of research interviewing:

1 Interviewing as semi-skilled labour. This idea encapsulates survey-type interviews, which are prevalent in commercial research and evidence-based practice, and are typified by routinized and standardised procedures to downplay, even try to eliminate, the role of the interviewer.
2 Interviewing as a skilled craft. This conception of interviewing acknowledges that the interviewer requires some level of skill and acknowledges the need for the interviewer to exercise some judgement in the process of the interview, and also for the interviewer to possess some knowledge of the subject matter of the interview.
3 Interviewing as requiring specialist expertise. Here the interviewer is expected to have a sound theoretical knowledge of both the practice of interviewing as well as the subject matter of the interview. The interviewer here is able to relate the knowledge arising from the interview to the wider context as a result of this subject-specific expertise.
4 Interviewing as an 'art'. This final category includes an element of creativity and spontaneity, a preparedness to break the rules, including use of innovative and unconventional techniques.

(Kvale and Brinkmann 2009: 85)

In developing this typology, Kvale and Brinkmann (ibid.: 86) observe the paradox that 'the less skill required of the interviewers, the closer the process comes to a mechanical conception of method, and the higher the social scientific status of the interview form. And, correspondingly, the more expertise required in the basic production of interview data, the less the scientific status of the knowledge produced'. This reflects the 'methodological imperialism' of positivistic approaches that we find across all disciplines.

The preceding discussion of the varied nature of qualitative interviewing as method leads to the issue of analysis. Unsurprisingly, different approaches to qualitative interviewing lead to different ways of approaching the analysis, although for the purpose of this chapter the focus is on more interpretive approaches.

Analysing qualitative data

It is not always possible to record interviews; indeed, interviewees may be reluctant to have their interview recorded for a variety of reasons, in which case it is advisable to take extensive notes and write up the interview as soon as possible after completion. Where interviews are recorded, interview transcripts should ideally record verbatim speech, including not only what is said, but also emphasis and hesitation. This can be hugely time consuming, but is an important part of immersing yourself in the interview data, and it is helpful to make notes while doing the transcription. Analysis of interview data is a skill that is always uncertain and very labour intensive. The subsequent coding, or classification, of the interview data will vary depending on the research question that underpins the study. In some studies, the phenomena of interest may not be entirely clear, which can make coding more difficult. For some studies, perhaps with only a small number of interviews, different coloured highlighter pens can function adequately as a means of distinguishing different themes within the data. More complex studies may benefit from the use of computer-assisted coding. Coding is particularly important where the research approach is grounded theory, as formulated by Glaser and Strauss (1967), who sought to develop explicit coding strategies to legitimise qualitative research at a time when it has less, and diminishing, respectability. Grounded theory seeks to develop theory inductively. Content analysis also entails systematic categorisation of texts, usually to reduce large volumes of qualitative data into smaller numbers of observations that can be quantified and then used for hypothesis testing: a more positivist approach to analysis.

The idea of coding or categorising data is to elicit meaning from it, and there are several approaches to this. The researcher can seek to condense meaning by paraphrasing interviewee responses into more manageable chunks while stopping short of attributing quantitative values as in content analysis. This is consistent with an approach that sees the researcher as separate from the data. Alternatively, the researcher may seek to interpret the interview texts using, for example, hermeneutic traditions as developed in the study of literary texts or legal texts. This quest for meaning brings to mind the miner and traveller analogies developed by Kvale and Brinkmann (2009). The researcher needs to decide whether he or she is trying to find the author's/interviewee's intended meaning or understanding as a nugget of knowledge, or develop a broader understanding of the matter under study. We need to confront the question also of whether there is only one correct interpretation of meaning, or a plurality of equally valid interpretations, the latter being more closely associated with a postmodern way of thinking. A belief that there is a 'real meaning' is consistent with the miner analogy. Another way of thinking about interview data, however, is, '[t]hat different interpreters construct different meanings in an interview study is not a problem, but a fruitfulness and virtue of interview research' (ibid.: 218).

Interviews are all about language and there are also different approaches to analysing language that can be drawn upon. Focus on the use of language, drawing from linguistics, can provide additional insights into 'generating and verifying the meaning of statements' (Kvale and Brinkmann 2009: 220). Conversation analysis is a specific form of studying interactive talk, focusing less on what is said and more on how it is said, for example the sequencing and turn-taking that arises in conversations. Narrative analysis looks at the stories being told and attempts to discern their structures and plots. Linguistics, conversation analysis and narrative analysis are relatively easy to define. More problematic, however, is discourse analysis, as discussed in the next section.

Discourse analysis

To many researchers, irrespective of years of experience, the term 'discourse' is shrouded in mystery. On a popular level it means 'what people say', but clearly in research methodology terms it has a different meaning that is not readily apparent, and seems to vary from discipline to discipline, and even within disciplines. Discourse analysis is a term applied to a variety of styles of analysis, although they all tend to share the common view that language is not a neutral means of describing the world. The purpose of this chapter is to try and unravel this mystery as much as possible, or at least shed some light on the different forms that discourse analysis can take.

Interest in discourse analysis has increased significantly in recent years, having originated in 'the linguistic turn' or the shift in emphasis to giving greater prominence to language, as a counter to positivism.

Gill (2000) proposes four main themes of discourse analysis. First, and most obviously, discourse analysis takes discourse itself as the object of inquiry, broadly conceived of as all forms of talk and text including natural conversations, but not to find out 'what really happened'. Second, language is seen as constructive, that it is possible to describe social phenomena in numerous ways depending on the orientation of the producer of the description and we use texts to construct our world. Third, discourse is very much a social practice that doesn't occur in a vacuum: '[p]eople use discourse to *do* things' (ibid.: 178) and use different accounts of events and activities depending on the context in which they are offered, for example depending on to whom we are speaking, or the occasion. Fourth, 'discourse analysis treats talk and text as *organized rhetorically*' (ibid.: 180), that is 'establishing one version of the world in the face of competing versions' (ibid.).

Alvesson and Karreman (2000: 1126) suggest that there are two main, quite different approaches to 'discourse'. The first of these is concerned with the study of social text, not just written but also talk, which can be analysed as a phenomenon 'distinct from other levels of social reality (such as the levels of meaning and practice)'. The second is a more constructivist approach which sees social reality as actually being shaped through language, that 'views discourses as general and prevalent systems for the formation and articulation of ideas in a particular period of time'.

These two very different ways of approaching 'discourse' lend themselves to different levels of analysis. In the first, discourse is used to understand local practices without reference to wider context; in the second, discourse is used to understand wider social and political dimensions. This second perspective is often, but not necessarily, associated with Foucault (see Chapter 14), for whom discourse 'arranges and naturalises the social world in a specific way and thus informs social factors'

(Alvesson and Karreman 2000: 1127–8). To help penetrate the different versions of discourse analysis, Alvesson and Karreman (2000) identify two key dimensions: the connection between discourse and meaning, and the formative range of discourse. Along this first dimension we can locate a range of positions from 'transient meaning' that relates to specific interactions, to 'durable meaning' that embraces language use and meaning beyond its temporal and specific use, including cultural orientations, sense-making and cognition. The relationship between discourse and meaning can be seen as tightly coupled or closely connected, which Alvesson and Karreman (2000) refer to as 'discourse determination' through a range of more loosely coupled positions to an extreme of seeing discourse as being separated from meaning, 'discourse autonomy' (ibid.: 1133).

The second dimension used to categorise varieties of discourse considers its formative range, that is, its scope and scale. A close-range view will focus on 'local, situational context' whereas at the other extreme discourse is viewed as universal, a 'grand narrative' approach. Alvesson and Karreman take these dimensions into a typology of discourse analysis as follows:

1 Micro-discourse approach – social texts, calling for the detailed study of language use in a specific micro context;
2 Meso-discourse approach – being relatively sensitive to language use in context but interested in finding broader patterns and going beyond the details of the text and generalising to similar local contexts;
3 Grand-discourse approach – an assembly of discourses ordered and presented as an integrated frame. A grand discourse may refer to/constitute organisational reality, for example dominating language use about corporate culture or ideology;
4 Mega-discourse approach – an idea of more or less universal connection of discourse material. Mega-discourse typically addresses more or less standardized ways of referring to/constituting a certain type of phenomenon e.g. business re-engineering, diversity or globalization.

(Alvesson and Karreman 2000: 1133)

This raises the question of whether, as researchers, we want to address more than one of these levels in the same study, to examine localised discursive practices but also consider the wider discursive context. Alvesson and Karreman suggest that this leads to a further question of rigour versus significance. There is a danger in myopic focus on the details of discourse, as seen with some forms of content analysis, which Alvesson and Karreman suggest can lead to 'linguistic reductionism' – a focus on specific language use that neglects broader patterns. On the other hand, there is also a danger in too wide a focus: '[i]nclinations to "jump over" language use in a social context and make broader statements about discourse at an aggregate level' (Alvesson and Karreman 2000: 1145). In this latter case, the use of discourse is perhaps misleading and what the researcher may be dealing with is ideology.

Gill (2000) discusses three broad theoretical traditions to help us discern the 'at least 57 varieties of discourse analysis'. First is critical linguistics, which is closely associated with linguistics, in particular semiotics and structuralism. This approach highlights the way in which 'particular linguistic forms ... can have dramatic effects on how an event or phenomenon is understood' (ibid.: 176). The second approach is influenced by speech-act theory, ethnomethodology and conversation analysis and stresses the 'functional or action orientation of discourse' (ibid.). Third is the tradition informed by post-structuralism, most prominently Foucault.

In 'doing' discourse analysis, Gill (2000: 182) suggests that we need to suspend our 'belief in the taken-for-granted', or in anthropological terms 'render the familiar strange', and adopt a sceptical stance to what we are reading, be it an already produced text or a transcript of an interview. 'What discourse analysts do is to produce readings of texts and contexts that are warranted by careful attention to detail and that lend coherence to the discourse being studied' (ibid.: 185).

'Discourse analysis does not set out to identify universal processes' (Gill 2000: 189). It is not concerned with generalisability. Indeed, Kvale and Brinkmann (2009: 228) go so far as to say that from a discourse analysis perspective, some common objections to the validity of qualitative research interviews dissolve. Reliability and validity in discourse analysis are less concerned with techniques and more concerned with the coherence and acceptability of the accounts produced. 'It is an *interpretation*, warranted by detailed argument and attention to the material being studied' (Gill 2000: 190).

Critical discourse analysis is concerned with texts in context, and in this way differs from traditional linguistics. It additionally adopts a 'critical lens, which is focussed on the way in which knowledge, subjects and power relations are produced, reproduced, and transformed within discourse' (Leitch and Palmer 2010: 1195).

Leitch and Palmer (2010) undertake an analysis of papers using a critical discourse analysis approach and identify nine methodological protocols related to conceptual definitions, data selection and data analysis, which they argue benefit the consistency and rigour with which critical discourse analysis is applied in organisation studies. In the same edition of the *Journal of Management Studies*, Chouliaraki and Fairclough (2010) counter Leitch and Palmer's recommendation for strict methodological protocols with an alternative conception of discourse that gives primacy to trans-disciplinarity over rigour. Both papers give a good flavour of the methodological debates surrounding critical discourse analysis within the field of organisation studies.

Deconstruction

Kvale and Brinkmann (2009: 230) observe that Jacques Derrida 'introduced the concept of deconstruction as a combination of "destruction" and "construction"'. It refers to a process by which text is taken apart and opened up to other understandings, not in a search for an underlying meaning but to expose the unspoken assumptions and to think about not just what is said, but also what is left unsaid. It can apply to both written text and also verbal texts, for example interview data, but more commonly is used to probe written texts. 'A deconstructive reading reveals the presuppositions and internal hierarchies of a text and lays open the binary oppositions built into modern thought and language such as true/false, real/unreal, subjective/objective' (ibid.: 230–1). Infanti (2004, 2005) explicitly uses deconstruction as an analytical technique to probe tax expenditure analyses and Circular 230, which governs the conduct of tax preparers in the USA, respectively.

Conclusion

This chapter has attempted to introduce at a basic level, and at the risk of over-simplification, some difficult concepts in relation to the gathering and interpretation of qualitative data. In broad terms, at one end of a spectrum we have an 'absolutist quest for one, and only one, objective meaning' (Kvale and Brinkmann 2009: 241). At the other is 'subjective relativism ... where everything can mean everything' (ibid.). These positions map onto the extremes of crude positivism and extreme social constructionism. In between is a huge variation in terms of approach to qualitative research interviews. In this, as in all methodologies, the researcher is urged to reflect on the philosophical underpinnings so as to remain consistent across a research project in terms of approach to data gathering as well as analysis.

References

Alvesson, M. and Karreman, D. (2000) 'Varieties of discourse: On the study of organizations through discourse analysis', *Human Relations* 53: 1125–49.

Burr, V. (2003) *Social Constructionism*, London: Routledge.

Chouliaraki, L. and Fairclough, N. (2010) 'Critical discourse analysis in organizational studies: Towards an integrationist methodology', *Journal of Management Studies* 47(6): 1213–18.

Gill, R. (2000) 'Discourse Analysis', in M.W. Bauer and G. Gaskell (eds), *Qualitative Researching with Text, Image and Sound*, Sage, pp. 173–89.

Glaser, B.G. and Strauss, A.M. (1967) *The Discovery of Grounded Theory: Strategies for Qualitative Research*, New York: Aldine.

Infanti, A.C. (2004) 'A tax crit identity crisis? Or tax expenditure analysis, deconstruction and the rethinking of collective identity', Working Paper 3, University of Pittsburgh School of Law Working Paper Series.

——(2005) 'From the Sidelines: A Deconstructionist view of circular 230', *Tax Notes* 107.

Kvale, S. and Brinkmann, S. (2009) *InterViews: Learning the Craft of Qualitative Research Interviewing*, 2nd edn, Thousand Oaks, CA: Sage.

Leitch, S. and Palmer, I. (2010) 'Analysing texts in context: Current practices and new protocols for critical discourse analysis in organization studies', *Journal of Management Studies* 47(6): 1195–212.

4

CASE STUDIES

Helen Rogers and Lynne Oats

A 'case study' typically refers to the study of a particular case in some depth. The extent of the depth varies among those who report using a case study approach. This chapter offers some examples of case study tax research and also discusses some of the challenges and problems posed by this approach.

The appropriateness of a case study approach depends on what is to be studied and the nature of the research questions. 'Case study is not a methodological choice but a choice of what is to be studied' (Stake 2000: 435). Typically, a case study approach has much to offer in situations where the research question is looking at *how* things work within organisations, e.g. accounting processes, management of tax compliance, implementation of new policy etc., and so requires a detailed examination of the setting and how procedures, and practices, evolve and become established.

Accordingly, a case study can be described as a 'research strategy which focuses on understanding the dynamics present within single settings' (Eisenhardt 1989: 534). Thus it is intensive research into a particular case, such as an organisation or company, and is a particularly useful tool to help to understand complex phenomena. Case study research can either involve looking at one case, i.e. a single case study, or a number of cases; a multiple case study. Different research methods, including quantitative and qualitative (or both combined) can be used within a case study approach. One of the leading exponents of case study research is Robert Yin (2009), whose book *Case Study Research: Design and Methods* provides a guide to the conduct of case study research with a very practical orientation, pitched at a consultancy level. McKerchar (2010: 101–12) describes a number of studies that have drawn on Yin's approach, which provides a bridge for those who wish to explore a phenomenon in close detail, but remain within a positivist frame, since his approach has much in common with scientific method (Outhwaite and Turner 2007).

Stake (2000) identifies three main types of case study: intrinsic, instrumental and collective. An intrinsic case study is one examined because it is intrinsically interesting for its own sake. An instrumental case study is one that is selected on the grounds that it will provide insight into an issue and/or support or revise a generalisation or theory. For example, Preston (1989) carried out a single case study, looking at a company being investigated by the Inland Revenue (as it then was) in the UK. A collective case study describes research into a number of different instrumental cases, selected to provide a better understanding of some general issue, phenomenon or theory. For example, Baldwin (1990) reports research involving case studies of four firms of different sizes within the UK construction industry. The research looked into the level of tax compliance costs and complaints about certain issues, to offer some suggestions about how help with tax compliance might be effectively targeted at small companies. These examples help to demonstrate that tax issues can be, and have been, researched using a case study approach.

Organisational case studies

In the area of accounting, and in particular management accounting, there has been an ongoing debate about the use of case studies, starting in the early 1980s, with many calling for the increased use of case studies in accounting research. For example, in 1983 Hopwood observed that, 'with accounting so intertwined with organisational functioning, it is surprising that so little is known of the organisational nature of accounting practices' (Hopwood 1983: 287), and concluded that 'much more needs to be known of the ways in which accounting reflects, reinforces or even constrains the strategic postures adopted by particular organisations and of the ways in which accounting relates to the structures' (ibid.: 302). Similar calls were made by others, including Kaplan (1983, 1984), Jensen (1983), Roberts and Scapens (1985), and Covaleski and Aitken (1986).

Following on from this, a great deal of management accounting-focused case study research work has been carried out and published in recent years, a source of much rich organisational data. This helps to demonstrate that the 'role of accounting and other controls cannot be understood in isolation, and that a more contextual approach is required' (Otley and Berry 1994: 46). While there has been a rise in case studies and fieldwork in management accounting, the debate continues, seeming to broaden from the objective of obtaining rich organisational detail to the wider use and benefits of such detail and more understanding of the specific contributions such case study research can make: i.e. a shift away from intrinsic case studies to instrumental and collective case studies.

One area of overlap between management accounting and tax is that of transfer pricing, a topic that has been the focus of several case studies in recent years. Reasons given for a case study approach in this context include: the ability to accommodate complexity; the opportunity for a rich investigation and description of transfer pricing in one organisation; and the limitations of alternative approaches when researching in this area. Van der Meer-Kooistra (1994) undertook a collective case study design, carrying out research into domestic (as opposed to cross-border) transfer pricing within Dutch multinational entities, looking in particular at the different factors that influence the way in which internal transactions of goods and services are coordinated by means of transfer pricing systems. From the different companies studied, Van der Meer-Kooistra found that changes in the characteristics of the internal transactions and in the organisational context caused changes in the transfer pricing system.

Colbert and Spicer in 1995 carried out a collective case study looking at domestic transfer pricing in four different US companies in the electronics sector, helping to develop a theory of transfer pricing from a transaction costs perspective. This is a useful starting point for further case study work into transfer pricing, although this research was only concerned with domestic transfers between various divisions of US companies. Looking at cross-border transactions, Elliott (1999), in an unpublished PhD thesis, carried out a case study into the management of international transfer pricing in a single, medium-sized, multinational group with a UK parent company. This case study looked at how the international transfer pricing policy was implemented and managed by investigating specific transactions at the subsidiary level.

A more recent case study has been carried out by Cools *et al.* (2007), examining transfer pricing policy in a single multinational group, considering both products and inter-group services. In particular it looked at the tensions between tax compliance and management control. The group studied had as one of its primary objectives compliance with the various rules, and made changes to the management control system to help to facilitate this compliance. Cools *et al.* concluded that changes to a company's management control system cannot be fully understood without considering the company's tax compliance process.

This chimes with an earlier organisational case study dealing with another aspect of tax practice. Preston (1989) presents an insightful account of the operations and accounting procedures of a record producing company and an interesting description of the Inland Revenue's investigation and the company's response to it. Preston used the case study approach to look at the ways in which investigations by the Inland Revenue heavily influenced the design, development and operation of a company's accounting system. This is a useful example of an instrumental case study: the case of an anonymised record producing company with a 'chaotic working environment' (ibid.: 393) and few accounting controls, is investigated. Preston does not claim that this 'seemingly anarchic' (ibid.: 392) case study company is typical or representative of other companies in any way; indeed, he acknowledges it as 'an unusual organisation in which to conduct research' (ibid.).

This unusual company is a source of rich organisational detail, enabling a good understanding of the particular case. However, Preston goes on to do more than provide such detail about a company and how it responds to an investigation from the Inland Revenue. There is a description and discussion of Inland Revenue practice such as the creation of databases and benchmark deviations from which might result a company being investigated, something which is of general relevance. Furthermore, the case is used to address interests and theories that are wider than the case itself, including the ideas of Foucault in respect of disciplinary technologies (see Chapter 14 for a discussion of Foucault). 'The application of … disciplinary techniques reveals connections … between the Revenue and accounting practice. Accounting practice is seen to be both the focus of the Revenue's gaze and a facilitative technology which renders the financial activities and accounting practice of individual organisations visible' (Preston 1989: 411). This case study suggests that the Revenue may 'exert an important influence upon a company's adoption and development of particular forms of accounting practice' (ibid.).

Law case studies: international tax law

Case studies, of course, do not necessarily have to relate to organisations. The 'case' may be an event or phenomenon as shown by Christians (2010), who analyses a number of research studies conducted by North American legal scholars in the area of international tax, concluding that there is room for improvement in relation to the way these studies are presented. Christians calls for legal scholars to draw on social science to make explicit the choice and purpose of case study research within tax law scholarship, and also to learn from the methodologies used in the social sciences, for example interview techniques and methods of analysing qualitative data. In conclusion, she states that 'in a world of complex economic, financial and social relationships, using qualitative socio-legal methods to study our cases represents our best hope of developing new knowledge and, with it, new and better theory for international taxation' (ibid.: 29). Arguably the same sentiments can be applied to many other areas of tax law and policy.

Difficulties with case studies

Given the scope that case study research offers, it is worth considering some of the reasons why researchers may choose not to adopt a case study approach. A key, practical deterrent to undertaking a case study can be the difficulty in obtaining sufficient access to an organisation in order to carry out the work in sufficient depth: in some cases it may not be possible to obtain access to carry out research work. Also there is sometimes a concern that, even if access is initially obtained, it might be withdrawn at any time, e.g. due to a change in personnel within the organisation or a change of strategy, leaving the researcher with incomplete data. This is a further practical deterrent: case studies are challenging to carry out in that they are very time consuming (for one or more researchers) and can involve financial cost in large geographically diverse organisations. This was specifically referred to by Colbert and Spicer (1995: 454) in their case study research of four divisionalised companies: 'the problems of access, cost and logistics in undertaking multiple case study research of this type should not be underestimated'.

However, aside from the practical problems of access, there is sometimes a reluctance to devote such cost and time to case study work, as the focus on one particular organisation can imply that there is specific organisational context. This leads on to a broad concern that research and conclusions from specific case study data cannot be generalisable. In summary, the main reasons frequently given for a case study approach being an inappropriate research design are problems with access and a perception of the lack of generalisability from case study data.

Access to organisations is often acknowledged as very difficult to obtain and often more so in the case of commercial organisations, when compared with public organisations. The general problem of access is frequently exacerbated in the case of tax research as this is typically a very commercially sensitive issue with very limited public disclosure required in the annual financial accounts. This problem can be partly overcome by undertaking not to disclose the identity of those being studied. Furthermore, it can help to provide reassurance about how much (or rather how little) time will be required from each individual, and that information given by individuals will be confidential. As is often the consequence of gaining access for an academic study, offering to give back to the organisation in the form of a final report and/or presentation of findings obtained during the case study can be useful. This can be attractive to some organisations, as the findings are likely to provide helpful insight into the organisation and are likely to be in respect of issues not typically addressed by consultants, or in the case of tax research, tax advisers.

Misunderstandings about case studies

Writing from a management background, Flyvberg (2006) addresses five common misunderstandings about case studies, as follows:

1. General, theoretical (context-independent) knowledge is more valuable than concrete, practical (context-dependent) knowledge.
2. One cannot generalise on the basis of a single case; therefore, the single case study cannot contribute to scientific development.
3. The case study is most useful for generating hypotheses – that is, in the first stage of a total research process – whereas other methods are more suitable for hypothesis-testing and theory-building.
4. The case study contains a bias towards verification – that is, a tendency to confirm the researcher's preconceived notions.
5. It is often difficult to summarise and develop general propositions and theories on the basis of specific case studies.

The ensuing discussion, in which Flyvberg answers each of these misconceptions, makes a powerful case for the role of case study research and is recommended reading for anyone who is uncertain about whether to embark on such a project. Due to space limitations, here we discuss just one of these misunderstandings, specifically the alleged problem of generalisability.

In terms of generalisability, certainly there is some trade-off between rich contextual detail and broad generalisability across a range of very different cases, i.e. a trade-off between studying cases in depth or in breadth, and a primary concern of case studies is explanation of context. However, as discussed before, rich organisational detail is valuable in itself. As a minimum, a single case study can be seen as a step (albeit small) towards generalisation, but any assessment of the way in which conclusions from case study research can be generalisable is contingent upon what is meant by 'generalisable'. Cooper and Morgan (2008) refer to Lindsay (2004), who describes two forms of generalisation: statistical (to populations) and empirical (across populations).

Typically in the case of the former, statistical studies generalise from a random sample to a wider population using statistical methods. However, there can be difficulties in statistical generalisations in the social sciences. MacIntyre (1990) traces this problem back to the difficulty of predicting human behaviour and thus the difficulty of making valid generalisations about human behaviour. This is exacerbated with regards to tax and accounting as laws frequently change and the social context of organisations and institutions also vary, both over time and between different organisations.

Not only does aggregated statistical information from a wide population lose any rich organisational detail, but it also loses sight of separate individual cases, which can be more interesting and relevant when looked at in isolation, as opposed to when combined with many others. This can be particularly relevant to tax: for example, a new tax might be regarded as 'revenue neutral' but there might be individual taxpayers paying much more or much less than previously.

'Large scale empirical studies rely on summary statistics which tend to see outliers and variance as a problem; case studies in contrast often specifically focus on the outliers and anomalies' (Cooper and Morgan 2008: 7). However, frequently it is research into these anomalies that can be relevant and such outliers can examine or test 'the boundary conditions of a theory' (ibid.: 10). For example, Baldwin's four case studies stemmed from a review of the Department of Trade and Industry report in 1985, *Burdens on Business*, based on statistics drawn from 200 different businesses. These statistics indicated that compliance burdens were distributed 'fairly evenly' across firms of different sizes in different sectors. Closer examination by Baldwin brought this into question and he investigated this further by carrying out case studies into four firms in the construction sector, indicating that the general statistical conclusions were not applicable to firms in the construction industry, suggesting reasons such as a recent significant change in VAT legislation applicable to the construction industry and the different possible ways of taxing labour employed in construction.

So statistical generalisation does have some disadvantages and this may be a reason to adopt a case study approach. Furthermore, it is possible to generalise from case study data in an empirical way, by contributing to and adding to theory. This can be done in different ways. For example, Flyvberg (2001, 2006) refers to Popper's test of falsification: if one observation does not fit with the proposition it is considered not generally valid and the theory must be either revised or rejected. Popper used the example of 'all swans are white' and asserted that one single observation of a black swan would falsify this proposition and consequently have general significance and stimulate further research and theory building.

Flyvberg offers the example of Galileo's rejection of Aristotle's laws of gravity, which was 'not based upon observations across a wide range, and the observations were not carried out in some numbers, it was a matter of a single experiment, a case study, if any experiment were conducted at all' (Flyvberg 2006: 74). He points out that once Aristotle's theory was falsified by Galileo, it was not necessary to carry out the experiment repeatedly using different objects, different heights and under varying weather conditions.

Lukka and Kasanen (1995) also point out that the use of statistical methods is only one possible way of generalising from data and argue that generalisation *is* possible from a case study by adding to theory. A case study that contributes to the development of a theory in some way, by definition has an element of generalisability: 'case observations are often part of theoretical studies in which a case is used as an illustrative device to support a theoretical analysis by examples, offering a practical forum to make the argumentation more concrete. The most fundamental feature of these studies is that their purpose is to argue something (e.g. a certain social theory) to be relatively widely valid i.e. to generalise' (ibid.: 78).

There are difficulties and limitations in carrying out case study research in organisations and in other settings. However, for many research questions, including some from the field of tax, these are outweighed by the potential benefits. There are opportunities to obtain rich, detailed, context-specific information in respect of complex issues, to help to understand the case and also go beyond pure description and to test, support, add to or generate theories that are generally relevant, beyond the case being researched. Preston's (1989) case study, for example, provided rich and sometimes fascinating organisational detail, but it did more than this: it supported and added to the existing theories and studies of disciplinary power. Thus, by doing so, this research achieves a real level of generalisability beyond the uniqueness of the specific case of the record producing company, demonstrating the important contribution that can be made by case study research.

References

Ahrens, T. and Chapman, C. (2006) 'Doing qualitative field research in management accounting: Positioning data to contribute to theory', *Accounting, Organizations and Society* 31: 819–41.

Baldwin, T. (1990) 'Taxation compliance costs: Implications for small business', *British Tax Review* 9: 319–30.

Christians, A. (2010) *Case Study Research and International Tax Theory University of Wisconsin Law School*, Legal Studies Research Paper Series, Paper No. 1110, papers.ssrn.com/sol3/papers.cfm?abstract_id = 1593722 (accessed 14 November 2011).

Colbert, G.J. and Spicer, B.H. (1995) 'A multi case investigation of a theory of transfer pricing process', *Accounting Organizations and Society* 20: 423–56.

Cools, M., Emmanuel, C. and Jorissen, A. (2007) 'Management control in the transfer pricing tax compliant multinational enterprise', *Accounting Organizations and Society* 33: 603–28.

Cooper, D. and Morgan, W. (2008) 'Case study research in accounting', *Accounting Horizons* 22(2): 159–78.

Covaleski, M. and Aitken, M. (1986) 'Accounting theories of organisations: Some preliminary considerations', *Accounting Organizations and Society* 11: 297–319.

Eisenhardt, K.M. (1989) 'Building theories from case study research', *Academy of Management Review* 14(4): 532–50.

Elliott, J. (1999) 'Managing international transfer pricing policies: A grounded theory study', unpublished PhD thesis, University of Glasgow.

Flyvberg, B. (2001) *Making Social Science Matter*, Cambridge: Cambridge University Press.

——(2006) 'Five misunderstandings about case study research', *Qualitative Inquiry* 12(2): 219–45.

Hopwood, A.G. (1983) 'On trying to study accounting in the contexts in which it operates, *Accounting Organizations and Society* 8(2/3): 287–305.

Jensen, M.C. (1983) 'Organization theory and methodology', *Accounting Review* LVII(2), April: 319–39.
Kaplan, R.S. (1983) 'Measuring manufacturing performance: A new challenge for managerial accounting research', *Accounting Review* 58(4): 686–705.
——(1984) 'The evolution of management accounting', *Accounting Review* July: 390–418.
Lindsay, R.M. (2004) 'Making progress in theory development in management accounting research by focussing on both context and patter: towards a more respectable role for case study research', unpublished paper, University of Western Ontario.
Lukka, K. and Kasanen, E. (1995) 'The problem of generalizability: anecdotes and evidence in accounting research', *Accounting Auditing and Accountability Journal* 18: 71–90.
McIntyre, A. (1990) *After Virtue: A Study in Moral Theory*, Guildford: Duckworth.
McKerchar, M. (2010) *Design and Conduct of Research in Tax, Law and Accounting*, Sydney: Thomson Reuters.
Otley, D.T. and Berry, A.J. (1994) 'Case Study Research in Management Accounting and Control', *Management Accounting Research* 5: 45–65.
Outhwaite, W. and Turner, S.P. (2007) 'Case Study', in W. Outhwaite and S.P. Turner (eds), *The Sage Handbook of Social Science Methodology*, London: Sage.
Preston, A.M. (1989) 'The Taxman Cometh: Some observations on the interrelationship between accounting and Inland Revenue practice', *Accounting Organizations and Society* 14: 389–413.
Roberts, J. and Scapens, R.W. (1985) 'Accounting systems and systems of accountability: Understanding accounting practices in organizational contexts', *Accounting Organizations and Society* 10(4): 443–56.
Scapens, R.W. (1990) 'Researching management accounting practice: The Role of Case Study Methods', *British Accounting Review* 22: 259–81.
Silverman, D. (2009) *Doing Qualitative Research*, 3rd edn, Thousand Oaks, CA: Sage.
Stake, R.E. (2000) 'Case Studies' in N.K. Denzin and Y.S. Lincoln (eds) *Handbook of Qualitative Research*, Thousand Oaks, CA: Sage.
Van der Meer-Kooistra, J. (1994) 'The coordination of internal transactions: the functioning of transfer pricing systems in the organizational context', *Management Accounting Research* 5(2): 123–52.
Yin, R. (2009) *Case Study Research: Design and Methods*, 4th edn, Thousand Oaks, CA: Sage.

5

DESIGNING AND ADMINISTERING SURVEYS

Margaret McKerchar

Introduction

When first asked to write a chapter on designing and administering surveys in the context of qualitative research I admit to being a little perplexed. As a 'seasoned' researcher, I would normally associate a survey as a research method (or strategy of inquiry) aligned more closely with quantitative research and the traditions of positivism, so I had to think more deeply about my contribution. Surveys (or questionnaires) are the oldest and most widely used method for collecting data in the social sciences and related applied fields (Neuman 2006: 272). They are typically used to make generalisations about a total population (that is too large to observe directly), based on data collected from a sample or subset of the same population. Surveys do have many and varied uses including describing the characteristics of the population; seeking explanations (such as cause and effect) for observations made; and/or forming the basis of an exploratory study (Babbie 2007: 244). They can be conducted by various means including electronic, telephone, in person or by postal mail, and can be used to collect both empirical and non-empirical data.[1]

The most distinguishing feature of a survey is its structural form, as this will reflect the underlying philosophical approach to the research and guide its design and conduct, and the nature of the knowledge claims made by the researcher. Structured or semi-structured surveys are generally considered to be methods used in quantitative research while unstructured surveys (or interviews) are generally used in qualitative research. Given that interviews are the subject of another chapter in this book, then the focus here must be on structured and semi-structured surveys (hereafter referred to simply as 'surveys') and by now you should be able to appreciate my dilemma. How can surveys be relevant to qualitative research? In addressing this question I have organised the chapter around two main themes. First, it is important to appreciate both what surveys are (and are not) and what they can (and cannot) be reasonably expected to do. That is, the limitations of surveys as a research method in the context of qualitative research need to be appreciated. The second theme then builds on the first by considering the opportunities that may exist for surveys to inform and/or enhance qualitative research. Before addressing these themes, it is clear that when it comes to designing research in taxation, the range and appropriateness of methodological approaches are not carved in stone. Scope exists both for innovation and to draw on best practice from a wide range of disciplines. For those who seek to push the conventional and/or disciplinary boundaries, the challenge is to convince others, namely the gatekeepers of knowledge, of the merit of their contribution. Having a sound and convincing rationale for the research design adopted is an elementary step in addressing this challenge. To build this step requires at least a basic understanding of research theory and its influence on the design and conduct of research, including the choice of method and the making of knowledge claims. Thus before exploring the two themes described in this section, some brief consideration first needs to be given to research theory.[2]

Theoretical considerations

At the outset, researchers need to have a clear understanding of the aim of their research (or the research question) and of their own beliefs about how knowledge is created and about reality. These beliefs, whether implicit or explicit, have a profound influence on the way research is designed and conducted.

The literature often portrays researchers as belonging to one of two fundamentally opposing camps (Sarantakos 2005: 31) or 'warring tribes' (Bryman 2008: 15–17), i.e. quantitative researchers or qualitative researchers. Quantitative researchers seek objective and absolute truth based on deductive reasoning and tend to use methodologies and methods that reflect the underlying principles of positivism. In contrast, qualitative researchers accept that truth is subjective and not absolute. They tend to rely more on inductive reasoning to build understanding and use methodologies and methods that reflect non-positivism or anti-positivism. Of course, this portrayal of only two tribes is overly simplistic and there are many other philosophical stances that could be characterised as being in the middle ground or even further afield.[3] Similarly, it is debatable exactly where legal research lies both in terms of geography and genealogy. Legal researchers have tended not to engage in the theoretical debate about research methodology to the same extent as have researchers from other disciplines, but there are elements of legal research that are consistent with the general principles discussed so far. For example, the black letter law approach to research reflects legal positivism (Perry 2009; Coleman 2009; and Peczenik 2004). Similarly, many examples exist of socio-legal or reform-orientated legal researchers adopting approaches to their research that reflect non-positivism to some extent (Flood 2005; Tooma 2008; and Bentley 2007). The key point from this discussion is that as a researcher you need to understand your own theoretical underpinnings when it comes to research and be explicit about them when you provide the rationale for your research design. Against this background, our attention now turns to surveys as a research method for the collection of data.

Surveys: design, conduct and limitations

As a research method, standardised surveys (and again the discussion herein is limited to structured and semi-structured surveys) are generally used by quantitative researchers: that is, those using deductive reasoning to determine the truth. This reflects the positivist view of a survey being more suited to the testing of theories than the uncovering of new hypotheses (Axinn and Pearce 2006: 4). Surveys have been widely used in tax research (for example McKerchar 1995; and McKerchar *et al.* 2008). They are regarded as an effective method for collecting data about self-reported behaviour or beliefs which typically are the 'what', 'when' and 'how' type of questions that describe the population and/or explain what is observed (Neuman 2006: 273), for example, 'what age group best describes you?', 'what records do you keep for tax purposes?', 'when did you last seek assistance from the tax authority?', and 'how do you update your professional knowledge?'

A structured survey tends to have mostly 'closed' questions where the respondent can choose from a limited range of set answers. In comparison, a semi-structured survey includes more 'open' (i.e. open-ended) questions where the respondent can provide an answer that is not pre-determined.[4] For example, in asking the question of a tax practitioner, 'how do you update your professional knowledge?', possible alternative answers might be 'professional journal', 'newspapers', 'television', 'colleagues', 'in-house training', but the reality is that there are many possible answers and the researcher may not be able to identify (or even want to list) them all. Providing the option for the respondent to supply a personalised answer can generate richer data and also minimise the risk of the researcher failing to identify all the possible answers. It can also contribute to keeping the survey instrument shorter and this is usually regarded as a desirable design feature.

It is important to recognise that the type of question (i.e. 'open' or 'closed') affects the nature of the data collected, but not the underlying nature of the research itself. That is, collecting qualitative data by means of an open question does make the research qualitative in nature. This is a very important distinction and one that is not always well understood. The quantitative researcher will seek to make statistical generalisations about the total population based on the sample and will be very concerned about the representativeness of the sample, the survey response rate and its impact on bias, the validity (i.e. correctness) of the survey and its reliability (i.e. dependability), as these factors will affect the level of confidence in the knowledge claims made based on the research. Further, the quantitative researcher will typically convert any qualitative data collected by the conduct of the survey to quantitative form (e.g. by coding, summarising and reduction), for the purposes of analysis. The quantitative researcher interprets the data with objectivity. In contrast, the qualitative researcher will seek to make analytical generalisations about the sample population based on the survey data, but is less concerned about representativeness, reliability and validity. Further, the findings presented will be expressed in terms of emerging theories and propositions and recognised as being subjective, rather than as the acceptance or rejection of hypotheses, in numerical or statistical form, or necessarily objective. That is, researchers will make very different knowledge claims based on their underlying philosophical approach to research, rather than on the nature of the data itself.

In spite of these differences in philosophical stances when it comes to research, there are some general principles that should be considered in the design and conduct of a survey. First, there is an art to both asking the right questions in a survey and then phrasing them appropriately if the results are to be meaningful (Neuman 2006: 272). To ask useful survey questions the researcher needs to have first identified the theories to be tested (in the case of the quantitative researcher), or the themes to be explored (in the case of the qualitative researcher), and this first requires a good understanding of the literature. The quantitative researcher will need to compose the survey questions in such a way as to allow for a causal relationship to be tested and robust conclusions to be drawn. De Vaus (2002) provides the following useful checklist (and extracted advice) for designing surveys that would be readily applicable in the context of tax research:

- Is the language simple? (i.e. Avoid jargon and technical terms)
- Can the question be shortened? (i.e. The shorter the question the less confusing and ambiguous it will be)
- Is the question double-barrelled? (e.g. How often do you visit your tax agent?)
- Is the question leading?
- Is the question negative? (e.g. Marijuana should not be legalised. Agree/Disagree)
- Is the respondent likely to have the necessary knowledge?
- Will the words have the same meaning for everyone?
- Is there a prestige bias in the question? (e.g. Exaggerate income)
- Is the question ambiguous?
- Do you need a direct or indirect question?
- Is the frame of reference for the question sufficiently clear?
- Does the question artificially create opinions?
- Is personal or impersonal wording preferable?
- Is the question wording unnecessarily detailed or objectionable?

The less ambiguous the survey questions, the greater is the internal validity of the instrument itself. However, even when the questions appear clear and unambiguous, it should never be assumed that respondents will interpret the questions in the way that was intended (Axinn and Pearce 2006). The piloting and pre-testing of a survey instrument can assist in improving its internal validity to some extent.

The type of questions also has implications for the analysis of data and its usefulness. While closed questions do make for easier data analysis, they still require the researcher to decide how many response choices should be given and what these choices are to be. Two response choices (i.e. yes/no, or agree/disagree) may be too limited to be very useful. For example, if the question asked was 'have you ever engaged in tax evasion?' a yes/no answer provides poorer information than if there were more alternatives from which to choose (e.g. never, very infrequently, occasionally, or regularly). These are not simple decisions, as the more alternatives that are provided, the more laborious is the survey for respondents and the honesty of answers may suffer as a consequence. When seeking data on respondents' attitudes it may be preferable to ask two questions: the first asking them to choose a position (with no middle ground option available, therefore establishing the direction of the attitude) and then to follow this with a question asking how strongly they feel about the choice (thereby establishing intensity) (Neuman 2006: 290). It is also preferable to ask respondents to rank rather than rate alternatives. For example, respondents may rate both tax evasion and perjury as serious crimes, but it may be more useful to know which they rank as the more serious.

The layout of the survey in terms of its visual appeal and ease of completion can impact on the response rate, so is of particular concern to the quantitative researcher. Other simple techniques such as a polite cover letter, a personalised request to participate in the survey, and clear and concise instructions, can make respondents feel that their contribution is valued and appreciated and thereby improve the response rate. Similarly, the length of the survey instrument can be expected to impact on the response rate. As a guide, postal surveys are typically four-to-eight pages in length. Where conducted in person, an hour is really the maximum time that should be anticipated for completion of a survey, and 30 minutes may well be the optimum length of a telephone survey.

In terms of the means of conduct of a survey, the researcher's decision may well be shaped by the availability of resources and the sensitivity of the questions. For example, a web-based survey may be less expensive to conduct and facilitate the ease of data analysis, but the response rate is generally lower than for mail-based surveys (for example, McKerchar 2005). A structured survey conducted in person is resource intensive but may be necessary if literacy levels are low (for example, see Yesegat 2008). There is also evidence that where the issue is sensitive, surveys that are self-administered (e.g. by mail or web-based) are more likely to increase the likelihood of honest responses compared to telephone or surveys conducted in person, as is providing explicit guarantees of anonymity and confidentiality. Similarly, asking questions to set the scene can improve the usefulness of the data collected, as can the phrasing of questions in a more neutral manner (i.e. depersonalising the behaviour), so that respondents feel they are not being judged as socially undesirable and/or lacking in knowledge (Neuman 2006: 283–5).

In the case of web surveys, it is useful to advise the respondent at the beginning how many questions there are and how long it should take to complete the survey. Using software that allows the respondent to see how much is still remaining, and gives them the option to come back to the survey later, may improve the response rate and the usefulness of the data collected. Another very distinct advantage of web surveys is that the data collected are usually provided in spreadsheet form, so there is no need to re-key the responses. This speeds up the data analysis process and reduces the likelihood of keying errors when compared to other forms of surveys. However, while a web-based survey may be fast and efficient, not everyone may have access to the survey and the response rate may be low.[5]

Other key decisions about the design of a survey include the sampling frame and size, and the recruitment of respondents. The sampling frame (i.e. the total population under consideration) is an important consideration because it needs to be relevant to the research if generalisations are to be made. While the qualitative researcher will not make statistical generalisations, they may well seek to make analytical generalisations and form theories so they too will consider the sampling frame – not so much its size, but its relevance given the research problem. Often it is very difficult to access the most appropriate population and researchers have to resort to electoral rolls, telephone directories, jury rosters and other publically available registers. Certainly in the case of tax research in Australia, there are examples of co-operation whereby access to relevant sample frames has been made available by the revenue authority under set conditions (see, for example, McKerchar *et al.* 2008).

The sample to be surveyed is a subset of the sample frame and its means of selection is an important consideration for the researcher as it has implications for the knowledge claims made. A quantitative researcher will usually prefer to have a random sample as this will better support (i.e. increase the reliability of) the statistical generalisations that are made to the population as a whole. Samples chosen by other means (such as convenience sampling, purposive sampling, or by snowball or chain sampling where one respondent is asked to recommend others who may be willing to participate in the research and so on) tend to be less representative of the total population and therefore affect the reliability of the findings of the research. The size of the sample does also have consequences for reliability of survey findings and in determining the optimal size the researcher will need to consider the likely response rate and the degree of accuracy required.[6]

A further and very important consideration in the design and conduct of a survey is the need to adhere to the principles of ethical research. For many tax researchers these principles will be institutional requirements and approvals need to be obtained in advance of the conduct of the survey (including any pilots). Most institutional ethics committees will require that participation in a survey is voluntary and on an informed basis, that confidentiality be maintained at all times, and that those recruited understand that they can withdraw their consent at any time.

It should be appreciated by now that it is quite easy to conduct a survey that yields misleading or worthless results (Neuman 2006: 272). A great deal can go wrong even where there has been careful planning. It is important to remember that structured and semi-structured surveys are powerful strategies for enabling statistical generalisations to large populations, but that they are considered to be weak in generating rich understanding of the intricate mechanisms that affect human thought and behaviour (Groves *et al.* 2004). As Neuman (2006: 273) explains, asking people the 'why' questions is problematic as they rarely understand the causes that shape their own beliefs or behaviour. For example, asking a survey respondent, 'why do your engage in tax evasion?' may not adequately capture the complexities of their behaviour. Similarly, asking respondents whether or not they had been unintentionally noncompliant in respect of their tax obligations is unlikely to produce meaningful results. Remember, the qualitative researcher is usually seeking deeper understanding of the processes and drivers of human behaviour, rather than any absolute or objective truth. Hence the structured (or semi-structured) survey may or may not be an appropriate method, depending on the purpose of the research and the methodological approach adopted.

Opportunities for the use of surveys in qualitative research

Once you understand what surveys are (and are not) and can (and cannot) do, you are better placed to identify the opportunities for their use in qualitative research. As was established at the beginning of this chapter, a survey can be used to describe a population, to explain or to explore. The 'explain' aspect is central to the establishment of causal relationships and this is primarily the domain of quantitative research. On the other hand, being able to 'describe' and/or 'explore' a population could be attractive to qualitative researchers. The description of the characteristics of a population can inform research (i.e. who appears most affected), as can an exploratory study. A survey can potentially allow a qualitative researcher to 'explore' the research problem in different and possibly larger contexts, to see the extent of the problem and appreciate its importance. The open-ended questions can generate new and at times unexpected responses that can lead to areas for further fruitful research. That is, a survey can provide insights to a qualitative researcher, but they will interpret the data from a different stance than will the quantitative researcher.

A survey can play an important role in research that reflects a more pragmatic philosophical stance (i.e. where the researcher is not necessarily wedded to either qualitative or quantitative approaches and instead draws freely from a mix of methodologies), which is usually driven by the research problem itself. For example, a survey as an exploratory study may identify the existence of relationships that could then be explored by qualitative research (for example, in-depth interviews) to understand more fully why they exist. The survey could also be an opportunity for respondents to self-identify if they are willing to participate further in the research (e.g. an in-depth interview to understand more fully the meaning of their responses).

Alternatively, a survey could be used subsequent to a method aligned to qualitative research (for example, a focus group) to determine the extent to which the findings of the qualitative research could be generalised to the broader population and thereby gauge the extent of the problem or issue. Another possibility is to use a survey as a means to validate (by triangulation) the findings derived from another method. Qualitative researchers (and more often those with leanings towards positivism) do at times adopt this triangulation technique as a 'reality check' to strengthen their findings and convince others of the merit of their research.

Concluding comments

Structured and semi-structured surveys are primarily the domain of quantitative researchers and there is indeed an art to their design if they are to be useful and provide meaningful outcomes. While qualitative researchers tend not to use structured and semi-structured surveys as their main method of data collection, they can nonetheless provide useful insights, particularly in terms of description and exploration. There are a variety of ways in which surveys can complement qualitative research, particularly in the case of mixed methodological research where one method can inform or validate another. Many people do feel more convinced by 'hard' and more objective evidence, and in this sense a survey can still be a useful method for a tax researcher who tends towards less positivist approaches but is mindful of disciplinary expectations and boundaries (even if seeking to challenge them). There does need to be context and understanding of the theoretical underpinnings of the research and realistic expectations about what any one method, or combination of methods, can contribute to advancing knowledge. Every research method has its strengths and weaknesses and these need to be recognised. The important message here is for qualitative researchers to consider the opportunities by which a survey can enhance the quality of their research and provide opportunities for greater innovation in research design.

Notes

1 It is acknowledged that this chapter draws heavily on McKerchar (2010).
2 For more detailed discussion see Crotty (1998), Neuman (2006) and McKerchar (2010).
3 For example, critical realism and pragmatism as methodologies lie in the middle ground, whereas anarchism represents a more extreme stance. See McKerchar (2010) for further discussion on specific methodological approaches relevant to tax, law and accounting.
4 In an unstructured survey (or interview) the researcher is not restricted to a set range of questions and thus can ask different questions of each respondent if desired. For example, additional questions could be asked of any one respondent to probe a particular response and questions may be tailored to the circumstances of the individual. Similarly, in an unstructured survey the questions themselves are typically 'open' rather than 'closed'.
5 See, for example McKerchar (2005). The response rate for an email survey of tax agents in Australia was 1 percent. The invitation to participate in the survey was sent to all registered tax agents by the Australian Taxation Office on behalf of the researcher.
6 See Fowler (2009) for a useful discussion on calculating optimal sample sizes for survey research.

References

Axinn, W.G. and Pearce, L.D. (2006) *Mixed Method Data Collection Strategies*, Cambridge: Cambridge University Press.
Babbie, E. (2007) *The Practice of Social Research*, 11th edn, Belmont, CA: Wadsworth.
Bentley, D. (2007) *Taxpayer Rights: Theory, Origin and Implementation*, Alphen aan den Rijn: Kluwer Law International.
Bryman, A. (2008) 'The end of the paradigm wars?' in P. Alasuutari, L. Bickman and J. Brannen, *The Sage Handbook of Social Research Methods*, London: Sage, pp.13–25.
Coleman, J. (2009) 'Beyond inclusive legal positivism', *Ratio Juris* 22 (3): 359–94.
Crotty, M. (1998) *The Foundations of Social Research*, Sydney: Allen & Unwin.
De Vaus, D.A. (2002) *Surveys in Social Research*, 5th edn, Sydney: Allen and Unwin.
Flood, J. (2005) 'Socio-legal ethnography', in R. Banakar and M. Travers (eds), *Theory and Method in Socio-Legal Research*, Oxford: Hart Publishing, pp. 33–48.
Fowler, F.J., Jr (2009) *Survey Research Methods*, 4th edn, Thousand Oaks, CA: Sage.
Groves, R., Fowler, F., Jr, Couper, M., Lepkowski, E., Singer, E. and Tourangeau, R. (2004) *Survey Methodology*, New York: Wiley.
McKerchar, M. (1995) 'Understanding small business taxpayers: Their sources of information and level of knowledge of taxation', *Australian Tax Forum* 12 (1): 25–41.
——(2005) 'The impact of tax complexity on practitioners in Australia', *Australian Tax Forum* 20 (4): 529–54.
——(2010) *Design and Conduct of Research in Tax, Law and Accounting*, Sydney: Thomson Reuters.

McKerchar, M., Hodgson, H. and Datt, K. (2008) 'Is there a perception of revenue bias on the part of the ATO in private binding rulings on large, complex issues?', *Australian Tax Forum* 23 (3): 309–32.

Neuman, W.L. (2006) *Social Research Methods*, 6th edn, Boston, MA: Allyn and Bacon.

Peczenik, A. (2004) 'Can Philosophy Help Legal Doctrine?' *Ratio Juris* 17 (1): 106–17.

Perry, S. (2009) 'Beyond the Distinction Between Positivism and Non-Positivism', *Ratio Juris* 22 (3): 311–25.

Sarantakos, S. (2005) *Social Research*, 3rd edn, Basingstoke: Palgrave Macmillan.

Tooma, R.A. (2008) *Legislating Against Tax Avoidance*, Amsterdam: IBFD.

Yesegat, W.A. (2008) 'Value added tax in Ethiopia: A study of operating costs and compliance', unpublished PhD thesis, University of New South Wales, handle.unsw.edu.au/1959.4/43317 (accessed 14 November 2011).

6

USING QUANTITATIVE APPROACHES

Margaret McKerchar

Introduction

In the broad context of social research, the distinction between quantitative and qualitative data is basically the distinction between numeric and non-numeric (typically textual) data.[1] Even observations that appear to be qualitative at the outset, such as a box ticked in a survey form, or responses to open-ended survey questions, are usually converted to a numeric form for analysis (Babbie 2007: 23). Without doubt, the quantification of data can make for easier analysis in that most of the techniques for analysing quantitative data are well established and, with computer assistance, are powerful tools, particularly for researchers with statistical skills. At the same time, it needs to be acknowledged that quantified data can lack depth of meaning and the drawing of useful insights and rich conclusions may not be simple at all.

The purpose of this chapter is to consider the different approaches that can be taken in interpreting data obtained using quantitative research methods, including the limitations of quantitative analysis when factors that are not easily quantified are brought into the analysis. Quantitative research methods used in tax research are primarily surveys and experiments, both of which are discussed in Chapter 5. It may be helpful at this stage to recognise that the literature also distinguishes at times between quantitative data and quantitative analysis, and qualitative data and qualitative analysis. The two types of data are reasonably straightforward concepts, as explained at the outset of this chapter. Quantitative analysis refers to the numerical examination and interpretation of observations, and qualitative analysis refers to the examination and interpretation of observations by non-numeric means (Babbie 2007: 410). Thus, the process of analysis can be distinguished from the form of the data. The distinction is important as it is possible to undertake quantitative analysis of qualitative data and, similarly, to undertake qualitative analysis of quantitative data (see Babbie 2007: 400; also Elliott 2005: 172). Against this background, discussion now turns to the techniques of quantitative analysis of data and how it can contribute to qualitative research.

Quantitative analysis

The prerequisite for quantitative analysis is that the data itself be in numeric form. As stated at the outset, virtually all data begin in qualitative form, so the process of quantification needs to take place before quantitative analysis can begin. This is usually done through a process of coding of data and the codes used are typically unique to a particular research project, or used to facilitate comparisons with other existing data.

Where a unique coding system is to be used, it is usually based on the data collection procedure or instrument. For example, survey instruments often include a combination of closed and open-ended questions. Closed questions (i.e. where the respondent is required to choose the most appropriate answer from a given range of alternatives) can come in different forms such as yes/no, agree/disagree, age groups, income groups, occupation groups, or scaled responses from strongly agree to strongly disagree. The researcher assigns a numeric code to each alternative and the responses are then coded and recorded accordingly.

Closed questions can include an open-ended response, such as 'other' which then normally allows the respondent to provide a unique answer. It is appropriate where not all possible responses can be anticipated, or where there could be so many as to make the survey instrument unwieldy to complete. Codes then need to be developed for both the designated and the 'other' responses. For example, the question could be: 'Who prepares your tax return?' The alternatives provided could be: 'self', 'spouse', 'other family member', 'tax practitioner', 'friend', and 'other' (with a request to then provide details). In this example codes 1–5 could be used for the designated responses and then for those who have answered 'other', a coding system would need to be devised and recorded based on the responses received. That is, the qualitative data is transformed to enable its analysis by quantitative means. If some of the 'other' responses were, for instance, 'neighbour', 'work colleague' or 'community helper', then codes 6–9 could be allocated to these. Usually a miscellaneous code is needed for those responses that are of small frequency and do not fit within other categories. That is, there may have to be some 'collapsing' of data. Ideally coding (at least in the first instance) should be as extensive as possible and where collapsing is necessary, it should happen at a later stage. For example, the responses to the same question above could be collapsed (which will require data recoding) into 'self', 'family', 'tax practitioner' and 'miscellaneous' to enable data analysis.

Coded data is then typically entered as a dataset into an electronic spreadsheet (for example, Microsoft Excel), or a statistical software package, such as SPSS (Statistical Package for the Social Sciences). Excel spreadsheets can be imported into SPSS and statistical add-in packages (for example, PHStat) are also available for Excel. As well as coding the responses, the individual respondents and the variables themselves are coded so that they can be located within the dataset. It goes without saying that coding does require well-organised and detailed record-keeping on the part of the researcher.

Depending on how many records there are in a dataset, a visual check of the coding of all entries may be possible to ensure the accuracy of the data, such as checking the columns to ensure that valid codes have been entered. Where a visual check of all records is not possible, you should consider at least doing an additional check of a range of randomly selected records (for example, every tenth record in the dataset). Extra time spent on improving the accuracy of the dataset prior to beginning analysis can save considerable time in the long run. Having to repeat analyses because of dataset inaccuracies can be very frustrating and is usually avoidable if sufficient care is taken when inputting data. Even worse, not spotting the error in the first place will lead to incorrect conclusions and, as a result, having your results publicly questioned.

The use of e-surveys (where the data is input into a spreadsheet automatically), and other methods of direct data entry such as optical scanning and bar-coding, can help reduce data entry errors, though this will depend on the extent of the controls in place (Neuman 2006: 346). For example, it is quite simple to control only a valid range of codes for each question (i.e. a yes/no question can only have one of two possible codes), but embedding controls for internal consistency (such as where a male respondent indicates that he is 20–25 years of age but has over 30 years in business) can be more demanding and it may be that visual scans of data will still be necessary. Once the dataset is complete, quantitative analysis can begin and this typically requires the use of a range of statistical analyses using descriptive and inferential statistics.

Descriptive statistics

Descriptive statistics refers to the simple manipulations of data undertaken to describe the basic patterns that exist and includes univariate, bivariate and multivariate statistics (Neuman 2006). Univariate statistics refers to manipulations in respect of one variable only, such as mean, median, mode, frequency distributions, and measures of dispersion including standard deviation. Bivariate statistics refers to manipulations of two variables and is typically undertaken to establish whether or not they are related. For example, the chi-square statistic ($\aleph^2$) is a measure of 'goodness of fit' appropriate for large samples and is used to determine whether or not to reject a null hypothesis (e.g. that there is no relationship between *x* and *y*). Researchers commonly use many other types of bivariate statistics, or measures of correlation, including Rho, which is also referred to as the Pearson correlation coefficient. Multivariate analysis refers to the statistical analysis of more than two variables simultaneously. It can be presented in simple form (e.g. tabular) or more complex forms including regression analysis.

Descriptive statistics cannot identify the direction of a relationship or its strength. That is, *x* and *y* may be related, but is *x* the cause (i.e. independent variable) of *y* (i.e. dependent variable) or is the relationship in the other direction? In non-experimental research, statistics are used to introduce control variables in order to gauge whether they influence the bivariate relationship being studied. For example, the researcher may test for a relationship between perceptions of fairness of a tax system and a taxpayer's income level, but there could well be other variables affecting these perceptions, including age, gender and level of education. These additional variables can either be controlled or their effects statistically removed. Multiple regression analysis is another way of introducing control variables and is often used in social research. The results can not only indicate how well a set of variables (with or without control variables) explains a dependent variable, but it can also measure the direction and size of the effect of each variable on a dependent variable. This form of multivariate analysis can be valuable for testing theories that state that multiple independent variables simultaneously cause one dependent variable (Neuman 2006: 369). For example, Torgler's (2007) study of tax morale (as the dependent variable) considers a wide range of independent variables, including moral rules and sentiments, perceptions of fairness, and the relationship between taxpayer and government.

Inferential statistics

Inferential statistics are the measures used for making inferences from findings based on sample observations to a larger population (Neuman 2006: 460). They rely on probability theory to formally test hypotheses and make more substantial claims beyond simply describing the observations, so care is needed in at least three respects. First, the sample must be drawn from the population about which inferences are being made. Second, inferential statistics assume that random sampling has been used as this, too, contributes to the representativeness of the observations. Third, inferences are made in the context of confidence levels (allowing for sampling errors), which need to be specified as they allow for inferences to be made about the statistical significance of the findings.

The power of inferential statistics is that they allow a researcher to state, with specific degrees of certainty, that specific sample results are likely to be true in a larger population. However, it needs to be recognised that the inferences may not always be correct. Apart from the three limitations discussed above, there are many aspects of the design and conduct of research that can impact on the accuracy of the inferential statistics. For example, both poorly worded survey questions and errors in data input can result in incorrect inferential statistics. Further, even if the researcher can design, measure, collect, code and calculate without errors, they still have to be able to interpret the results if the correct conclusions are to be drawn (Neuman 2006: 374). That is, the analysis of data stills needs to be linked back to theoretical concepts and how the research contributes to the existing body of knowledge.

Contribution of quantitative analysis to qualitative research

The various statistical analyses discussed above are the main techniques used in quantitative analysis. However, it needs to be recognised that qualitative researchers adopting interpretive approaches will generally not be concerned with undertaking statistical analysis of data simply because such an approach conflicts with their underlying philosophical beliefs about the creation of knowledge and the nature of truth. The interpretive qualitative researcher is not seeking objectivity or to prove or disprove hypotheses. Similarly, the qualitative researcher is not seeking to make statistical generalisations, but analytical ones.

How then can quantitative analysis contribute to interpretive qualitative research? One obvious possibility is that researchers who are more philosophically pragmatic may adopt mixed methodological approaches to their research and employ methods from different paradigms, including both quantitative and qualitative. In these cases the findings from the quantitative component (such as a structured survey) could be derived by quantitative analysis and used to inform or validate the qualitative component of the research. Another possibility is that some quantitative analysis techniques, such as content analysis, may offer some potential to qualitative researchers in terms of the systematic managing and categorising of data (Bryman 2008: 274). Content analysis is a means by which data contained in documents and texts (such as court transcripts, parliamentary *Hansard*, interview transcripts and field notes) are systematically coded, categorised and then quantified. These data can then be analysed to identify patterns and build theories, thereby informing the qualitative research. That is, the analysis does not extend to the testing of theories and hypotheses and remains consistent with the philosophy of qualitative research. A further possibility for quantitative analysis to contribute to qualitative research is evidenced by qualitative researchers with leanings towards positivism (for example, see Miles and Huberman 1994), who adopt more structured approaches to the analysis of qualitative data by using coding and different means of data display such as matrices, but resist extending the analysis to the quantification of data.

The coding of data is the constant theme in these various approaches to quantitative analysis of data. Earlier in the chapter the coding of open-ended questions in a structured survey (i.e. a quantitative research method) was considered. As discussed in Chapter 3, the purpose of coding in qualitative research is similar in that the researcher seeks to organise the data into categories on the basis of themes, concepts, or similar features that will allow for a reduction of data into a more manageable form to enable analytical (rather than statistical) generalisations to be made. The process of coding remains one whereby data is disassembled and reassembled (Ezzy 2002: 94).

Interpretive qualitative researchers generally start with a more fluid approach to coding in that they are not necessarily seeking yes/no responses or responses within a pre-determined range. They record the data in the field in their raw form, not just what was said, but will also record details of the setting, the body language of the interviewee, the emotions expressed and so on. These recordings may be in the form of field notes, which may then be transcribed more fully and additional information (such as the researcher's impressions) included. These data are then coded iteratively and systematically by passing over it several times with each pass representing a stage of greater refinement as more sense is made of its meaning (see, for example, Strauss 1987). Again, the qualitative researcher is not seeking the objective truth, but an interpretation of the truth. The more systematic and transparent the process of data coding, the more robust and replicable is the research, and the greater the credibility given to its findings. In this sense, aspects of quantitative analysis may help qualitative researchers seeking to convince others of the merits of their research.

However, researchers do need to appreciate that barriers exist between quantitative analysis of data and qualitative research, even if they are not insurmountable. While it appears to be acceptable to engage in qualitative analysis of quantitative data, quantitative analysis of qualitative data still remains a contentious area and should be approached only after careful consideration (Babbie 2007: 400). Bryman (2008: 598–9) makes three pertinent observations related to the quantification of qualitative data that are relevant here.

First, in the thematic analysis of qualitative data, some implicit quantification does take place as the researcher looks for the number of occurrences or repeats of a theme or code, which are then given greater prominence when building theories. Second, there is considerable evidence of quasi-quantification in qualitative research when researchers use terms such as 'many', 'rarely' and so on. Bryman believes that some limited amount of quantification may be more appropriate than the use of these imprecise terms when alluding to quantity. Third, Bryman observes that the extent of anecdotalism often evident in qualitative research makes it appear less rigorous, and that some limited quantification of data may help to address this perceived shortcoming. In other words, Bryman advocates that some quantification of qualitative data may be worth consideration, but only to the extent that it enhances the qualitative research.

Concluding comments

Quantitative analysis techniques are typically not used by qualitative researchers but they do offer the potential to inform and enhance social research. These techniques rely mainly on the coding of data as the first step in the process of making meaning. Various statistical analyses are available that enable the researcher to make statistical generalisations about broader populations, though the reliability of these will depend on a range of factors including the means of sample selection, the size of the sample, the wording of the questions posed and so on. However, given that interpretive qualitative researchers are generally not intent on proving or disproving hypotheses or making statistical generalisations, their use of statistical analysis is usually limited. Still, by undertaking systemic and iterative coding of data, some of the techniques of quantitative analysis do offer the potential to qualitative researchers to inform or enhance their findings. It is important to remember that different research methods do create different expectations when it comes to the nature of the knowledge claims that can be reasonably made and that researchers need to exercise care in this regard.

Note

1 It is acknowledged that McKerchar (2010) has been relied upon substantially in the writing of this chapter.

References

Babbie, E. (2007) *The Practice of Social Research*, 11th edn, Belmont, CA: Thomson Wadsworth.

Bryman, A. (2008) *Social Research Methods*, 3rd edn, Oxford: Oxford University Press.

Elliott, J. (2005) *Using Narrative in Social Research*, London: Sage.

Ezzy, D. (2002) *Qualitative Analysis: Practice and Innovation*, Sydney: Allen & Unwin.

McKerchar, M. (2010) *Design and Conduct of Research in Tax, Law and Accounting*, Sydney: Thomson Reuters.
Miles, M. and Huberman, A. (1994) *Qualitative Data Analysis: An Expanded Sourcebook*, 2nd edn, Thousand Oaks, CA: Sage.
Neuman, W. (2006) *Social Research Methods*, 6th edn, Boston, MA: Pearson Education.
Strauss, A. (1987) *Qualitative Analysis for Social Scientists*, Cambridge: Cambridge University Press.
Torgler, B. (2007) *Tax Compliance and Tax Morale: A Theoretical and Empirical Analysis*, Cheltenham: Edward Elgar.

7

ETHNOGRAPHY AND TAX COMPLIANCE

Karen Boll

Introduction

> An ethnography is the study of an intact cultural group in a natural setting over a prolonged period of time, primarily by collecting observational data, but [it] can also include data collected by focus groups or in-depth interviews ... Given its conditions of conduct, its application to tax research is limited.
>
> *(McKerchar 2008: 14)*

Tax researcher Margaret McKerchar is right in stating that ethnographic studies today have had limited application within tax research. In fact, it is hardly possible to find studies within the tax field that directly employ an ethnographic approach. However, this state of affairs need not characterise the future of tax research. For instance, if we look at the field of tax compliance research the approach is relevant. An advantage of using ethnography to study tax compliance is that such a study opens up the possibility of analysing the practicalities, artefacts, exciting small details and expressions that are part of tax compliance as it is played out on a daily basis in businesses. Most tax compliance researchers – i.e. social psychologists, economists and statisticians – use a quantitative framework for their research. This means that they use surveys, experiments and questionnaires to analyse tax compliance. This also means that their research tends to be quite distant from the actual locations wherein tax compliance is played out in practice. One wonders if these analysts have ever been in a business office? Or have they ever been sitting behind the desk approving invoices? Probably not. Conducting an ethnographic study of tax compliance means to pay attention to how these very practical and complex elements of being compliant to the letter of the tax law are put together and worked out in the daily running of a business. These practicalities are almost always erased in quantitative tax compliance research where the focus typically is on how morals, norms and values influence tax compliance in more abstract ways (Ahmed and Braithwaite 2005; Alm *et al.* 2010; Ashby *et al.* 2009;

Kirchler 2007; Kornhauser 2007). In this respect, ethnographic research presents an opportunity to complement the current research by opening up an understanding of the concrete practicalities of tax compliance. This chapter therefore argues that ethnography is a highly relevant research approach for the tax field.[1]

The outline of the chapter is as follows. First, the chapter juxtaposes 'conventional' ethnography with 'recent' ethnography. This illustrates some of the specific characteristics of present-day ethnography which also applies when doing ethnography of tax compliance. Also, it should fend off some of the stereotypes about what ethnography is, which might hinder both researchers and informants in engaging in ethnographic research. Second, the chapter introduces the way in which the author has studied tax compliance by means of ethnography. It provides an idea of how an ethnographic study of tax compliance can be played out and which difficulties using the approach also prompt for the researcher. Finally, it refers to a number of related studies which might serve as inspiration for doing further ethnographic research on tax compliance.

Ethnography

The term ethnography denotes a qualitative research method for generating and analysing empirical material. Ethnography usually implies a combination of field techniques such as note-taking, audio-recording, interviewing, examining written material, observation and participant observation. These techniques are rooted in the ideal of studying the everyday context:

> People's actions and accounts are studied in everyday context, rather than under conditions created by the researcher – such as experimental setups or in highly structured interview situations. In other words, research takes place 'in the field'.
>
> *(Hammersley and Atkinson 2007: 2)*

The notions of 'everyday context' and 'in the field' are core concepts within ethnography as it is seen as central to grasp the practices, actions and concrete doings of the people studied. This is in contrast to research that relies on surveys and questionnaires where there is no direct aim of understanding the context wherein the phenomenon under study takes place. Furthermore, ethnographers are not necessarily interested in the 'polished' accounts of what people believe they do – which is reflected by a tick in a questionnaire – but they are interested in the enacted practices themselves in a specific field site. It is through the observations of these that knowledge as to how the phenomenon under study operates, changes and reproduces is created. In spite of the centrality of the focus on the field, there are within ethnography itself divergent views on what constitutes the field. Below, the 'conventional' and 'recent' views are presented.

Conventionally, ethnography was developed within anthropology and involved the idea of a relatively long stay in a field site usually located outside the Western world. The field site was seen as a 'container' of information about social relations and culture, which the ethnographer could 'harvest' during the fieldwork. Basically, the ethnographer was supposed to be 'living with a group of people … in order to document and interpret their distinctive way of life, and the beliefs and values integral to it' (Hammersley and Atkinson 2007: 1). This way of doing ethnography was suited to study cultures that were relatively well-defined in a single location, for instance in a village or a neighbourhood. Also, the informants in these studies were often characterised by being relatively powerless in relation to the ethnographer. They had, of course, something to say about how the ethnographer could conduct his or her fieldwork in their community, but nearly no power as to how the ethnographer represented them in writing (Forsythe 2001: 121).

Today, much ethnography, at least the ethnography dealt with in this chapter, is based on other assumptions about the field and about the relationship between ethnographer and the subjects under study. For instance, ethnography is increasingly conducted in Western societies and within powerful groups. This can include phenomena such as tax practices, bureaucracy, law-making or accounting. The ethnographer does not necessarily travel halfway around the globe but might go the local tax office to conduct fieldwork. In these cases the ethnographer does not necessarily 'study down' on powerless groups such as indigenous people or minorities. Instead, the ethnographer 'studies up' on powerful people like politicians, law-makers, tax inspectors, accountants, or other academics (Forsythe 2001: 119). This alters the relationship between the ethnographer and the informants since both often have stakes involved in the research. The ethnographer might be dependent on funding or salary from the people studied. Also the studied might be affected by the way the ethnographer represents them in analysis, as the analysis might be critical towards taken-for-granted perceptions, organisational arrangements or beliefs. Thus, compared with 'conventional' ethnography, the ethnographer and the people studied are now increasingly engaged in new ways that influence the way the study is conducted and perceived.

Furthermore, many of the objects that now are being studied ethnographically cannot be found in one single, well-defined location. Instead, they are dispersed over several places. For instance, studying law-making could imply focusing on the parliament, group meetings of politicians, law-makers in ministries, the citizens affected by the law, or on the groups lobbying for the law. This illustrates that law-making cannot be situated in one single location. Consequently, much recent ethnographic fieldwork is conducted as 'multi-sited', meaning that the researchers follow the object of study in different sites where it presents itself (Marcus 1995).

Finally, today research sites are seen less as containers of culture that can be neutrally observed. The ethnographer is not merely 'a walking tape recorder' documenting everything that happens (Forsythe 2001). Instead, the ethnographer actively participates in constructing the site and study object by the choice of locations to go to and with the choice of theoretical approach. Hence the researcher does not 'harvest' empirical material but he or she actively constructs the empirical material based on the theoretical assumptions from which the study departs. Concerning the theoretical aspect of ethnography the authors behind the edited book *Ethnographies Revisited: Constructing Theory in the Field* (Puddephatt *et al.* 2009) write: 'Theory tends to hold an ambivalent place in ethnographic research … many prefer not to trouble themselves about theoretical issues, or treat theory as a general evil to be avoided' (ibid.: 3). However, this chapter argues that understanding theory is pivotal in doing ethnography, as ethnography is not just a data-harvesting technique but also always a thorough theoretical endeavour.

These characteristics of ethnography are relevant considerations when aiming at conducting an ethnographic study of tax compliance. Below this is illustrated by looking at how an ethnographic study of tax compliance can be done. The reflections are based upon the author's ethnographic fieldwork of tax compliance practices. The study was conducted in Denmark in 2009–10 and was part of the author's PhD project (Boll 2011).

Doing an ethnographic study of tax compliance

Locating tax compliance in space and time

Conducting an ethnographic study of tax compliance requires reflection as to where and when to find this object of study. For a 'conventional' ethnographer this might be the least challenging thing to do when starting a study. The object of study might be indigenous people or a suburban culture that can be investigated by going to a specific village, island or neighbourhood. The object of study is defined in a single location that the ethnographer can visit. Studying tax compliance 'locating the location' is more difficult as there is no single obvious site wherein tax compliance practices take place. When I initiated my ethnographic study of tax compliance I therefore started out by reflecting upon where to go to observe tax compliance.

Are tax compliance practices to be found in business offices in the form of bookkeepers' filing invoices? Are tax compliance practices enacted as business owners have meetings with accountants? Are they played out when tax inspectors come on unannounced walk-ins? Or is tax compliance played out in the tax administration's bureaucratic procedures? Which of these locations and events – business offices, meetings with accountants, unannounced walk-ins or bureaucratic procedures – are the most relevant settings for tax compliance? Which of these places should and could I visit to observe tax compliance in action? The different locations where tax compliance is present illustrates that I have come to think of tax compliance as a dispersed practice. This realisation inspired me to plan a 'multi-sited' ethnography in which I investigated multiple locations where tax compliance occurs.

Initially, I visited a number of small and medium-sized businesses where I assumed I could find and observe tax compliance practices. I observed and interviewed business owners and bookkeepers. I sat beside the bookkeepers and saw how they used their computers, ring binders, plastic pockets, colour pens and calculating machines to manage tax compliance. I first considered longer fieldwork in just one business to investigate how tax compliance plays out in a single business. However, this plan was changed because I became concerned about spending too much time in the business at times when the business did not do anything related to tax. I learned that many small and medium-sized businesses do not perform tax compliance every day: they register, document, file and pay on specific, appointed dates. This was one of my first ethnographic insights. I risked sitting for hours and days unable to observe tax compliance practices. Instead, I decided to visit several businesses and to ask the bookkeepers to tell more about and show me the work they do related with tax compliance.

Also, I gained the opportunity to follow a project in a local Danish tax office during a ten-month period. This project was about fraud with invoices when used cars are sold at auctions. During this fieldwork I sat in on project group meetings and noted down what happened. I came to understand how the tax inspectors represented the businesses that they wished to regulate. I went on visits to businesses and an auction house with the tax inspectors. I followed the tax inspectors as they interviewed bookkeepers and inspected the bookkeeping in the businesses. I observed meetings with citizens suspected of fraud. These people were summoned to the local tax office to account for their car sales and private finances. Also, I read all meeting minutes, reports, case descriptions and other official documents connected to the project.

As the examples show, studying tax compliance has meant studying a number of different sites where tax compliance is found, be it in the business, an auction house or in the meetings in the local tax office. My object of study is enacted in multiple locations and was studied via multi-sited ethnography where I 'follow people, connections, associations and relationships across space' (Falzon 2009: 2). The examples should also demonstrate that tax compliance practices are not solely dispersed in time over several locations but they are also dispersed in time. The study object cannot be found everyday but is played out at specific dates and times. For instance, practices concerning value-added tax (VAT) are only performed at specific times during the month and year when VAT reporting is done.

After conducting the ethnographic fieldwork one might ask what kind of material has been generated. Upon what does the ethnographer actually base his or her analysis? When quantitative researchers do their analysis they typically have a set of questionnaires or experiments that need to be analysed. This is the empirical material on which they rely and which they analyse. The empirical material of an ethnographic study has a different character. In my case it consisted of notes from the fieldwork. I have a vast amount of handwritten notes describing situations I observed during the fieldwork. It consists of printed materials such as emails, letters, minutes and the case workers' descriptions of their cases. It features photos of places where my fieldwork took place, for instance the tax office, the auction house and the bookkeepers' offices. In addition it also consists of transcriptions of interviews and supplementary descriptions of the interview situations. Finally, it consists of official strategies of how the Danish tax authority is working with tax compliance and information on how it tries to influence tax inspectors and businesses to comply. I have assembled this material in six ring binders which is now the sum of my empirical basis for the analysis of tax compliance practices.

Access, 'studying up' and studying the mundane

To continue with the focus on investigating tax compliance it is also necessary to consider issues of access. Tax authorities might be hesitant about giving an ethnographer access to case work concerning specific businesses and they might be unwilling to let the ethnographer participate in checks because of confidentiality.[2] Also, the businesses involved might be reluctant to engage with an ethnographer. This may be because they wish to protect business strategies. They may think it takes up too much time or they cannot see the purpose of having an ethnographer 'hanging around'.

A central dimension here is 'studying up' and accessing something that is very different from the 'conventional' ethnographic study object. In my experience that the people studied in relation to tax compliance – auditors, bookkeepers, tax inspectors and academics – have their own established methods and approaches on which they rely for analysis. This is typically auditing, accounting, statistics and law. From their perspective there is not a huge need for an ethnographic study of their practices as they are already 'knowledgeable'. Furthermore, they might very well hold an impression of ethnography as a study of something exotic and remote. They relate ethnography to 'conventional' ethnography and do not identify themselves with an 'indigenous' or 'exotic' study object. They might be puzzled as to how sitting for several hours in a tax office observing mundane case work can be part of an academic study. They may also become uncomfortable with the situation as they feel monitored by the ethnographer. People like tax inspectors and auditors are also powerful informants. I have experienced objection to my analysis of their practices and I have been made fun of as the 'silly academic' who believes it is possible to learn anything about tax compliance through an ethnographic study. As informants might be suspicious towards the ethnographic method and towards themselves as study objects it is even more important to justify the study to them. I justified my study by explaining that an ethnographic study produces knowledge about what constitutes tax compliance. This can complement knowledge about how tax compliance is understood as a legal and technical practice. This justified my research to a large extent. However, it is clear that some still saw the research as less relevant and interesting.

Analysing data

In the first part of this chapter I used Puddephatt *et al.* (2009) to highlight the fact that theory plays a particular role in ethnography. Regarding theory, they write:

> [T]heoretical frames can often provide a context and a trained sociological eye to approach and interpret the social patterns, viewpoints, and behavior of the groups we observe in unique, imaginative, and penetrating ways.
>
> *(Puddephatt* et al. *2009: 2)*

Thus theory can help the researcher to focus on certain interpretations and analyses. Furthermore, in this understanding of theory a theoretical basis always influences how the empirical material is generated. Observations are not 'neutral' but they have a certain 'theory-laden' character (Knorr-Cetina and Mulkay 1983: 4). This means that whether the researcher is inspired by pragmatism, symbolic interactionism, constructivism, grounded theory or the like, these theoretical assumptions influence how the empirical material is generated.[3] Each of such theoretical approaches equips the researcher with certain assumptions and a lens, which give a 'theory-laden' character to what the researcher observes during fieldwork. It is important that such assumptions behind the research are clarified before starting the ethnographic study, as they guide what the researcher focuses on as well as how the ethnographic descriptions and analyses are made.

It is important to note that my own fieldwork on tax compliance practices was informed by constructivism and more particularly by Actor-Network Theory (ANT). This approach urged me to focus on certain elements in relation to tax compliance practices, for instance how non-human actors are involved in enacting tax compliance, how tax compliance is not solely a social matter and how ideas about tax compliance travel from a business setting to the tax authority (for more information on ANT see Chapter 16). Had I, for instance, studied tax compliance using a Foucauldian lens the focus would have been otherwise. In such a case the focus would probably have been on discourse and the tax authority as a disciplinary power.

The point I wish to raise here is again that the ethnographer is not a 'walking tape recorder' neutrally documenting reality. Rather, the ethnographic observations are influenced by the theoretical perspective to which the ethnographer subscribes. This also means that two ethnographies on the same subject may be dissimilar. McKerchar suggests that what characterises interpretivism/qualitative research is that 'interpretivism provides an understanding of social reality that is based on the subjective interpretation of the researcher' (McKerchar 2008: 7). In my understanding of ethnography, saying that ethnographies are dissimilar does not mean, as McKerchar indicates, that analysis is based on different 'subjective interpretation'. On the contrary, the ethnographic observations differ as they rely on different theoretical frames and different conceptualisations of the field and its sites.

In summary, what should be illustrated so far is that doing ethnographic fieldwork is a practical activity. It is an activity that involves finding places to go, times to go, writing field notes and gaining access to field sites. Furthermore, doing ethnography should also be understood as a reflexive activity. It requires reflection upon one's own theoretical assumptions and on how the generated material should be analysed. My hope is that ethnography in the future will be used more in tax compliance research. Using an ethnographic approach holds the potential for creating knowledge about the practicalities of tax compliance which are aspects currently absent in tax compliance research. The chapter should also illustrate that today ethnography is much more than just a study of an intact cultural group in a natural setting over a prolonged period of time, which is the 'conventional' perception of ethnography. As shown here ethnography provides an alternative approach to study tax compliance practices which generates central insights for both academics and tax-regulating authorities.

Ethnography of tax and related research areas

To end this chapter, these last paragraphs provide an overview of a number of relevant studies that might inspire ethnographic studies of tax. First of all it should be mentioned that there are not many (if any) researchers who have conducted ethnographic studies of tax compliance or tax in general. However, there are researchers who have looked at tax from a social science perspective and who focus on the social and institutional aspects of tax which are some of the key aspects of an ethnography. See, for instance, Mulligan's (2008) study of understanding tax planning in practice; Lamb's (2001) study of the Carlyles' income taxes, which focuses on an 'understanding of taxation as a social and institutional practice that relies on accounting and entails accountability' (ibid.: 273); Waller's (2006) study of tax morale among used-car dealers; Ashby and Webley's (2008) study of the taxpaying culture in the hairdressing/beauty industry; Preston's (1989) study of the record company Axis; Pentland and Carlile's (1996) study of auditing as an expression game; and Carrol's (1987) study of compliance as a decision-making process. To describe these studies as ethnographic is an exaggeration of their approach as they primarily use interviews, and only then build their analysis on observations, but they are the nearest one can get to ethnographic studies of tax.

To broaden the perspective, it should be mentioned that there are two areas related to tax where ethnographic approaches are more widely used. These are critical-accounting studies and social studies of finance. Within the former, ethnographic studies that in different ways illustrate accounting practices have been conducted in a steel mill (Ahrens and Mollona 2007), in the Caterpillar plant (Miller and O'Leary 1994, 2002), and in a psoriasis clinic (Frandsen 2009). Within the latter, MacKenzie has in recent years been the main advocator of social studies of finance, which has yielded a number of ethnographic studies, for instance a study of a French strawberry market (Garcia-Parpet 2007), and a study of the Chicago Stock Exchange (MacKenzie and Millo 2003).

For anyone considering ethnography as an approach to their research, it is advisable to look at other studies such as these, but there is certainly considerable scope for this way of researching to add to our understanding of how tax works in the field.

Notes

1 The author of the chapter has also conducted fieldwork focusing on suburban identity, minority cultures and organisational changes. It is her experience from these studies and from a Master's degree in ethnology that the author draws upon when arguing that ethnography can be applied to the field of tax compliance.

2 In the present case access was made easier as I had been employed at the Ministry of Taxation prior to starting my PhD study. In this way the decision-makers knew me and they were keen to get the study started to see what would be the result of an ethnographic study of tax compliance.

3 For more examples of theoretical approaches that can be used in tax research, see McKerchar (2008).

References

Ahmed, E. and Braithwaite, V. (2005) 'Understanding small business taxpayers: Issues of deterrence, tax morale, fairness and work practice', *International Small Business Journal* 23(5): 539–68.

Ahrens, T. and Mollona, M. (2007) 'Organisational control as cultural practice: A shop floor ethnography of a Sheffield steel mill', *Accounting, Organizations and Society* 32(4–5): 305–31.

Alm, J., Martinez-Vazquez, J. and Torgler, B. (2010) *Developing alternative frameworks for explaining tax compliance*, New York: Routledge.

Ashby, J.S. and Webley, P. (2008) '"But everyone else is doing it": a closer look at the occupational taxpaying culture of one business sector, *Journal of Community & Applied Social Psychology* 18(3): 194–210.

Ashby, J.S., Webley, P. and Haslam, A.S. (2009) 'The role of occupational taxpaying cultures in taxpaying behaviour and attitudes', *Journal of Economic Psychology*, 30(2): 216–27.

Boll, K. (2011) Taxing Assemblages Laborious and Meticulous Achievements of Tax Compliance. PhD thesis, IT University of Denmark.

Carroll, J.S. (1987) 'Compliance with the Law: A decision-making approach to taxpaying', *Law and Human Behavior* 11(4): 319–35.

Falzon, M.-A. (ed.) (2009) *Multi-sited Ethnography: Theory, Praxis and Locality in Contemporary Research*, Farnham: Ashgate.

Forsythe, D. (2001) *Studying Those Who Study Us. An Anthropologist in the World of Artificial Intelligence*, Stanford, CA: Stanford University Press.

Frandsen, A.-C. (2009) 'From psoriasis to a number and back', *Information and Organization* 19 (2): 103–28.

Garcia-Parpet, M.-F. (2007) 'The social construction of a perfect market: The strawberry action at Fontaines-en-Sologne', in D. MacKenzie, F. Muniesa and L. Siu (eds), *Do Economists Make Markets? On the Performativity of Economics*, Princeton, NJ: Princeton University Press, pp. 20–54.

Hammersley, M. and Atkinson, P. (2007) *Ethnography: principles in practice*, third edn, London and New York: Routledge.

Kirchler, E. (2007) *The Economic Psychology of Tax Behaviour*, New York and Cambridge: Cambridge University Press.

Knorr-Cetina, K.D. and Mulkay, M. (eds) (1983) *Science Observed. Perspectives in the Social Study of Science*, London: Sage Publications.

Kornhauser, M.E. (2007) 'Normative and cognitive aspects of tax compliance: Literature review and recommendations for the IRS regarding individual taxpayers', in N.E. Olson (ed.), *National Taxpayer Advocate – 2007 Annual Report to Congress*, Research Studies and Reports, Vol.2, Taxpayer Advocate Service, pp. 138–80.

Lamb, M.A. (2001) '"Horrid appealing": accounting for taxable profits in mid-nineteenth century England, *Accounting, Organizations and Society* 26(3): 271–98.

MacKenzie, D. and Millo, Y. (2003) 'Constructing a market, performing theory: The historical sociology of a financial derivatives exchange', *American Journal of Sociology* 109(1): 107.

McKerchar, M.A. (2008) 'Philosophical paradigms, inquiry strategies and knowledge claims: Applying the principles of research design and conduct to taxation', *eJournal of Tax Research* 6(1): 5–22.

Marcus, G.E. (1995) 'Ethnography in/of the World System: The Emergence of Multi-Sited Ethnography', *Annual Review of Anthropology* 24(1): 95.

Miller, P. and O'Leary, T. (1994) 'Accounting, "economic citizenship" and the spatial reordering of manufacture', *Accounting, Organizations and Society* 19(1): 15–43.

——(2002) 'Rethinking the Factory: Caterpillar Inc', *Journal for Cultural Research* 6(1): 91–117.

Mulligan, E. (2008) *Tax Planning in Practice: A Field Study of US Multinational Corporations*, Warwick Business School, University of Warwick.

Pentland, B.T. and Carlile, P. (1996) 'Audit the taxpayer, not the return: Tax auditing as an expression game', *Accounting, Organizations and Society* 21(2–3): 269–87.

Preston, A.M. (1989) 'The taxman cometh: Some observations on the interrelationship between accounting and Inland Revenue practice', *Accounting, Organizations and Society* 14 (5–6): 389–413.

Puddephatt, A.J., Shaffir, W. and Kleinknecht, S.W. (eds) (2009) *Ethnographies Revisited: Constructing Theory in the Field*, London and New York: Routledge.

Waller, V. (2006) *Tax Morale Amongst Used Car Dealers*, Regulatory Institutions Network, Australian National University.

8

MORAL REASONING IN TAX PRACTICE

The development of an assessment instrument

Elaine Doyle, Jane Frecknall Hughes and Barbara Summers

Introduction

Ethics is an important issue in tax practice, with ethical dilemmas involving tax issues being identified by members of the American Institute of Certified Public Accountants as posing the most difficult ethical or moral problem for them (Finn *et al.* 1988: 607–9). Cognitive developmental psychologists believe that before an individual reaches a decision about how and whether to behave ethically in a specific situation, ethical or moral reasoning takes place at a cognitive level. The psychology of moral reasoning aims to understand how people think about moral dilemmas and the processes they use in approaching them. Kohlberg (1973) developed a six-stage model of moral reasoning based on concepts of social cooperation and justice. James Rest (1979a) subsequently developed a test, named the Defining Issues Test (DIT), which is based directly on Kohlberg's model and measures moral reasoning. The DIT is "a broad, general measure of moral reasoning" (Fisher 1997: 143), acceptable in dealing with personal issues in a social context (Fraedrich *et al.* 1994). However, concern has been expressed that it does not, and cannot, fairly represent the reasoning used in facing ethical dilemmas in a business context (Trevino 1986, 1992; Weber 1990; Elm and Weber 1994; Fraedrich *et al.* 1994; Welton *et al.* 1994; Dellaportas *et al.* 2006).

Investigating moral reasoning in a particular context, therefore, requires an instrument that uses dilemmas from that context. This chapter describes the process of developing such an instrument, using a tax context-specific adaptation of Rest's well-known and validated DIT, to examine the ethical reasoning of tax practitioners.[1] The development of this instrument was part of a larger project which combined the newly developed context-specific instrument with the short version of the original DIT (to investigate moral reasoning in the social and tax contexts), and disseminated it to both tax practitioners and non-tax specialists (the control group) in order to examine the moral reasoning of tax practitioners relative to non-specialists in both contexts. The use of a control group addressed one of the gaps in prior DIT research carried out on professionals. A control group was considered critical in this study to allow the results to be interpreted in relation to tax practitioners. For example, if tax practitioners should reason differently in social and tax contexts this cannot be attributed to their professional status unless we know how those outside the profession behave; the result might just reflect the reasoning norms of society at large.

The development of the tax-context instrument itself is the primary focus of this chapter.

The Defining Issues Test

Kohlberg's model of ethical cognition (stage-sequence theory), upon which the DIT is based, sets out three developmental levels through which individuals move as they develop and experience social interaction: the 'pre-conventional morality' level, the 'conventional morality' level, and the 'post-conventional morality' level (although not all individuals reach this level). Within each of the three levels there are two developmental steps, resulting in a total of six stages. The DIT is a self-administered, multiple-choice instrument, making use of social ethical dilemmas used by Kohlberg in his original analysis, (e.g. 'Heinz and the drug', see Appendix A). Rest (1979a) developed this test based on an interpretation of the stages in Kohlberg's theory (see Table 8.1).

Table 8.1 Six stages of ethical reasoning

Pre-conventional: Focuses on the individual	Stage one	The morality of obedience: do what you are told
	Stage two	The morality of instrumental egoism and simple exchange: let's make a deal
Conventional: Focuses on the group and relationships	Stage three	The morality of interpersonal concordance: be considerate, nice and kind: you'll make friends
	Stage four	The morality of law and duty to the social order: everyone in society is obligated to and protected by the law
Post-conventional: Move towards universalism and thus strive towards general norms	Stage five	The morality of consensus-building procedures: you are obligated by the arrangements that are agreed to by due process procedures
	Stage six	The morality of non-arbitrary social co-operation: morality is defined by how rational and impartial people would ideally organise co-operation

(Adapted from Rest 1994)

Participants taking the DIT are presented with either six (long-form DIT) or three (short-form DIT) ethical dilemmas stated in third-person form. The dilemmas are presented as narratives describing the circumstances of the third party who must make a decision about how to act in the scenario. After reviewing the dilemmas, participants choose what the actor should do in the circumstances from three alternatives offered: 'take the action', 'do not take the action', or 'cannot decide'. They are then asked to rate the importance of 12 statements relating to the particular dilemma (known as the 'items for consideration'), indicating how important each is (in their opinion) in making the decision described in the scenario using a five-point scale (great importance, much importance, some, little or no importance). The 12 statements were constructed by Rest to represent issues that would be prevalent for individuals at particular stages of ethical development. The participant is asked to select the four items that he/she considers to be of most importance to the decision and to rank these in order of importance (first through fourth). This part of the test produces the score which is usually the focus of analysis in DIT research, the P score. The P score measures the percentage of responses at stages five and six made by an individual across the three (or six) cases. The P score thus measures the comprehension and preference for the principled level of reasoning (Rest *et al.* 1999).

Context-specific tests

As mentioned in the introduction, many researchers contend that a test of moral reasoning based entirely on dilemmas in a social context cannot necessarily reflect moral reasoning in business contexts (Weber 1991; Ponemon 1993; Dellaportas *et al.* 2006). This has led to the development of context-specific instruments based on the DIT in a number of areas.[2] This use of the DIT as a basis for context-specific instruments also offers a potential opportunity to compare results across studies, and this in turn brings methodology into focus: instruments need ideally to be developed and administered in such a way that comparability with the original DIT and with each other is valid.

Many of the papers reporting use of a context-specific DIT, however, devote only a small amount of coverage to the actual process of test development, having their primary focus on delivering results in domain-specific ethics rather than on methodology. As it stands, the development of context-specific instruments does show some variation which has not been explored. In this context, this chapter examines briefly the characteristics and the nuances of the DIT and identifies the issues of concern in developing a context-specific DIT, and in the use of such instruments in domain and group comparisons. It then describes the process that was undertaken to develop a tax practice-context version of the DIT.

The properties of the DIT

Rest (1979b: Ch. 4) gives very specific guidance on how the DIT is constructed and the rationale behind the structure of the test. These properties need to be preserved in context-specific tests if the integrity of the test is to be retained.

It is important that moral judgement scenarios be framed in terms of the third person or in terms of what a hypothetical person would do (Rest 1979b: Ch. 4). Rest (ibid.: 69) warns that more than one test dilemma is needed, recommending that enough data be collected 'so that a general picture emerges that is not overly influenced by an idiosyncratic subject-situation interaction or by fluctuations in the subject's thinking'. He also suggests building in some diversity to the dilemmas used so that the P score is based on a representative sampling of possible situations.

For studies making comparisons between contexts, one aim may be to produce similarity between the two, so that different biases and influences on the results do not impair the comparison. Scenarios also need to be as realistic as possible, so that they invoke the domain being studied clearly, contributing to the ecological validity of the test.

The 'items for consideration' used in the DIT are designed to reflect factors that would be considered by individuals at particular stages of moral development. Rest (1979b: 90) suggests that these need to be short and cryptic. Short statements, using fragments of a line of ethical argument (rather than providing a complete logical argument), should be recognisable by someone who understands the line of thinking. The items should also be comparable in length, sentence complexity and vocabulary, and should avoid building an argument for one course of action over another.

In addition to items for consideration derived from the dilemma, Rest (1979b: 91) also includes meaningless but complex sounding items ('M' items – standing for 'meaningless'). These are scattered throughout the list of considerations as a trap for participants who opt for particular considerations because of their apparent complexity, pretentiousness and sophistication rather than because of their meaning. Should a participant select too many M items his/her test is regarded as invalid. Rest (1990: 4.2) also specifically includes some items (known as 'A' items) reflecting an 'anti-establishment' orientation. The A viewpoint typically condemns tradition and the existing social order for its arbitrariness or its corruption by the rich for the exploitation of the poor.

Rest (1979b) places a great degree of importance on the ordering of the items for consideration. Although it is common in other sorts of instrument, Rest does not see random ordering as optimal, recommending that low stage considerations appear early on the list, followed by a mix of considerations. Considerations at stages five and six should only be introduced after the fourth consideration on the list, and even then, should be mixed with considerations at stages three and four. The rationale for this is to introduce lower-stage ideas early in the list, so that less ethically developed participants can find their own ideas quickly and might therefore be less likely to project their thinking to a higher-stage item.

The DIT does not contain equal numbers of considerations at each stage of moral reasoning. The long-form DIT uses six scenarios, each with 12 considerations. No stage one considerations are included, on the basis that the reading level and general personal development required to take the test instrument would virtually eliminate the possibility of finding stage one participants (Rest 1979b). Similarly, there are very few stage two considerations. It is expected that participants' reasoning will cluster around stages three, four and the principled stages, and these should have roughly equal numbers of considerations (ibid.).

An analysis of previous studies shows a variety of approaches in terms of the number of scenarios, numbers of items for consideration, and items for consideration at each stage of reasoning included.[3] When undertaking comparative studies, however, many studies use the original DIT and a context-specific test so that reasoning over both social and work contexts can be compared. When taking this approach comparability of treatment in each context is important, as any variations can otherwise be put forward as explanations for significant results. If the original DIT is used as one comparison context, following Rest's approach would be necessary for the instruments developed for other contexts to maximise comparability. In particular, issues can arise if the number of items at each stage or the percentage of items at stages five and six differ from those in the original DIT. This is because the P score is the percentage of the overall score arising from these stages, and thus variations that affect its upper or lower limit can impact on comparability. Although weighted calculations can address this to some extent, differing contexts for judgement are still present and, as shown by Parducci (1968), the way a particular stimulus is judged can depend on the other stimuli in its context.

The development of the tax-specific test

There is a lack of information on the development process for scenarios in context-specific tests based on the DIT that have been developed in previous studies. However, a starting point for developing any such instrument is the relevant literature (see, for example, Marshall *et al.* 1998), followed by an exploration of issues with practitioners to develop an understanding of the types of ethical dilemmas that are actually encountered in practice. This was done in this study by means of semi-structured interviews with tax practitioners.

After undertaking a thorough review of the scenarios already developed for previous studies and the dilemmas discussed with and shared by interviewees, four dilemma types were selected and moulded into short vignettes. Although only three would be used in the new test, it was considered prudent to develop an extra scenario to allow the possibility of a scenario proving unsuitable in pilot testing. Following Sims (1999), the scenarios were written in a general manner to allow the respondents to be able to imagine themselves in the situation depicted by each scenario. As another aim of the larger study was to make a comparison between tax practitioners and non-specialists, particular attention was paid to language, and the use of tax jargon was eliminated to make the scenarios as clear as possible to non-specialists.

Once the tax-specific scenarios were initially drafted, a small focus group of a tax faculty (who all had a tax-practice background) was convened to read and debate whether a real ethical dilemma existed within each scenario, and whether the scenarios were realistic. A tax academic from another Irish university was also consulted for her views on the scenarios. The academics were invited to suggest other scenarios that might be suitable for use in a tax-specific DIT. On the basis of this feedback, three of the original scenarios were amended slightly, one of the scenarios was rejected and two new scenarios were drafted.

One of the difficulties in designing the scenarios was to balance realism with the need to represent a genuine ethical problem, while keeping the scenarios easy to read and understand. The DIT scenarios themselves describe situations that, while conceivable, are not common. In order to ensure that the scenarios were realistic in a tax-practice context, and following the example of Reckers *et al.* (1994), who had their scenarios reviewed by a number of professionals, the revised set of five scenarios was distributed to 30 tax practitioners working in firms of different sizes. The practitioners were asked, for each scenario, to give their views on the following (using a five-point Likert scale):

- how easy the scenario was to read and understand;
- the degree to which the scenario presented an ethical dilemma for the tax practitioner concerned;
- the realism of the scenario.

They were then asked to list the types of issues that they might consider if they were faced with the scenario and had to decide upon a course of action.

Although all scenarios scored highly in terms of readability and understandability, there was some variation in their ratings for presenting a dilemma and for realism. The two scenarios with the combined lowest scores for degree of dilemma presented and realism were eliminated. These scenarios were the two that had been developed after consultation with the tax academics. The three remaining original scenarios were amended further to reflect some of the comments made by practitioners. Finally, one entirely new scenario, based on a real situation, was developed after in-depth discussions with two of the tax practitioners who were anxious to contribute. While this was not tested on the 30 pilot tax practitioner participants, its realism cannot be questioned.

Four robust scenarios thus emerged from the consultation and discussion outlined above, three of which had been through a number of rounds of alteration. One of the scenarios was eventually eliminated because it was quite similar to one of the others. The three remaining scenarios were finally further refined so that, to the maximum degree possible, they mirrored the three original short-form DIT scenarios in the sense of the psychological responses triggered by each story.

Once the scenarios themselves were drafted, a list of 'items for consideration' for each scenario needed to be developed. It was critical that the 12 considerations drafted to follow each of the tax-specific scenarios echoed Kohlberg's different stages of moral reasoning, to ensure comparability. The items themselves, however, also needed to be relevant to the tax-specific scenarios developed and flow naturally from them. They also needed to be drafted consistently with the wording and format of the DIT items for consideration at each stage of ethical development.

Following the example of Fisher (1997), the items for consideration for the tax scenarios were informed by comments gathered during interviews with tax practitioners on their perceptions of the dilemmas they raised. Four tax academics (referred to above) also contributed their views on the issues that a tax practitioner might consider when faced with the specific dilemmas, and the survey of tax practitioners elicited their views.

The number of considerations at each stage of ethical reasoning was matched to the DIT. In other words, when drafting the 12 considerations for the capital allowances scenario (see Appendix B), one stage-two item, three stage-three items, two stage-four items, two stage-five items, one stage-six item, one anti-establishment item and two meaningless items were included, in order to exactly match the number of items at each level in the Heinz scenario. The considerations at each stage were also listed in exactly the same order as those in the DIT scenarios. The range of issues put forward in the consultation made this possible without any items seeming contrived.[4]

Once the finalised tax scenarios and the items for consideration for each were drafted, a panel of three tax academics and one currently practising tax practitioner were asked independently to code the items, indicating the stage of moral development that they felt each represented. This was done using the table reproduced as Table 8.1 as a guide. While there was a very high level of consistency between the stages identified by the independent coders and the researcher (80 per cent), the items for consideration were altered slightly to address any ambiguities in the stages identified by the panel.

Finally, following some of the prior research involving the development of context-specific DITs in the accounting and auditing area (Welton *et al.* 1994; Thorne 2000; Massey 2002), the tax-context test instrument was validated by two recognised DIT scholars.[5] This provided a further check on the reliability with which the items were coded. Some further modifications were made to the scenarios and the items for consideration on the basis of the feedback from the DIT scholars. The full research instrument, consisting of the short-form DIT, the specific tax test and a demographic questionnaire, was then pilot tested on a small group of tax practitioners and non-specialists.

Table 8.2 summarises the process of developing both scenarios and items for consideration.

If comparisons are to be made between contexts and groups, another issue that needs to be addressed is the potential for order effects. If all participants were to answer the DIT scenarios first and then the tax scenarios, differences might arise because the first set of scenarios primed participants to think in a particular way. A counter-balanced design was therefore used, with one version of the instrument having the DIT scenarios first, and the other the tax scenarios. This facilitates checking for order effects and adopting an averaged view in comparative analysis. As the literature does not indicate that the scenarios for the DIT are presented in different orders to sets of participants, further order randomisation within each context was not used, to retain comparability.

Conclusion

This chapter has discussed the development of a context-specific research instrument, designed to test the ethical reasoning process of tax practitioners and non-tax specialists in a tax context, in line with the recognition in the literature of a need for domain-specific tests. The research instrument is based on the general socio-ethical

Table 8.2 Summary of the development process

1	Literature review of prior studies in accounting and tax either utilising scenarios or indicating ethical issues facing tax practitioners.
2	Identification of some common themes.
3	Interviews with practitioners on the types of ethical scenarios encountered in a tax context.
4	Drafting of four scenarios based on the literature review and interviews.
5	Discussion of draft scenarios with four tax academics, with amendments as a result of their feedback. One of the original scenarios was dropped and two new scenarios developed.
6	Views on the five scenarios elicited from 30 tax practitioners covering: 1 the clarity and readability of the scenario; 2 the degree to which it would present an ethical dilemma in tax practice; and 3 the realism of the scenario.
7	The practitioners were also asked to list the types of issues they would consider if faced with each of the five dilemmas (to gather data that would inform the development of the 'items for consideration').
8	On the basis of this consultation with tax practitioners, three of the five scenarios were further strengthened, two were dropped and a new scenario was developed.
9	Three scenarios were selected that best matched the type of psychological responses triggered in the three original DIT scenarios being used.
10	Items for consideration were drafted for each scenario based on issues raised by tax practitioners in step 3, tax academics in step 5, and tax practitioners in step 7.
11	A panel of three tax academics and one practising tax practitioner independently coded the items for consideration following each tax scenario, linking each back to the ethical reasoning stage detailed in Table 8.1.
12	Two recognised DIT scholars reviewed the scenarios and items for consideration.
13	The completed instrument consisting of instructions, three DIT scenarios, three tax-context scenarios and a demographic questionnaire was pilot tested with both tax practitioners and non-specialists.

reasoning test, the DIT, as developed by Rest (1979a, 1979b).

In order to allow for comparisons of reasoning in the tax versus the general social context, the newly developed tax test was combined with the short-form DIT. This chapter explored the methodological issues in developing context-specific versions of the DIT, including a consideration of the issues that arise in comparative studies. The considerations that shaped the development of the original DIT by Rest have been explored and utilised to produce tax-specific scenarios that mirror as exactly as possible the three original scenarios in the short-form DIT, in terms of psychological triggers and the number and nature of scenarios. The process of validating different elements in the research instrument has been explored, and a significant contribution has been made to the DIT literature by giving explicit detail on how the tax-specific test has been authenticated.

The analysis of previous studies shows a variety of approaches in the number of scenarios, items for consideration and the number of items for consideration at each stage of reasoning. This variation suggests that a discussion of methodological issues for context-specific and comparative work is both timely and useful in the development of future instruments. This chapter thus provides information that can facilitate future comparisons of ethical reasoning between social and professional contexts, and between professional contexts.

Appendix A

DIT scenario one: Heinz and the drug (Rest 1986)

(Note that the stages placed after the items for consideration are not present in the instrument used with participants.)

In a small European town a woman was near death from a rare kind of cancer. There was one drug that doctors thought might save her. It was a form of radium that a pharmacist in the same town had recently discovered. The drug was expensive to make, but the pharmacist was charging ten times what the drug cost to make. He paid £200 for the radium and charged £2,000 for a small dose of the drug. The sick woman's husband, Heinz, went to everyone he knew to borrow the money, but he could only get together about £1,000, which is half of what it cost. He told the pharmacist that his wife was dying and asked him to sell it cheaper or let him pay later, but the pharmacist said, 'No. I discovered the drug and I'm going to make money from it'. So Heinz got desperate and began to think about breaking into the man's store to steal the drug for his wife.

Should Heinz steal the drug?

Should steal it ☐ Can't decide ☐ Should not steal it ☐

Rate the following 12 items in terms of importance	*Great*	*Much*	*Some*	*Little*	*No*
Whether a community's laws are going to be upheld (Stage 4).					
Isn't it only natural for a loving husband to care so much for his wife that he'd steal? (Stage 3)					
Is Heinz willing to risk getting shot as a burglar or going to jail for the chance that stealing the drug might help? (Stage 2)					
Whether Heinz is a professional wrestler, or has considerable influence with professional wrestlers (M item).					
Whether Heinz is stealing for himself or doing this solely to help someone else (Stage 3).					
Whether the pharmacist's rights to his invention have to be respected (Stage 4).					
Whether the essence of living is more encompassing than the termination of dying, socially and individually (M item).					
What values are going to be the basis for governing how people act towards each other (Stage 6).					

(continued)

Rate the following 12 items in terms of importance	*Great*	*Much*	*Some*	*Little*	*No*
Whether the pharmacist is going to be allowed to hide behind a worthless law which only protects the rich anyway (A item).					
Whether the law in this case is getting in the way of the most basic claim of any member of society (Stage 5).					
Whether the pharmacist deserves to be robbed for being so greedy and cruel (Stage 3).					
Would stealing in such a case bring about more total good for the whole society or not? (Stage 5)					

From the list of questions above, select the four most important:

Most important item	1	2	3	4	5	6	7	8	9	10	11	12
Second most important item	1	2	3	4	5	6	7	8	9	10	11	12
Third most important item	1	2	3	4	5	6	7	8	9	10	11	12
Fourth most important item	1	2	3	4	5	6	7	8	9	10	11	12

Appendix B

Tax-DIT scenario one: capital allowances

Anne is a tax practitioner with an accounting firm. She is working on a capital allowances claim to benefit one of her firm's corporate clients that is in financial distress. Despite profitable trading, the client has suffered severe cashflow problems as a result of adverse economic conditions. The capital allowances claim relates to a new factory building and will significantly reduce taxable corporate profits (and thus the tax the client has to pay). To be eligible for capital allowances the factory has to be in use at the end of the client's financial year. Without the reduction in tax from the capital allowances, it is unlikely that the company will survive, which will result in 5,000 employees losing their jobs.

It is now a month since the client's financial year end and Anne has asked the financial controller for documentary evidence that the factory was in use at the end of the financial year. The financial controller sends her a copy of the minutes of the latest directors' board meeting. The last item on the board minutes notes that the factory premises became fully operational on the last day of the financial year. However, Anne is convinced that this was not the case as she drives past the factory every evening and it is clearly unoccupied. However, she also knows that the company will not survive if the capital allowances cannot be claimed.

Should Anne file a tax return claiming capital allowances for the financial year?

She should ☐ Can't decide ☐ She shouldn't ☐

Rate the following 12 items in terms of importance	*Great*	*Much*	*Some*	*Little*	*No*
Would it be fair to all the taxpayers who have met the legal requirements to claim capital allowances if one client is permitted to claim allowances without meeting the criteria?					
What impact will the company's demise have on the accounting firm Anne works for?					
Under self-assessment, once Anne has the proper documentation on file her position is covered regardless of whether the building is actually 'in use'.					
Whether Anne's notification juxtaposes immediate Revenue authority cognisant of the client's actions.					
Whether Anne and the financial controller are close friends.					
Isn't a tax practitioner required to file an accurate tax return?					
Aren't capital allowances the essence of alternative displacement?					
Which values best determine how tax practitioners should interact with their clients and engage with the tax legislation?					
Whether a tax system that includes random and meaningless definitions ought to be completely abandoned.					
Whether the saving of 5,000 jobs will bring about the best result for society as a whole.					
Whether the firm's reputation will be damaged if the claim is subsequently challenged.					
Whether it is socially acceptable for management inadequacies to deprive employees of their opportunity to earn a living.					

From the list of questions above, select the four most important:

Most important item	1	2	3	4	5	6	7	8	9	10	11	12
Second most important item	1	2	3	4	5	6	7	8	9	10	11	12
Third most important item	1	2	3	4	5	6	7	8	9	10	11	12
Fourth most important item	1	2	3	4	5	6	7	8	9	10	11	12

Notes

1 The process is outlined in more detail in Doyle *et al.* (2009).

2 For example, in business-related areas there are accounting-specific tests (Welton *et al.* 1994; Thorne 2000, 2001); broad business dilemmas and auditing scenarios (Weber 1991; Massey 2002); management vignettes (Loviscky *et al.* 2007); and a test of tax compliance (Fisher 1997).

3 For a comprehensive analysis see Doyle *et al.* (2009).
4 Rest (1979b: 94) notes that if considerations are contrived (say to produce particular numbers at a particular stage) the instrument will be less functional because participants will not be attracted to artificial considerations.
5 Professor Dawn Massey (Fairfield University, USA), and Professor Linda Thorne (York University, Canada).

References

Dellaportas, S., Cooper, B.J. and Leung, P. (2006) 'Measuring moral judgement and the implications of cooperative education and rule-based learning', *Accounting and Finance* 46(1): 53–70.

Doyle, E., Frecknall Hughes, J. and Summers, B. (2009) 'Research methods in taxation ethics: Developing the Defining Issues Test (DIT) for a tax specific scenario', *Journal of Business Ethics* 88(1): 35–52.

Elm, D.R. and Weber, J. (1994) 'Measuring moral judgment: The moral judgment interview or the defining issues test?' *Journal of Business Ethics* 13(5): 341–55.

Finn, D.W., Chonko, L.B. and Hunt, S.D. (1988) 'Ethical problems in public accounting: The view from the top', *Journal of Business Ethics* 7(8): 605–15.

Fisher, D. (1997) 'Assessing taxpayer moral reasoning: The development of an objective measure', *Research on Accounting Ethics* 3: 141–71.

Fraedrich, J., Thorne, D.M. and Ferrell, O.C. (1994) 'Assessing the application of cognitive moral development theory to business ethics', *Journal of Business Ethics* 13(10): 829–38.

Kohlberg, L. (1973) *Collected Papers on Moral Development and Moral Education*, Cambridge, MA: Laboratory of Human Development, Harvard University.

Loviscky, G.E., Trevino, L.K. and Jacobs, R.R. (2007) 'Assessing managers' ethical decision-making: An objective measure of managerial moral judgment', *Journal of Business Ethics* 73 (3): 263–85.

Marshall, R.L., Armstrong, R.W. and Smith, M. (1998) 'The ethical environment of tax practitioners: Western Australian evidence', *Journal of Business Ethics* 17(12): 1265–79.

Massey, D.W. (2002) 'The importance of context in investigating auditors' moral abilities', *Research on Accounting Ethics* 8: 195–247.

Parducci, A. (1968) 'The relativism of absolute judgements', *Scientific American* 219(6): 84–90.

Ponemon, L.A. (1993) 'Can ethics be taught in accounting?' *Journal of Accounting Education* 11 (2): 185–209.

Reckers, P., Sanders, D. and Roark, S. (1994) 'The influence of ethical attitudes on taxpayer compliance', *National Tax Journal* 47(4): 825–36.

Rest, J. (1979a) *Defining Issues Test*, Minneapolis: University of Minnesota Press.

——(1979b) *Development in Judging Moral Issue*, Minneapolis: University of Minnesota Press.

——(1986) *DIT: Manual for the Defining Issues Test*, Minneapolis: University of Minnesota Centre for the Study of Ethical Development.

——(1990) *DIT Manual*, 3rd edn, Minneapolis: University of Minnesota Press.

——(1994) 'Background: Theory and Research', in J.R. Rest and D. Narvaez (eds), *Moral Development in the Professions,* Hillsdale, NJ: Lawrence Erlbaum Associates, pp. 1–26.

Rest, J., Narvaez, D., Bebeau, M. and Thoma, S. (1999) *Postconventional Moral Thinking: A Neo-Kohlbergian Approach*, Mahwah, NJ: Lawrence Erlbaum Associates.

Sims, R. (1999) 'The development of six ethical business dilemmas', *Leadership & Organization Development Journal* 20(4): 189–97.

Thorne, L. (2000) 'The development of two measures to assess accountants' prescriptive and deliberative moral reasoning', *Behavioral Research in Accounting* 12(1): 139–69.

——(2001) 'Refocusing ethics Education in accounting: An examination of accounting students' tendency to use their cognitive moral capability', *Journal of Accounting Education* 19(2): 103–17.

Trevino, L.K. (1986) 'Ethical decision making in organizations: A person-situation interactionist model', *Academy of Management Review* 11(3): 601–17.

——(1992) 'Moral reasoning and business ethics: Implications for research, education, and management', *Journal of Business Ethics* 11(5–6): 445–59.

Weber, J. (1990) 'Managers' moral reasoning: Assessing their responses to three moral dilemmas', *Human Relations* 43(7): 687–702.

——(1991) 'Adapting Kohlberg to enhance the assessment of managers' moral reasoning', *Business Ethics Quarterly* 1(3): 293–318.

Welton, R.E., Lagrone, R.M. and Davis, J.R. (1994) 'Promoting the moral development of accounting graduate students: An instructional design and assessment', *Accounting Education* 3(1): 35–50.

PART II
Possibilities of social theory

The aim of this Part is to introduce some possibilities in terms of using social theory to enhance our understanding of tax. It does not purport to be in any way an exhaustive survey; rather it is a somewhat eclectic selection of theoretical perspectives, chosen largely because they are not prominent in the current body of tax research, yet are deserving of greater consideration for the insights they potentially bring. Space precludes discussions of more widely used theoretical framings such as feminist-inspired work, but this is dealt with in a burgeoning tax literature, emanating mainly from North American tax law scholars. This neglect of other theoretical work should not be interpreted as a view that they are not important, but rather reflects the proclivities of my own research trajectory and interests.

The first set of chapters in this part deals with institutional theory. This is a problematic area of theorising, because of the many and varied approaches across different disciplines, and also across time and space. Chapter 9 attempts to map the terrain of the different strands of institutionalism, and Chapters 10 and 11 then describe two particular forms: new institutional sociology, which is used extensively in management and organisational studies, and historical institutionalism, which emanates largely from political science and is an important strand of the new fiscal sociology. In Chapter 23 Gitte Heij demonstrates how these two strands of theory can be brought together to form a theoretical framework for understanding tax policy developments.

Chapter 12 provides a brief overview of two different theoretical frameworks that both look at the role of experts and knowledge expertise, specifically communities of practice and epistemic communities. These theories have developed in completely different areas, yet have some commonalities, and both (not necessarily together) can fruitfully be used to analyse tax issues.

The next three chapters are largely concerned with theories of power: Chapter 13 with the work of Pierre Bourdieu, Chapter 14 with that of Michel Foucault, and Chapter 15 with Stephen Lukes. Tax policy and practice is imbued with power relations that are frequently neglected, or taken for granted, in tax scholarship, and these three approaches to thinking about power can provide us with new ways of analysing tax at all levels from the most practical to the most abstract policy questions.

The final chapter in this part describes Actor Network Theory, which was previously introduced by Karen Boll in her earlier chapter on ethnography. Once again it has been chosen for inclusion in this volume because it has not been utilised to any great extent, yet arguably holds great promise for research that is concerned with tax practices as enacted in society, but breaking free from traditional rationalist and functionalist ways of thinking.

9
VARIETIES OF INSTITUTIONALISM

Lynne Oats

When researchers approach institutionalism as a theoretical framework for their research, it soon becomes apparent that there are numerous versions, with considerable variations in the way the concept has been appropriated within different academic disciplines, and with confusing conceptual overlaps, often with different terminology describing similar phenomena. Within sociology, economics and political science there is talk of 'old' and 'new' institutionalisms, but these appear to be, and indeed are, different, in some cases moving (from old to new) in completely different directions.

The aim of this chapter is to provide some modest, and very basic, guidance as to the various forms of institutionalism, before introducing two specific forms in the following two chapters. Tax researchers to whom institutional analyses appeal should, of course, delve much more deeply into these different varieties, and more deeply still into the form finally chosen to support an analysis. This chapter draws heavily on the work of Peters (2005), a political scientist and Scott (2008), a sociologist, both of whom are highly recommended as providing useful overviews of institutional theory, old and new. Peters (2005) describes institutions as structural features of society that may be formal (e.g. with legal frameworks) or informal (with shared norms) that entail predictable, patterned interactions with some degree of temporal stability and that affect individual behaviour. Scott (2008: 48) defines institutions as comprising 'regulative, normative and cultural cognitive elements that, together with associated activities and resources, provide stability and meaning to social life'.

Given the focus of this book on fieldwork, some varieties of institutionalism are arguably less relevant, and will be mentioned only in passing, starting with a cursory examination of economics.

Both old and new institutionalisms in economics are interested in a broad range of institutions, not just economic but also political and social. Old (economic) institutionalism took a holistic perspective, and was broadly concerned with the relationship between institutions and economic behaviour, bringing into view a wide variety of institutions from states to social norms. Although prominent in the early part of the twentieth century, institutionalism was overtaken, and indeed smothered, by neoclassical economics. Schumpeter, who of course recognised the importance of tax as an institution, was a prominent part of this old school, and the renewed interest in fiscal sociology, which owes its origins in part to Schumpeter, is a welcome addition to new directions in tax scholarship (see Martin *et al.* 2009). New (economic) institutionalism, which emerged in the 1970s, adopts a more narrow view based on rational choice theory and methodological individualism. Ronald Coase (1937), a leading light of new institutional economics, was dismissive of old institutionalism and began to focus on the way in which institutions affected economic transactions, one significant branch of new institutional economics being transaction cost economics, popularised by Oliver Williamson (1985). This strand of theory retains the neoclassical economic concern with individuals as the key analytical focus, taking an atomistic and functionalist approach. Another strand of new institutional economics concerns itself with more macro-analyses bringing into focus politics, culture and law in terms of their effects on economic processes.

In political science, old institutionalism has a long and distinguished history and according to Peters (2005) has a number of defining features. First is a concern with the central role of law as the chief mechanism by which governments can influence the behaviour of the governed. Old institutionalism in political science is also concerned with structure, to the extent that structure is considered to be determinative of behaviour, structure in this sense referring to more formal features of the political system such as constitutions. Like old institutional economics, old institutionalism in political science takes a holistic view, looking at political systems in the round and extending to (descriptive) comparative analyses. The final two defining characteristics of old institutionalism in Peters' (ibid.) view are explorations of the historical foundations of contemporary politics and a strong normative concern with good government. As Scott (2008: 7) observes, traditional institutionalism within political science was largely non-theoretical and was challenged in the mid-twentieth century by behaviouralist concerns to develop a more theoretical political science with a focus on power and behaviour, for example voting behaviour.

New institutionalism in political science emerged not so much as a reaction to perceived deficiencies in old institutionalism, but rather a reaction to the behavioural trend that emerged in the mid-twentieth century and affected a number of disciplines, paving the way for rational choice. 'New' within this discipline is actually (and confusingly) two quite different strands of theoretical development. On the one hand, rational choice theorists draw on economic (neoclassical) work, including transaction cost economics, and can thus be seen as allied to new economic institutionalism. It is concerned with individuals, and sees institutions as being deliberately constructed by individuals to further their own interests. In this version of new institutionalism, methods such as game theory are used to model, for example, coordination mechanisms. Rixen (2008: 16) observes that 'rational choice intuitionalism asks why institutions exist and why they take the form they do … The short answer is that … institutions are instruments to overcome problems of collective action'. This approach fully embraces rational choice theory and considers institutions to be 'the object of states' strategic choices' (ibid.: 17). It is argued that game theory bridges the distinction between structural and actor-centred approaches (see also Levi 1989).

The other key strand of new institutionalism in political science is historical institutionalism. Within this strand, theorists are also (obviously) concerned with the state, but in particular the distribution of power among actors. Unlike rational choice versions of institutionalism, historical institutionalists see institutions as both constraining behaviour and enabling it. Analyses within this framework usually take the form of detailed accounts of specific institutions. Another important distinction is that historical institutionalists reject the notion that social conditions are the result of aggregated individual actions (see Immergut 1998). In Chapter 11 Lisa Marriott explains historical institutionalism in more detail, which she used to underpin her analysis of tax policy-making in the context of tax and retirement (see Chapter 25). Immergut (1998) suggests that the bifurcation of the terrain of institutionalist analysis in political science into two orientations – rational choice versus interpretation – can be overcome through the combination of elements of rational choice, sociological institutionalism and historical institutionalism. Her main point is that institutionalists in political science of both varieties need to pay more attention to questions of power (see Chapter 15 for a discussion of different approaches to analysing power). However, whether it is possible (or even desirable) to create a synthesis between rational choice conceptions of society and more cultural and interpretivist approaches is actually more contentious than Immergut (ibid.) seems to admit.

In sociology, arguably the youngest of the three disciplines considered here, there has been greater consistency over time in terms of the level of attention paid to institutions, and here the transition from 'old' to 'new' varieties of institutionalism seems to be more muted, with more continuities than discontinuities. Scott (2008: 8–9) identifies Herbert Spencer as the originator of 'the most influential conception of institutions pervading mainstream sociology throughout the twentieth century'. Spencer 'viewed society as an organic system evolving through time' (ibid.: 8). In Europe, Karl Marx was influential in terms of the development of institutional theory, along with Durkheim and Weber. At the risk of gross oversimplification, for Marx structures of oppression arise from human ideas and activities. Durkheim's formulation places emphasis on collective, symbolic, representations and shared cognitive frames. Weber did not explicitly refer to institutions but his overriding concern was the way cultural rules define structures in society and govern behaviour. In the USA Talcott Parsons was influential, and saw institutions as a system of norms regulating relations between individuals. The shift to new institutional sociology was influenced by a number of scholars including Mead, Schutz, Bourdieu, and Berger and Luckmann. The contribution of Bourdieu to social theory is explored in more detail in Chapter 13. The new institutionalism in sociology 'comprises a rejection of rational-actor models, an interest in institutions as independent variables, a turn towards cognitive and cultural explanations, and an interest in properties of supra-individual units of analysis that cannot be reduced to aggregations or direct consequences of individuals' attributes or motives' (DiMaggio and

Powell 1991: 8). New institutional sociology embraces the 'importance of culture, particularly for how the social world is constituted and cognized by social actors' (Carruthers 1995: 315). Seminal works include Meyer and Rowan (1991), who subvert the rational choice emphasis on formal procedure by considering the mythical and ceremonial aspects of organisational life and the way in which what actually happens in organisations is often decoupled from the formal rules. DiMaggio and Powell (1991) introduce the notion of isomorphism to help to understand the way in which organisations emulate each other.

In Chapter 10 Emer Mulligan explains in more detail new institutional sociology as it is used in organisational theory. Importantly, she shows how new institutional sociology can fruitfully be extended to incorporate the insights from socio-legal studies. Early versions of new institutional scholarship have been criticised for their treatment of law as exogenous, leading to a new strand of theorising that highlights law's endogeneity. This development is particularly pertinent for tax scholars, given the centrality of law to our field of enquiry. The way in which this theoretical strand was operationalised in her fieldwork study of US multinationals is then described in Chapter 24.

So where does this brief overview leave us in terms of the varieties of new institutionalism?

Peters (2005) identifies six varieties of (new) institutional theory, as follows:

- Normative institutionalism, as advanced by March and Olsen (1984), which emphasises the ways in which institutions shape the behaviour of their members.
- Rational choice institutionalism sees institutions as systems of rules and incentives from which behaviour derives and develops functionalist models.
- Historical institutionalism takes as a point of departure, predictably, the initial policy choices which then shape subsequent developments.
- Empirical institutionalism, which is concerned with the structure of government, and which, it is argued, makes a difference to policy choices.
- International institutionalism is also concerned with structure and is exemplified in international regime theory.
- Societal institutionalism takes as its focus relationships between state and society.

Scott (2008) is critical of Peters' typology, suggesting that it overemphasises differences in methodologies and/or topics of analysis. Hall and Taylor (1996) condense these categories into three – historical, rational choice and sociological – institutionalisms. The important thing to note is that each of these various strands of institutional theory carries its own philosophical underpinnings and ways of expressing its concepts.

Some varieties of institutionalism are not entirely compatible, and caution is needed when attempting to draw on disparate strands of theory, particularly those based on rational-actor models of society with those based on social constructionism. In Chapter 23 Gitte Heij demonstrates how historical institutionalism can be successfully synthesised with new institutional sociology to produce a theoretical framework for analysing tax policy developments.

References

Carruthers, B.G. (1995) 'Accounting, ambiguity and the new institutionalism', *Accounting, Organizations and Society* 20(4): 313–28.

Coase, R. (1937) 'The nature of the firm', *Economica* 4: 386–405.

DiMaggio, P.J. and Powell, W.W. (1991) 'Introduction', in W.W. Powell and P.J. DiMaggio (eds), *The New Institutionalism in Organizational Analysis*, Chicago, IL: University of Chicago Press, pp. 1–38.

Hall, P.A. and Taylor, R.C.R. (1996) 'Political science and the three new institutionalisms', *Political Studies* 44: 952–73.

Immergut, E.M. (1998) 'The theoretical core of the new institutionalism', *Politics and Society* 26(1): 5–34.

Levi, M. (1989) *Of Rule and Revenue*, Berkeley and Los Angeles: University of California Press.

March, J.G. and Olsen, J.P. (1984) 'The new institutionalism: organizational factors in political life', *American Political Science Review* 78: 738–49.

Martin, I.W., Mehrotra, A.K. and Prasad, M. (eds) (2009) *The New Fiscal Sociology: Taxation in comparative and historical perspective*, New York: Cambridge University Press.

Meyer, H.D. and Rowan, B. (1991) 'Institutionalised organisations: Formal structure as myth and ceremony', in W.W. Powell and P.J. DiMaggio (eds), *The New Institutionalism in Organizational Analysis*, Chicago, IL: University of Chicago Press.

Peters, B.G. (2005) *Institutional Theory in Political Science*, 2nd edn, London and New York: Continuum.

Powell, W.W. and DiMaggio, P.J. (eds) (1991) *The New Institutionalism in Organizational Analysis*, Chicago, IL: University of Chicago Press.

Rixen, T. (2008) *The Political Economy of International Tax Coordination*, London: Palgrave Macmillan.

Scott, W.R. (2008) *Institutions and Organizations: Ideas and Interests*, 3rd edn, London: Sage Publications.

Williamson, O. (1985) *The Economic Institutions of Capitalism*, New York: Free Press.

10

NEW INSTITUTIONAL SOCIOLOGY AND THE ENDOGENEITY OF LAW

Emer Mulligan

A significant body of scholars in the sociology/organisational theory domain has contributed to the theoretical debate on institutional theory (see Powell and DiMaggio 1991) for important contributions by Powell, DiMaggio, Meyer and Rowan, Scott, and Zucker).[1] The move towards new institutional sociology, classified as an interpretive perspective (Covaleski *et al.* 1996), or a normative cultural perspective that 'stresses the impact of cultural rules, models, and mythologies on organizational structures and practices' (Edelman and Suchman 1997: 493), represents a changing emphasis in perspective from efficiency (concerning technical environments), to legitimacy (concerning institutional environments). A key objective of the contributors to the new institutional sociology (NIS) perspective is to 'develop robust explanations of the ways in which institutions incorporate historical experiences into their rules and organizing logics' (DiMaggio and Powell 1991a: 33).

There is no agreed definition of institutions in the literature. Scott provides a comprehensive, 'omnibus conception' of institutions, as follows:

> Institutions are social structures … composed of cultural-cognitive, normative, and regulative elements, that together with associated activities and resources, provide stability and meaning to social life. Institutions are transmitted by various types of carriers, including symbolic systems, relational systems, routines, and artifacts … operate at multiple levels of jurisdiction.
>
> *(Scott 2008: 48)*

Institutions therefore, he explains, exhibit resistance to change and tend to be transmitted over time, to be maintained and reproduced (Zucker 1991). An institutional perspective must also 'encompass associated behavior and material resources … rules norms and meanings arise in interaction, and they are preserved and modified by human behavior' (Scott 2008: 49).

Similarly, Meyer and Rowan (1991: 42) describe institutionalisation as involving 'the process by which social processes, obligations or actualities come to take on a rule like status in social thought and action'.

DiMaggio and Powell (1991a: 15) state that 'taken-for-granted scripts, rules, and classifications are the stuff of which institutions are made'.[2] Subsequently, however, Powell (1991: 183), in attempting to refine and sharpen some arguments he earlier made with DiMaggio, recognised that 'we need an enhanced understanding of both the sources of heterogeneity in institutional environments and the processes that generate institutional change'. Powell (1991) outlined some key sources of heterogeneity, which explain in part why despite similarities in the external environment facing organisations, and many isomorphic forces potentially at play, the practice and process differ. These include: different resource environments, differences in industry structure and how organisations relate to the state, partial or fragmented governance, professional and occupational diversity. Also importantly, as recognised by Powell (1991: 200), 'not all forms of social change can be explained from an institutional point of view'.

In the accounting literature, Dillard *et al.*, advocates of the new institutional sociology perspective, state that institutional theory is:

> primarily concerned with an organization's interaction with the institutional environment, the effects of social expectations on the organization, and the incorporation of these expectations as reflected in organizational practices and characteristics.
>
> (*Dillard* et al. *2004: 508)*

They believe it is 'a way of thinking about formal organization structures and the nature of the historically grounded social processes through which these structures develop' (ibid.: 508).

While some new institutional sociology-based research focuses on how institutions undergo change over time, an equally valid pursuit is to establish what 'institutions' are in action in a given field, and to get the perspective of arguably powerful actors in that field, (in terms of creating and maintaining and changing institutions), as to how these institutions are then maintained.

Three common themes, namely legitimacy, isomorphism and decoupling, permeate early new institutional sociology-based research and these are outlined in turn.

Legitimacy

Legitimacy is a core concept within new institutional sociology. This concept is rooted in the idea that organisations need to be socially acceptable and credible in order to survive in their social environment (Scott 2008). Suchman defines legitimacy as:

> a generalized perception or assumption that the actions of an entity are desirable, proper, or appropriate within some socially constructed system of norms, values, beliefs, and definitions.
>
> *(Suchman 1995: 574)*

According to Scott (2008: 59), legitimacy is 'a symbolic value to be displayed in a manner such that it is visible to outsiders'. The use of language is very important here, whereby terms such as 'symbol', 'value' and 'display' suggest that how an organisation or indeed an individual is perceived by various constituents within its/his/her extant environment is, first, very important for survival, and second, does not necessarily reflect the reality. Carruthers (1995: 317) refers to the effective survival strategy of 'achieving legitimacy in the eyes of the world, state, powerful professions, or society at large'. Managing how an organisation or an individual is perceived by the complex set of external constituents, with many and sometimes conflicting views or 'competing sovereigns' (Scott 2008: 60) on what constitutes legitimate behaviour, is truly a challenging task. How this is accomplished, along with its importance and implications for practice and policy, merits investigation.

Dillard *et al.* (2004) refer to the economic and political context of market capitalism which delivers the primary legitimising characteristic of economic efficiency. Importantly, Scott (2008) recognised the restricted conception posited by new institutional sociology theorists in the earlier days, himself included (Scott and Meyer 1991: 135), which viewed institutional processes as opposing efficiency concerns, whereas subsequent research sees institutional processes as 'shaping and interacting with interest-based efforts. Institutional structures do not frustrate but frame rational decision making'. Powell (1991: 183) maintained that 'institutional and competitive processes are not necessarily oppositional'. Covaleski *et al.* (1996: 10) describe the general theme of the institutional perspective as: 'an organization's survival requires it to conform to social norms of acceptable behavior as much as to achieve levels of production efficiency'. Hopper and Major summarised this issue well:

> Leading NIS researchers now recognize that institutional and economic pressures are not mutually exclusive or oppositional, can confront organizations simultaneously, and prevail on both public and private organizations.
>
> *(Hopper and Major 2007: 63)*

Covaleski *et al.* (1996) also refer to formal organisational structures and how structures that adhere to the norms and behavioural expectations in the extant environment effectively prevents the organisation from being questioned about its conduct. The need to establish procedural legitimacy may be greater among organisations the processes of which have a high degree of arbitrariness, which makes them more vulnerable to attacks on their work arrangements and procedures (Scott 1987). The procedures themselves, providing a form of scientific rationality, are seen as primary legitimating characteristics which establish appropriateness and rationality:

> Organizations are driven to incorporate the practices and procedures defined by prevailing rationalized concepts of organizational work and institutionalized in society. Organizations that do so increase their legitimacy and their survival prospects, independent of the immediate efficacy of the acquired practices and procedures.
>
> *(Meyer and Rowan 1991: 41)*

Institutional isomorphism

Inextricably linked with legitimacy is the second theme within the NIS literature, namely *institutional isomorphism,* which constitutes the adaptation of institutional practice by an organisation, which ultimately 'promotes the success and survival of organizations' (Meyer and Rowan 1991: 49).[3] Covaleski and Dirsmith (1988: 563) describe the effort within isomorphism as being 'directed at building both an agreed-upon knowledge base and rational-appearing tools of practice'. DiMaggio and Powell (1991b: 66) contend that institutional isomorphism 'is a useful tool for understanding the politics and ceremony that pervade much modern organizational life'. They identify three classifications of isomorphism, i.e. coercive, mimetic and normative. Scott's (2008) typology refers instead to three 'pillars of institutions' which provide bases of legitimacy, namely regulative systems, normative systems and cultural-cognitive systems. Scott's three pillars clearly equate with DiMaggio and Powell's classifications of isomorphism. There is also some degree of overlap with the three processes referred to by Meyer and Rowan (1991) that generate rationalised myths of organisational structure: the elaboration of complex relational networks, the degree of collective organisation of the environment and leadership efforts of local organisations.

While distinguishing between different types of isomorphism may be useful, such a distinction may not always be easily made and indeed these three forces of isomorphism are not necessarily mutually exclusive. For example, Edelman and Suchman (1997: 497) state that 'the literature increasingly suggests that multiple isomorphic pressures may operate together in any particular historical instance'.[4] Each classification does offer potential in terms of understanding the external forces at play. A prominent source of coercive isomorphism comes from legislation, which contains rules, and sanctions. Due to the ambiguity of some laws, their existence alone, per se, does not constitute a source of organisational isomorphism and one may have to 'explore the complex ways in which organizations may mediate the impact of legal mandates and may construct the meaning of legal compliance' (Suchman and Edelman 1996: 941). Suchman and Edelman posit that institutional theory 'obscures the extent to which law is, in reality, obscure, fragmented and highly ambiguous' (ibid.: 929). As noted by Scott (2008: 54), 'many laws are sufficiently controversial or ambiguous that they do not provide clear prescriptions for conduct'. This clearly calls into question Fligstein's (1991: 314) conclusion that 'the state can actually set the rules of the game for any given organizational field … It can, therefore alter the environment more profoundly and systematically than other organizations'.

Normative isomorphism, however, is concerned with specifying how things should be done. It 'stems primarily from professionalization' (DiMaggio and Powell 1991b: 70) and is thereby concerned with pursuing legitimate means to achieve objectives. They refer to the important mechanisms of 'filtering of personnel',[5] 'occupational socialization',[6] and similarly identify two important sources of normative isomorphism relating to professionalisation:

> One is the resting of formal education and of legitimation in a cognitive base produced by university specialists; the second is the growth and

> elaboration of professional networks that span organizations and across which new models diffuse rapidly.
>
> *(DiMaggio and Powell 1991b: 71)*

This classification is concerned with professional ethics and unveils, for example, the 'rules specifying how the game is to be played, conceptions of fair business practices … how the specified actors are supposed to behave' (Scott 2008: 55). Normative isomorphism assumes the provision of guidance on moral governance to achieve the legitimacy objective.

The mimetic sources of isomorphism differ from the other two as they revolve around 'the shared conceptions that constitute the nature of social reality and the frames through which meaning is made' (Scott 2008: 57), and are less tangible perhaps than the other two. Carruthers (1995: 317) posits that '[O]rganizational fads and fashion seem likely to spread through mimetic isomorphism'. Mimetic isomorphism recognises the influence of external cultural frameworks and is particularly present in uncertain environments: 'It is a response to uncertainty' (DiMaggio and Powell 1991b: 69). This modelling 'may be diffused unintentionally, indirectly through employee transfer turnover, or explicitly by organizations such as consulting firms or industry trade associations' (ibid.).

Of potential significance in the context of interpreting ambiguous regulations, Carruthers (1995: 317) states: 'There is reassurance if not actual safety in numbers, and in the absence of a compelling reason to strike out on their own, organizations do what others are doing'. Specifically in relation to new ideas, the concept of 'diffusion of innovation' comes into play and perhaps the idea, for example, 'that organizations imitate others whom they perceive to be successful or prestigious' (Scott 2008: 162). Equally it is the case that 'diffusion occurs only if new ideas are compellingly presented as more appropriate than existing practices' (Greenwood *et al.* 2002: 60).

Decoupling

The third early theme within the NIS literature is decoupling, 'which is treated as a hallmark of institutional conformity' (Scott 2008: 173). It refers to the situation in which the formal organisational structure or practice is separate and distinct from actual organisational practice; i.e. the practice is not integrated into the organisation's managerial and operational processes. The decoupling process:

> relies on both societal and organizational actors functioning in an atmosphere of confidence and good faith and not taking the institutionalized structures too seriously.
>
> *(Covaleski and Dirsmith 1988: 563)*

According to Meyer and Rowan (1991), such formal structures constitute 'powerful myths', which are often in conflict with efficiency criteria. There may be therefore a formal and an informal structure with:

> the former reflecting officially sanctioned offices and ways of conducting business, the latter, actual patterns of behavior and work routines. An uneasy tension exists between these structures.
>
> *(Scott 2008: 153)*

Scott goes on to point out that such formal structures are 'ceremonial' and while they 'signal conformity', some organisations buffer internal units, allowing them to operate independent of these pressures. As posited by Meyer and Rowan:

> to maintain ceremonial conformity, organizations that reflect institutional rules tend to buffer their formal structures from the uncertainties of technical activities by becoming loosely coupled building gaps between their formal structures and actual work activities.
>
> *(Meyer and Rowan 1991: 41)*

Edelman and Suchman (1997: 496) noted that 'regardless of the underlying motivation, the decoupling of ceremony from substance arguably undercuts and marginalizes the role of law in organizational life'.

As noted by Covaleski *et al.* (1996), Zucker (1991: 11) argued that 'the rationalization in formal control systems is an important part of a network of political and power relations which are built into the fabric of social life, a process of transforming the moral into the merely factual'. There is some obvious overlap between the theoretical constructs of decoupling and legitimacy-seeking behaviour. Are formal structures and processes, which might secure organisational legitimacy, reflecting the practical activity of the organisation? Meyer and Rowan (1991) posit that they may not be, as the practical demands for efficiency may conflict with the need to be seen to conform to society's expectations. According to Scott:

> it is a truism of modern organization studies that organizations are highly differentiated, loosely coupled systems in part because they must relate to many and different environments.
>
> *(Scott 2008: 157)*

Meyer and Rowan (1991: 44) identify the professions (which would include tax professionals) as an example whereby elements of its formal structure 'are highly institutionalised and function as myths'.[7] Such professionalisation 'binds both supervisors and subordinates to act in good faith' (ibid.: 58).

While Carruthers cautions against over-emphasising the degree of decoupling, his description is rich:

> Formal plans, decision-trees, econometric forecasts, specification of contingencies and alternatives, quantitative estimates, and the ample use of accounting information all help to enhance the *post hoc* legitimacy of a decision. New institutionalists claim that these rationalized features usually

> do not determine how the decision was made, for they concern how the decision gets presented to the outside world after the fact.
>
> *(Carruthers 1995: 322)*

He does go on to warn that some audiences (the tax authorities perhaps) are mindful of decoupling, 'especially if it becomes too extreme' (ibid.: 323).

The next section addresses the different 'levels of analysis' at which new institutional sociology-based research has been carried out, focusing in particular on the importance of identifying and understanding the potential impact that the members of the 'organisational field' can have on practices and processes.

Levels of analysis

New institutional sociology-based research has been carried out at different levels of analysis. While there is not a consensus on exactly how many levels of analysis exist, the three levels of social systems put forward by Dillard *et al.* (2004) are capable of encapsulating the many and varied actors involved in a given field, and an understanding of the level, means and extent of interactions between actors at all levels provides an insightful perspective on, inter alia, the construction of the 'social reality' within which these actors operate. The three levels of social systems – 1 economic and political, 2 organizational field, and 3 organizational level – map well onto other typologies used in new institutional sociology.[8] Dillard *et al.*'s framework facilitates understanding of both the context and processes associated with creating, adopting and discarding institutional practices.[9] Establishing who the constituents are at each level in itself is an important first step and as DiMaggio and Powell (1991b: 65) pointed out in relation to the structure of the organisational field for example, 'it must be defined on the basis of empirical investigation'.[10] 'The concept of organizational field is central to institutional theory' (Greenwood *et al.* 2002). DiMaggio and Powell (1991b: 65), who posit that the virtue of the organisational field unit of analysis lies in its directing attention 'to the totality of relevant actors', define the organizational field as:

> Those organizations that, in the aggregate, constitute a recognized area of institutional life: key suppliers, resource and product consumers, regulatory agencies, and other organizations that produce similar services or products.
>
> *(DiMaggio and Powell 1991b: 64)*

Scott's description of the field helps to explain how actors contained therein could indeed create their own 'social reality' over time:

> The notion of field connotes the existence of a community of organizations that partakes of a common meaning system and whose participants interact more frequently and fatefully with one another than with actors outside of the field.[11]

DiMaggio and Powell refer to four parts of the process of institutional definition:

> An increase in the extent of interactions among organizations in the field; the emergence of sharply defined interorganisational structures of domination and patterns of coalition; an increase in the information load with which organizations in a field must contend; and the development of a mutual awareness among participants in a set of organizations that they are involved in a common enterprise.
>
> *(DiMaggio and Powell 1991b: 65)*

Upon examination of the above passage, Barley and Tolbert (1997: 95) posited that 'in their early work, institutionalists explicitly postulated that institutions exhibit an inherent duality: they both arise from and constrain social action'.

New institutional sociology theorists identify types of institutional influences that potentially have strong effects at all levels of analysis, namely the nation-state, the professions, international organisations and associations, and cultural frameworks (Scott 2008; DiMaggio and Powell 1991b). Notably, DiMaggio and Powell (1991b: 64) see the state and the professions as having become 'the great rationalizers of the second half of the twentieth century', and are therefore being held responsible for bureaucratisation and other forms of homogenisation emerging. The importance of recognising the existence and impact of the organisational field is of particular relevance in the sometimes uncertain terrain of tax laws and the interpretation thereof. DiMaggio and Powell state that:

> highly structured organizational fields provide a context in which individual efforts to deal rationally with uncertainty and constraint often lead, in the aggregate, to homogeneity in structures, culture and output.
>
> *(DiMaggio and Powell 1991b: 64)*

While the latter essentially reflects how institutional isomorphism leads at times to homogeneity, it does not explain institutional change or entrepreneurship. It is important, therefore, to note the role of individual agency also. Scott emphasises the varied and complex interrelations that exist between professional and political actors. Particularly relevant to the tax domain, he goes on to state:

> In some instances, the professional associations and practitioners have been so effective in staking out and defending their jurisdictional claims against competitors that they have been invited to assist the state in exercising control over all providers of designated services.
>
> *(Scott 2008: 129)*

Power

An extremely important and relevant extension (in the context of the tax arena) of new institutional sociology, considers the role of certain actors and organisations, the 'power' they have in terms of maintaining and creating institutions in the tax planning domain, the source of such power and the ways in which they use this power, along with the associated implications. As noted by Covaleski *et al.* (2007b: 8), 'institutionalization as a process may be profoundly political and reflects the relative power of organized interests'.

There have been a number of calls for addressing power within the new institutional sociology perspective. Perrow (1985: 154) was concerned that power and group interest had lost out to 'cultural myths and symbols' within institutional theory. Covaleski and Dirsmith (1988: 562–3) refer to the institutionalist perspective's assumption of passivity and lacking 'consideration of the active agency by which various social actors may construct, change, and enforce' societal expectations and being 'inattentive to power and self-interest in terms of both societal and organizational actors'. Dillard *et al.* (2004: 522) refer to the 'neglect of power, special interest and the political nature of organizations', as a limitation of prior institutional theory research, and importantly posit that '[a] significant element of institutionalization is an ongoing product of the political efforts of actors to accomplish their ends' (ibid.: 510). Carruthers (1995: 324–5) also refers to this call among institutionalists for 'greater attention to issues of politics, power and conflict … and to focus on myth and ceremony is to overlook power and control'. Actors may be able (individually or collectively) to use their power to impact on the social world by getting the rules of the game changed, impacting on accepted practice and resource distribution, thereby creating and maintaining institutions.

Scott (2008: 75) notes this important progression by institutional theorists towards giving 'more attention to the ways in which both individuals and organizations innovate, act strategically, and contribute to institutional change'. He posits that there has been an increase in attention given to 'the play of power and the role of agency in institutional analysis' (ibid.: 193). Powell (1991: 191) recognises 'the exercise of power' as an avenue of institutional reproduction: 'Elites may be both the architects and products of the rules and expectations they have helped devise'. Such elites tend to be 'knowledge experts' and/or skilful negotiators. Covaleski *et al.*'s (2005: 135) study posited the reinforcement of the notion that, after negotiations, 'the form the resulting institution takes depends on the relative power of the actors who support, oppose, or otherwise strive to influence it'.[12]

As noted by Scott (2008), some theorists in the institutional theory domain have begun to widen their theoretical frames, which incorporate multilevels and recursive models. In the context of such a highly regulated domain as tax, extending new institutional sociology in a way that embraces the work of some legal scholars (such as Edelman and Suchman 1997) brings some valuable additional insight. Extending new institutional sociology in this way responds to any shortfalls considered to exist within the new institutional sociology framework (as described thus far) by legal scholars:

> who complain that institutionalists too often embrace a legal formalism stressing the external, objective, rational nature of law. Rather, as Suchman and Edelman (1996; see also Edelman and Suchman 1997) propose, laws

> and regulations are socially interpreted and find their force and meaning in interactions between regulators and the regulated.
>
> *(Scott 2008: 169)*

This extension recognises the 'endogenous process' of law-making which is further addressed below.

Endogeneity of law[13]

Traditionally, the view of new institutional sociology theorists has been to interpret 'governmental regulations as an exogenous force shaping the behavior of those regulated' (Dirsmith *et al.* 2007: 10). The endogeneity of law perspective instead pays attention to active agency and the play of power and politics in the context of understanding the social construction of meaning of tax laws.

According to Edelman *et al.*, law is rendered 'endogenous' whereby:

> organizations are both responding to and constructing the law that regulates them … the content and meaning of law is determined within the social field that it is designed to regulate.
>
> *(Edelman* et al. *1999: 407)*

They examined the construction of the meaning of compliance with European employment opportunity law through consideration of the interactions between organisations, the professions and the courts, and they posit that their arguments in this context should be applicable to other areas (such as tax law). Such interactions, according to Edelman *et al.* (1999), result in the development of a particular 'ideology of rationality over time'.[14] This endogeneity of law perspective therefore particularly challenges the effectiveness of the state/government as a source of coercive isomorphism. This may arise largely due to the sometimes ambiguous and uncertain nature of the meaning of tax laws. Edelman *et al.* (ibid.: 408) thereby extend the new institutional sociology perspective by seeking to 'specify how the diffusion of institutional structures affects their market rationality'. There is a strong connection here with some of the writings by McBarnet and Whelan, in particular, when McBarnet and Whelan (1992) refer to the role of the regulated in actively resisting law having some explanatory power in terms of understanding the ineffectiveness of law (on-the-books). Such resistance amounts in part to the playing out of the game, and the social construction of the meaning of law, within this endogeneity of law framework.

Suchman and Edelman (1996: 938) posit that the interplay between organisations and their legal environment (e.g. tax legislators/legislation) results in a relationship that is a 'highly endogenous and reciprocal one', which suggests that corporate interests and professionals play a role in tax policy development.[15] They call on institutionalists to 'consider how organizations *mediate*, not just respond to, law' (ibid.: 933), and emphasise the political process that precedes law-making.[16] As taxation is an area of law regulating organisations, it is therefore:

> especially open to social construction because corporate lobby is usually successful in softening regulation that infringes on corporate interests, thus producing broad, vague mandates.
>
> *(Edelman* et al. *1999: 407)*

It is not only possible to describe the 'endogenous process' associated with any one piece of specific tax legislation, but also to examine the existence at all of this process generally within the tax domain, and the extent to which various actors believe they shape tax policy through such a process.[17] Their strategic responses could be categorised as one of Oliver's (1991) five strategic behaviours, namely acquiescence, compromise, avoidance, defiance and manipulation. Manipulation is arguably the:

> most active response to such regulatory pressures because it is intended to actively transform or exert power over the content of the regulation of the governmental agencies that interpret and enforce them.
>
> *(Covaleski* et al. *2005: 125)*

Suchman and Edelman (1996) assert that the reciprocal relationship between law and organisations appears at intra-organisational, organisational and environment levels. In relation to the first of these, they make an important point in the context of addressing why and how laws such as tax become perceived to be 'important' or high profile or embedded within an organisation:

> Political considerations will move certain camps within the organization to portray a particular legal threat as uniquely fearsome or to portray a particular solution as uniquely effective. If the organization acts on these alarms, and if other organizations imitate its actions, the standards for compliance in the organizational field are likely to strengthen, and the law may matter more than the rules on paper would suggest.
>
> *(Suchman and Edelman 1996: 939)*

Organisations tend to define the law through their practices regarding compliance, usually resulting in 'prevailing industry practices' (ibid.: 939). Finally, at the environmental level they assert that the speed at which standards of practice emerge and stabilise 'depends quite intimately on the structure of communication channels in the interorganizational environment' (ibid.: 940). They suggest accordingly that the presence of professional networks and trade publications in a sector leads to experiencing the law as more concrete and binding compared to sectors where such features do not exist.

Suchman and Edelman (1996) refer to the 'New Institutionalism' organisational theories as providing an appropriate backdrop for synthesising an integration of the sociology of law and sociology of organisations. Of particular relevance in a tax context, where the regulatory environment is often ambiguous, Edelman and Suchman (1997: 480) refer to law developing meaning 'through its interpretation by organized professions, and it develops substance through its application by organizational compliance officers'.

They argue 'that organizations construct and configure legal regimes even as they respond to them' (ibid.: 484), and that it is rare for regulations to 'emerge independently of the organizational actors whom they ostensibly govern' (ibid.: 488).

The notions of 'complex networks of power' and organisations working together as members of trade associations and industry working are central to the endogeneity of law perspective. Equally important is the notion that organisations sometimes actively seek the implementation of certain types of regulations to obtain certain advantages. Edelman and Suchman (1997: 489) observe: 'a great deal of lawmaking seems to respond primarily to the parochial interests of targeted firms, industries, and sectors'. The endogenous relationship continues beyond regulation into compliance. Organisations themselves have an influence here in often being the creators of processes and procedures which are accepted by the regulators and ultimately become the only acceptable processes. Some aspects of new laws therefore may be implemented in practice not through 'hard enforcement' but the favoured 'informal enforcement methods such as education, persuasion, negotiation and publicity' (ibid.: 490). There is a wealth of expertise on tax matters on both the regulator and regulatee sides, but an interesting aspect to examine is the extent to which the regulated depend on/use the expertise of the regulated to help them create/amend tax laws, and in so doing how influential certain taxpaying organisations are on the tax regulatory process. This essentially addresses the issue of who is more powerful in terms of tax knowledge production. The wider implications of where such power resides should be addressed.

Edelman *et al.* suggest that while organisations might seek to respond rationally to law,

> the definition of rationality is constructed and evolves at the environmental level, driven by institutionalized stories about the value of particular organizational structures and actions.
>
> *(Edelman* et al. *1999: 411)*

Inextricably linked with new institutional sociology, Edelman and Suchman refer to the 'culturalist' accounts of law and organisations calling:

> attention to the important role of professional discourses in constructing the meaning of initially ambiguous laws, in determining the situations to which legal reasoning applies, and more generally, in advocating for the legality and legitimacy of particular worldviews.
>
> *(Edelman and Suchman 1997: 499)*

In describing the cultural (which maps well onto the new institutional sociology) perspective on the regulatory environment, Edelman and Suchman (1997) argue that the social construction of meaning often takes place at the organisational field level, which ultimately points to the relationship between law and organisations being 'not so much reciprocally causal as endogenously coevolutionary' (ibid.: 501). Karayan and Swenson (2007: 30) describe tax rules as 'social constructs resulting from political processes', which are essentially a combination of official and unofficial actions taken by different government representatives over time. Such social construction (through dialogue, litigation, etc.) thereby explains the transition from 'law-on-the-books' to 'law-in-action',[18] which has significant explanatory power. Edelman and Suchman see this as a rather messy process, whereby the legal rules and organisational practices move 'in tandem' and:

> as the underlying belief system permeates both the legal and the organizational worlds, the boundaries between these realms become increasingly ambiguous.
>
> *(Edelman and Suchman 1997: 502)*

Similarly, Suchman and Edelman (1996: 922) describe the relationship between organisational practice and legal mandate as one that 'evolves collectively over time, may be collaborative rather than confrontational, and involves normative and cognitive as well as instrumental dynamics'. They also state that, 'the law is made as it is enforced, often with as much input from those who are its targets as from those who are its custodians' (ibid.: 934).

The institutionalised relationships among the social actors within an organisational field (upon which an organisation can rely) have been identified as a resource termed 'social capital' (Covaleski *et al.* 2005). They identified the hiring of a former Revenue official (an external social actor) as being an essential part of a company's strategy in helping to 'orchestrate the company's efforts'.[19] This person brought real knowledge to the table but was also (and arguably more cynically) a part of the 'impression management' exercise being undertaken by the company. For both reasons, he and the company for which he worked held and exercised this 'power' in advancing their vested interests, their action representing the 'strategic manipulation of institutional logics by skilled entrepreneurs' (ibid.: 144). Another source of power demonstrated in this case was the 'threat' that if the company did not essentially get what it wanted, it would have to withdraw company expansion and do it elsewhere.

In some contrast the notion of 'symbolic capital' put forward by Covaleski *et al.* (2005), drawing on Bourdieu (see Chapter 13), refers to a form of power, 'linking the various forms of capital available to an organisation by exploiting inherent defects in their logics; controlling the language used within the field of social actors, strategically redirecting key definitions, and shaping the social setting to serve vested interests' (ibid.: 3–4). Whatever source of power is used by companies when negotiating on the meaning of laws, Covaleski *et al.* suggest that '[w]hat is needed is the resolve of politicians at multiple (e.g. local and state), reinforcing levels of government who are unafraid of face to face confrontations with regulatees (Frug 1984), and who will back government agencies in the enforcement of legal provisions of whatever level of specificity is applied in order to make New Public Management efforts work' (Covaleski *et al.* 2005: 143). Interestingly in this case, where uncertainty of the law was expected to be at a minimum, the resolve of the company and its CEO resulted in outcomes that did not reflect 'the form abided by the letter or spirit of the law as written' (ibid.). Importantly, they conclude that, 'the construct of uncertainty is a rich and multi-faceted variable which lies at the core of many complex organisational and political relationships characterising the New Public Management' (ibid.).

Covaleski *et al.* (2007b), in demonstrating the endogeneity of law process, highlight not only the role played by regulatees in shaping the meaning of the laws by which they are governed, but also how 'regulators anticipate this regulatee response and seek to contain its effect in their strategic development and implementation of new regulations' (ibid.: 1). The latter, which they describe as a 'second order effect', suggests essentially some form of pre-emptive strike on the part of the regulator being built into the process, which in itself signifies a negotiation process, and sets the scene for an interesting and insightful perspective to be gained in relation to how 'shared meanings' of tax laws, and appropriate processes and practice, might come to be in the tax organisational field. This second order effect may well come into play and be facilitated in the context of new tax laws during the period between a government announcement around some new proposed tax laws and their being enacted.

Clearly the call for law and society scholars to engage with NIS scholars (Suchman and Edelman 1996) is recognised and welcomed by the new institutional sociology theorists. Scott posits that institutional theory will:

> benefit greatly by continuing to cultivate connections with law and society scholars ... students of society and accounting ... all of these communities bring theoretical insights and useful methodologies to our understanding of institutions and institutional change processes.
>
> *(Scott 2008: 199–200)*

This chapter highlights the benefits of interweaving two strands of theory originating in different (sub)disciplines, in this case new institutional sociology and law and sociology. This is not without difficulties, particularly as each tradition will have its own way of explaining often similar issues, and the specialist terminologies can be difficult to penetrate. In Chapter 24 the way in which these two theoretical strands were combined and intertwined with the literature on tax planning is described. This produced a powerful conceptual model that was used to help to understand the dynamics of tax planning in multinational companies, but could equally be used in other tax settings.

Notes

1 A number of contributions to Powell and DiMaggio (1991) were originally published elsewhere (such as the *American Journal of Sociology*) in the late 1970s/early 1980s. They were republished (amended in some cases) in this 1991 publication.

2 According to DiMaggio and Powell (1991a: 9), NIS in organisational analysis 'takes as a starting point the striking homogeneity of practices and arrangements found in the labor market, in schools, states, and corporations'.

3 DiMaggio and Powell (1991b) also recognise competitive isomorphism but contend it does not present a fully adequate picture of the modern world of organisations, so they focus on institutional isomorphism, as does this study.

4 Further analysis of the three classifications here, however, will focus on how they are different to each another. Scott (2001) emphasised also that his typology was not intended to rule out 'inter-pillar communication'.

5 Occurs through hiring individuals from firms in the same industry, through the recruitment of fast-track staff from a narrow range of training institutions, etc.
6 Takes place in trade association workshops, employer-professional-school networks, trade magazines, etc.
7 Meyer and Rowan (1991: 44) continue: 'these are occupations controlled not only by direct inspection of work outcomes but also by social rules of licensing, certifying, and schooling'.
8 Scott (2001), for example, identifies six levels, i.e. world system, society, organisational field, organisational populations, organisation, and organisational subsystem.
9 However, as noted by Scott (2001: 126), 'to attend too rigidly to the distinction between levels of analysis is to ignore the ways in which social phenomena operate as nested, interdependent systems, one level affecting the others'.
10 Scott and Meyer's (1991) definition of 'societal sector' is similar to DiMaggio and Powell's definition of 'organisational field'.
11 This quotation is reproduced in Scott (2008: 86), from one of Scott's earlier publications (1994).
12 Covaleski and Dirsmith (1988), Barley and Tolbert (1997), DiMaggio (1988), Covaleski *et al.* (2007a), Covaleski *et al.* (2007b), DiMaggio and Powell (1991a), Dillard *et al.* (2004) and Covaleski *et al.* (2005), go some way to address 'power'.
13 See Hopper and Major (2007) for an alternative extension of NIS, incorporating economic, labour process and actor network theories.
14 They reviewed data from the professional personnel literature, the courts and a national sample of organisations.
15 See Roberts and Bobek (2004).
16 See Radielli (2005) for a discussion of taxation research as political science research.
17 See Kelly (2003) for an illustration of the endogenous process in the context of a specific tax law related to dependent care expense accounts and employer-sponsored childcare centres.
18 The focus on law-in-action is within the Law and Society tradition of research according to Suchman and Edelman 1996.
19 This study demonstrated how a Tax Incremental Financing programme was manipulated by the regulated company through its strategic action. This official was the architect of various state policies when working with the Revenue.

References

Barley, S.R. and Tolbert, P.S. (1997) 'Institutionalization and structuration: Studying the links between action and institution', *Organization Studies* 18: 93–117.

Carruthers, B.G. (1995) 'Accounting, Ambiguity, and the New Institutionalism', *Accounting, Organizations and Society* 20: 313–28.

Covaleski, M.A. and Dirsmith, M.W. (1988) 'An institutional perspective on the rise, social transformation and fall of a university budget category', *Administrative Science Quarterly* 33: 562–87.

Covaleski, M.A., Dirsmith, M.W. and Samuel, S. (1996) 'Managerial accounting research: The contributions of organizational and sociological theories', *Journal of Management Accounting Research* 8: 1–35.

Covaleski, M.A., Dirsmith, M.W. and Mantzke, K. (2005) 'Institutional destabilization and the new public management: The case of tax incremental financing', *International Journal of Public Policy* 1: 122–46.

Covaleski, M.A., Dirsmith, M.W. and Weiss, J.M. (2007a) 'Welfare reform budgeting: The power and politics of becoming taken for granted', University of Wisconsin, Working Paper (on file with author).

——(2007b) 'The market based delivery of welfare: A field study of on-going institutional processes', University of Wisconsin, Working Paper (on file with the author).

Dillard, J.F, Rigsby, J.T. and Goodman, C. (2004) 'The making and remaking of organization context', *Accounting, Auditing and Accountability Journal* 17: 506–42.

DiMaggio, P.J. (1988) 'Interest and agency in institutional theory', in L.G. Zucker (ed.), *Institutional Patterns and Organizations: Culture and Environment*, Cambridge: Ballinger, p. 3–21.

DiMaggio, P.J. and Powell, W.W. (1991a) 'Introduction', in W.W. Powell and P.J. DiMaggio (eds), *The New Institutionalism in Organizational Analysis*, Chicago, IL: University of Chicago Press, pp.1–38.

——(1991b) 'The iron cage revisited: institutional isomorphism and collective rationality in organizational fields', in W.W. Powell and P.J. DiMaggio (eds), *The New Institutionalism in Organizational Analysis*, Chicago, IL: Chicago University Press, pp. 63–82.

Dirsmith, M.W., Huddart, S. and Jagolinzer, A.D. (2007) 'Insider trading: The endogenization of securities laws in a highly institutionalized organizational field', Penn State University, Working Paper (on file with the author).

Edelman, L. and Suchman, M.C. (1997) 'The legal environment of organizations', *Annual Review of Sociology* 23: 479–515.

Edelman, L., Uggen, C. and Erlanger, H.S. (1999) 'The endogeneity of legal regulation: Grievance procedures as rational myth', *The American Journal of Sociology* 105: 1–23.

Fligstein, N. (1991) 'The structural transformation of american industry: An institutional account of the causes of diversification in the largest firms 1919–79', in W.W. Powell and P.J. DiMaggio (eds), *The New Institutionalism in Organizational Analysis*, Chicago, IL: University of Chicago Press.

Frug, G. (1984) 'The ideology of bureaucracy in American law', *Harvard Law Review* 97: 1276–388.

Greenwood, R., Suddaby, R. and Hinings, C.R. (2002) 'Theorizing change: The role of professional associations in the transformation of institutionalized fields', *Academy of Management Journal* 45: 111–40.

Hopper, T. and Major, M. (2007) 'Extending new institutional analysis through theoretical triangulation: Regulation and activity-based costing in Portuguese telecommunications', *European Accounting Review* 16: 59–97.

Karayan, J.E. and Swenson, C.W. (2007) *Strategic Business Tax Planning*, Hoboken, NJ: John Wiley & Sons.

Kelly, E.L. (2003) 'The strange history of employer-sponsored child care: Interested actors, uncertainty, and the transformation of law in organizational fields', *American Journal of Sociology* 109(3): 606–49.

McBarnet, D. and Whelan, C.J. (1992) 'Regulating accounting: Limits in the law', in M. Bromwich and A. Hopwood (eds), *Accounting and the Law*, Hemel Hempstead: Prentice Hall.

Meyer, J.W. and Rowan, B. (1991) 'Institutionalized organization: Formal structure as myth and ceremony', in W.W. Powell and P.J. DiMaggio (eds), *The New Institutionalism in Organizational Analysis*, Chicago, IL: Chicago University Press, pp.41–62.

Oliver, C. (1991) 'Strategic responses to institutional processes', *Academy of Management Review* 16: 145–79.

Perrow, C. (1985) 'Review: Overboard with myth and symbols', *American Journal of Sociology* 91: 151–55.

Powell, W.W. (1991) 'Expanding the scope of institutional analysis', in W.W. Powell and P.J. DiMaggio (eds), *The New Institutionalism in Organizational Analysis*, Chicago, IL: University of Chicago Press.

Powell, W.W. and DiMaggio, P.J. (eds) (1991) *The New Institutionalism in Organizational Analysis*, Chicago, IL: University of Chicago Press.

Radielli, C. (2005) 'Taxation research as political science research', in M. Lamb, A. Lymer, J. Freedman and S. James, *Taxation An Interdisciplinary Approach to Research*, Oxford: Oxford University Press.

Roberts, R.W. and Bobek, D.D. (2004) 'The politics of tax accounting in the United States: Evidence from the taxpayer Relief Act of 1997', *Accounting Organizations and Society* 29: 565–90.

Scott, W.R. (1987) 'The adolescence of institutional theory', *Administrative Science Quarterly* 32 (4): 493–511.

——(2008) *Institutions and Organizations*, Thousand Oaks, CA: Sage Publications.

Scott, W.R. and Meyer, J.W. (1991) 'The Organization of societal sectors: Propositions and early evidence', in W.W. Powell and P.J. DiMaggio (eds), *The New Institutionalism in Organizational Analysis*, Chicago, IL: University of Chicago Press.

Suchman M.C. (1995) 'Managing legitimacy: Strategic and institutional approaches', *Academy of Management Review* 20(3): 571–610.

Suchman, M.C. and Edelman, L.B. (1996) 'Legal rational myths: The new institutionalism and the law and society tradition', *Law and Social Inquiry* 21: 903–41.

Zucker, L.G. (1991) 'The role of institutionalism in cultural persistence', in W.W. Powell and P.J. DiMaggio (eds), *The New Institutionalism in Organizational Analysis*, Chicago, IL: University of Chicago Press.

11
HISTORICAL INSTITUTIONALISM

Lisa Marriott

This chapter explores the historical institutionalism 'branch' of new institutional theory. Historical institutionalism is often used for analysis of policy development and political structures. The theory has particular relevance for tax policy; as well as being focused on the policy process, researchers utilising an historical institutionalist approach are 'primarily interested in understanding and explaining specific real world political outcomes' (Steinmo 2001: 1). Thus, using historical institutionalism as a theoretical framework can assist with providing insights into the key explanatory variables in the tax policy process.

The chapter commences with a discussion on 'what is historical institutionalism'. Thelen (2002: 92) provides a good starting point when she suggests that historical institutionalism has 'something to do with history and something to do with institutions'. The first section of this chapter expands on this and outlines some of the key features of historical institutionalism. The advantages and limitations of the theoretical framework are subsequently provided, together with a brief synopsis of some of the literature that has successfully used historical institutionalism to analyse tax policy development.

Historical institutionalism

Historical institutionalism is described by Steinmo (2008a) as an approach to studying politics, and by Peters *et al.* (2005: 1276) as 'a leading approach to institutional analysis, and, indeed, a prominent approach within political science more generally'. While perhaps best known among the political science discipline, the theoretical framework has demonstrated utility outside of this field, with successful studies undertaken in sociology, taxation and public policy, to name just a few.

A feel for what is important in historical institutionalism can be seen from two commonly used phrases among the historical institutionalist community: 'institutions matter' (e.g. Ma 2007: 63), and historical institutionalists 'take history seriously' (e.g.

Pierson and Skocpol 2000: 5; Steinmo 2008a: 166). The historical component emphasises that 'political development must be understood as a process that unfolds over time', while the institutional influence 'stresses that many of the contemporary implications of these temporal processes are embedded in institutions' (Pierson 1996: 126).

A feature of historical institutionalism is the claim that institutions influence how groups define their political interest and how individuals shape their preferences, which, in turn, impacts on the distribution of power and the direction adopted by political actors. This is achieved by limiting the 'set of policy ideas that political elites find acceptable' (Campbell 1998: 378) and thereby restricting the policy ideas that are considered. However, institutional theorists agree that institutions do not determine behaviour (e.g. Immergut 1998); instead they provide the contextual environment from within which analysis of choice can be made, thereby privileging certain policy options above others.

One of the strengths of historical institutionalism is that it does not claim that institutional constraints are the only influence on policy outcomes; instead it is open to the myriad other variables that play a role in policy formation. Furthermore, it welcomes the complex interplay of political, social and economic variables in explaining policy outcomes. This contributes to the theoretical framework's utility in explaining large, 'real-world' events that have evolved from a complex set of interacting variables. By way of illustration of this point, historical institutionalism has been used to explain case studies as diverse as the evolution and demise of authoritarian regimes, the origins of welfare states, the development of economic and tax regimes, and the causes of social revolutions (Pierson and Skocpol 2000: 1).

Historical institutional scholars typically adopt a broad definition of institutions, generally including formal and informal norms, rules, and accepted practices. Moreover, institutions are not limited to state institutions: they can be a variety of interest groups, public institutions or private organisations.

Features of historical institutionalism

A number of features combine to result in an historical institutional approach to research. The key features are the focus on history and timing, path dependency, punctuated equilibrium, critical junctures, and an emphasis on the importance of ideas and power relations. These features are discussed in the following sections.

Historical process

It is perhaps appropriate to commence discussion on the features of historical institutionalism with what may be considered the key component of the theoretical framework: history. It may be self-evident, but historical institutionalism places considerable emphasis on historical process. This is captured by Immergut, who writes:

> our understanding of particular events and developments is constrained by the large role played by chance. Quirks of fate are responsible for

> accidental combinations of factors that may nevertheless have lasting effects. In addition, self-conscious political actors ... can divert the supposedly ineluctable march of progress onto unexpected paths. Such contingent developments stand beyond logic and can only be grasped through historical analysis.
>
> *(Immergut 1998: 20)*

It is important also to note that this historical component is 'not just looking at the past, but looking at processes over time' (Pierson and Skocpol 2000: 5). The value of adopting an historical approach to assist in the understanding of policy evolution stems from the need to know why an event occurred, or did not occur, and why 'certain structures or patterns take shape in some times and places but not others' (ibid.: 4). Ma (2007: 63) suggests that historical institutionalism's primary interest is in 'historical processes, legacies and contingencies'. The contingencies, in particular, can be seen in another important component of historical institutionalism: path dependency. This is discussed in the next section.

Path dependency

Path dependency is a fundamental feature of historical institutionalism. Path dependency suggests that earlier policy choices have a continuing, or constraining, influence over future policy choices (Peters 1999: 63). The concept of path dependency within historical institutionalism does not suggest that these paths cannot be changed; instead, considerable political pressure is required to achieve change. As noted by Bulmer (2009: 309), path dependency 'highlights how political processes entail trajectories that are difficult to reverse because they are underpinned by mechanisms of positive feedback and increasing returns, as reflected in sunk costs and vested interests'.

Lecours (2000: 516) suggests that the attention paid by historical institutionalists to 'the contingencies of history and complex patterns of causality' leads them to the path dependency position. Thus, the focus on historical events is likely to effectively highlight the long periods of policy stability, followed by potentially transformational change. However, these periods of stability may be interrupted by periods of swift and sudden change, known as punctuated equilibrium: this is discussed in the following section.

Punctuated equilibria

Peters *et al.* (2005: 1289) observe that historical institutionalism frames change as punctuated equilibria: 'the assumption is that policies remain in equilibrium for a long (but unspecified) period of time until they are shifted from that path and a new equilibrium is achieved'. When used within studies of policy development, punctuated equilibria can indicate different rates of change in social and political structures over time (Krasner 1984: 240). As Krasner highlights, it is important to distinguish between periods of policy creation and those of policy stasis. The factors that explain why a set of arrangements is created may be quite distinct from those that explain why it has endured over time; for example, punctuated equilibrium tends to indicate that new structures may evolve during times of crisis with periods of stasis prominent during other periods.

As noted by Thelen (2002: 99), punctuated equilibrium suggests that institutions either break down or continue to exist as a result of an 'exogenous shock or environmental shift'. In historical institutionalism these significant events are known as critical junctures: these are discussed in the subsequent section.

Critical junctures

Critical junctures are a key component of historical institutionalism. They are infrequent events, described as 'turbulent formative moments' (Peters *et al.* 2005: 1276) and 'brief phases of institutional flux … during which more dramatic change is possible' (Capoccia and Kelemen 2007: 341). One of the important points about critical junctures is that they may place an organisation on a policy path that then becomes difficult to change: 'these choices close off alternative options and lead to the establishment of institutions that generate self-reinforcing path-dependent processes' (ibid.: 341).

Historical institutionalism's focus on critical junctures is claimed to have the benefit of highlighting the 'overarching contexts and interacting processes that shape and reshape states, politics, and public policymaking' (Pierson and Skocpol 2000: 1). The investigation of critical junctures in historical institutionalism highlights the turning points that shape the future of policy.

Timing

The importance of timing in historical institutionalism originates from the focus on historical processes. As suggested by Heclo (1974: 14), in order to appreciate the cumulative effect of institutions on social policy it is necessary to investigate historical processes over time, rather than investigating events in isolation. In addition, critical junctures occur infrequently in history, thus the inclusion of a significant period of time in the analysis ensures that important events are not overlooked through the investigation of an isolated occurrence.

Thelen (2002: 97) suggests that 'the emphasis on timing and sequencing in historical institutional research is also motivated by the insight, borne out in a number of studies, that when things happen, or the order in which different processes unfold, can itself be an extremely important part of the causal story'. The benefit with the emphasis on timing may assist with observance of the often slow-moving occurrence of significant policy changes.

Power relations

An important feature of historical institutionalism is its focus on power and, in particular, power imbalances among individuals and social groups. Hall and Taylor argue that historical institutionalism has been particularly focused on the way in which institutions distribute power unevenly across groups, writing:

> Rather than posit scenarios of freely-contracting individuals, for instance, they are more likely to assume a world in which institutions give some groups or interests disproportionate access to the decision-making process; and, rather than emphasise the degree to which an outcome makes everyone better off, they tend to stress how some groups lose while others win.
> *(Hall and Taylor 1996: 940)*

Immergut (1998: 22) uses the example of how political institutions and government policies may facilitate the organisation of interests by recognising particular interest groups or recognising the legitimacy of particular claims. As institutional factors impact on the political and policy-making processes, the result is that some interests will be privileged at the expense of others.

Ideas

In recent times there has been greater attention paid to the concept of ideas within historical institutionalism. At one level, the influence of ideas is self-evident; as noted by Campbell (2002: 29), individual actors carry certain ideas into the policy-making process. There is general agreement among researchers that policy ideas are formulated within an institutional context (e.g. Steinmo 2008b: 231) and, therefore, institutions can influence the ideas that are heard. This is referred to by Campbell (2002: 30) as 'institutional filtering'. Therefore, in order to understand policy outcomes, it is necessary to explore historic policy ideas and their evolution in practice.

Hall (1992: 91) suggests that interests and ideas interact in a number of ways, including providing incentives to encourage certain forms of behaviour and in making 'the expression of political views more or less viable for certain groups', thereby affecting the power held within certain institutions and the privileging of certain ideas above others. Ideas may also help in communicating the need for change and how this change can be structured. Blyth (2002: 38) suggests that 'change can reconstitute those interests by providing alternative narratives through which uncertain situations can be understood'. Thus, a benefit from utilising ideas to validate change is in both defining the policy issue and also in providing a solution to the issue.

Benefits of historical institutionalism

A number of benefits are attributed to the use of historical institutionalism as a theoretical framework. Perhaps the most significant of these is the claim made by Pierson and Skocpol (2000: 3) that historical institutionalism 'makes powerful contributions to ... understandings of government, politics, and public policies'.

It is frequently claimed that historical institutionalism has greatest utility in comparative, historical studies that explain macro-level policy differences in countries. The framework allows for contemplation of a wide range of institutional influences, many of those outside the traditional realm of institutional theory, therefore allowing for a rich and deep explanation of policy evolution. The inclusion of a wide range of influences facilitates analysis of the interactions between variables.

In addition, historical comparative studies undertake to explain institutional influence over both the policy process and the policy outcome. Historical institutionalism assists by facilitating an explanation of differences seen over time and between nation-states. Immergut (1998: 30) suggests that 'by tracing changing definitions of interests through time and across cultures, the impact of institutions on the construction of interests can be studied without imposing arbitrary, "objective" definitions of interests'. Thus, the adoption of historical institutionalism as a theoretical framework allows issues of representation and political bias to be highlighted and analysed, together with the influence of interested parties.

An important factor in policy analysis is to understand those institutions that are privileged in the policy process, as well as those groups that struggle to have their voices heard. Historical institutionalism assists in this understanding, with its focus on power relations and ideas.

Pierson and Skocpol (2000: 6) claim that the systematic tracing of the development of social processes can make an important contribution to supporting claims about social causation. The investigation of a small number of cases avoids reliance on single institutional effects in isolation. The detail gained from the analysis can assist with evaluating claims about causality. Pierson and Skocpol (ibid.) suggest that 'without the kind of attentiveness to temporally specified process that is a distinctive hallmark of historical institutionalist scholarship, important outcomes may go unobserved, causal relationships may be misunderstood, and valuable hypotheses may never receive consideration'.

A significant difference between historical institutionalism and other theoretical frameworks is the importance of explanation of events and, moreover, explaining through empirical explanations, rather than theorising. It is often said of historical institutionalism that it is not a 'theory in search of evidence' (e.g. Steinmo 2001: 2). Campbell (1997: 23) suggests that historical institutionalism incorporates a wide range of motivations as a result of subscribing to an inductive methodology. Thus, 'rather than deducing interests from micro-analytic first principles ... [historical institutionalists] prefer to identify the motivation, interests, and identities of organizational actors by sifting through the empirical record first and generalizing about it later'. This focus on empirical evidence results in meaningful analysis and positive contributions in the form of explanations of 'real world' events.

Limitations of historical institutionalism

A common criticism of historical institutionalism is that it does not effectively explain change (e.g. Peters 1999: 68; Rothstein 1996: 153) and, more specifically, institutional change. A premise of institutional theory is that institutions and policy choices are enduring, based on decisions made at inception. Peters *et al.* (2005: 1278) further suggest that it 'has difficulty in properly conceptualizing and accounting for political conflict'. As Peters *et al.* (2005) observe, an historical institutional account should adequately account for change, and the adoption of punctuated equilibrium is viewed by Peters *et al.* as unsatisfactory for explaining the often gradual change in policy; instead, it is better suited for explaining the persistence of policy. However, a contrary view is expressed by Lecours (2000: 514), who suggests that historical institutionalism places emphasis on 'unexpected developments and incongruities as opposed to continuity and regularities and is therefore philosophically able to deal with change'. Furthermore, the suggestion is made by Steinmo (2008a: 169) that the adoption of ideas as an important explanatory variable among the historical institutionalist community has resulted in an increased ability to explain institutional change. It is also notable that researchers have successfully utilised historical institutionalism in explaining change, such as Immergut's (1992) investigation of national health insurance politics.

While historical institutionalism is notable for the absence of a motivation to discover general laws of history (e.g. Steinmo 2008a), it is frequently criticised for this approach. As noted by Thelen (2002: 94), 'the more empirical and contextualized approach to theory construction is something for which historical institutionalists have been criticized, particularly by proponents of "general theory-building"'. Thelen and Steinmo (1992: 12) suggest that 'historical institutionalists lack the kind of universal tool kit and universally applicable concepts on which ... more deductive theories are based'. Thelen continues to comment that 'the search for middle range theory is thus driven less by a disdain for theory than the conviction that deeper understanding of causal relations (i.e. good theory) can often be achieved through a more intense and focused examination of a number of carefully selected casts' (Thelen 2002: 95). Accordingly, while perhaps being a shortfall of historical institutionalism, the lack of focus on writing general theory may also be considered a strength of the approach.

Historical institutionalism in practice

Historical institutionalists have produced a number of prominent tax policy studies. This section provides a selection of the seminal tax literature using historical institutionalism. While this section is limited to research on tax policy, many researchers in other disciplines contribute significantly to the broader policy literature (e.g. Hall 1992; Immergut 1992; Mahoney 2000: Pierson 1994; and Skocpol 1992).

Steinmo (1993) uses an institutional approach to highlight how the preferences, strategies and power of actors are defined by the institutional context. Steinmo finds that the structure of economic and political institutions shape the strategic choices of those involved in tax policy formulation. In addition, Steinmo suggests that differing political and economic institutions present interested parties with different incentives in relation to tax policy compromises, which have the potential to influence the range of policy outcomes seen.

Later research undertaken by Steinmo and Tolbert (1998) investigates the influence of institutional variation in shaping tax policy. This research produces similar results to Steinmo (1993) and indicates that countries with highly concentrated large unions and national collective bargaining have distinctive spending policy outcomes.

Steinmo and Tolbert show that in countries where business and labour groups are highly organised and integrated into government decision processes, tax policy choices are made with the consent of labour and business interests.

Research undertaken by Radaelli (1999) uses an institutional approach to analyse the tax system in the US and suggests that the fragmented US tax system may be explained by institutional analysis when looking at the divided political system. Radaelli refers to the multiple veto points within the system that provide opportunities for interest groups to influence the policy direction.

Eccleston (2004) uses an historical institutionalist approach to consider the extent to which institutional variables influenced the politics of tax reform in Australia. Eccleston (ibid.: 24) suggests that institutional variables have a significant impact on state capacity and policy outcomes, claiming that 'the institutional structure of the state not only shapes the decision-making authority of executive government, but also has a profound impact on patterns of state-society relations – the so-called institutional basis of relational capacity'. Eccleston (ibid.: 176) concludes that Australia's historically fragmented state structure, liberal political culture and absence of interest group capacity restricted the creation of 'coalitions capable of enhancing the capacity of the state'.

Research by Steinmo (2008b: 198) investigates tax reforms in the late twentieth and early twenty-first centuries and suggests that the context from within which policy is made impacts on the context of the future policy-making environment. Steinmo suggests that tax policy was the 'leading edge in these new political tides. In short, old policies created new problems. New ideas were introduced to help solve these new problems'.

Conclusion

Historical institutionalism has become one of the most influential theoretical perspectives in social policy research over the past two decades (Beland 2005: 1). The historical institutionalist approach has been successfully used for analytical purposes over a wide range of disciplines and subjects and provides a positive contribution to research through 'improving qualitative inquiry' (Immergut and Anderson 2008: 362).

The key features of historical institutionalism are complementary, with path dependency, punctuated equilibrium and critical junctures all contributing to explanations of policy evolution. When combined with an historical approach, incorporating the elements of power and ideas, the output produces a strong contribution to the literature, with robust explanations of policy development.

References

Beland, D. (2005) 'Ideas and social policy: An institutionalist perspective', *Social Policy and Administration* 39(1): 1.

Blyth, M. (2002) *Great Transformations: Economic Ideas and Institutional Change in the Twentieth Century*, Cambridge: Cambridge University Press.

Bulmer, S. (2009) '*Politics in Time* meets the politics of time: Historical institutionalism and the EU timescape', *Journal of European Public Policy* 16(2): 307–24.
Campbell, J. (1997) 'Recent trends in institutional political economy', *The International Journal of Sociology and Social Policy* 18(7/8): 15.
——(1998) 'Institutional analysis and the role of ideas in political economy', *Theory and Society* 27: 377–409.
——(2002) 'Ideas, Politics, and Public Policy', *Annual Review of Sociology* 28: 21.
Capoccia, G. and Kelemen, R.D. (2007) 'The study of critical junctures: Theory, narrative and counterfactuals in historical institutionalism', *World Politics* 59: 341–69.
Eccleston, R. (2004) *The Thirty Year Problem: The Politics of Australian Tax Reform*, Australian Tax Research Foundation Study No. 42.
Hall, P.A. (1992) 'The movement from Keynesianism to Monetarism: Institutional analysis and British economic policy in the 1970s', in S. Steinmo, K. Thelen and F. Longstreth (eds), *Structuring Politics: Historical Institutionalism in Comparative Analysis,* Cambridge: Cambridge University Press.
Hall, P.A. and Taylor, R.C. (1996) 'Political science and the three new institutionalisms', *Political Studies* 44(5): 936.
Heclo, H. (1974) *Modern Social Politics in Britain and Sweden: From Relief to Income Maintenance*, New Haven, CT: Yale University Press.
Immergut, E.M. (1992) 'The rules of the game: The logic of health policy-making in France, Switzerland, and Sweden', in S. Steinmo, K. Thelen and F. Longstreth (eds), *Structuring Politics: Historical Institutionalism in Comparative Analysis,* Cambridge: Cambridge University Press.
——(1998) 'The theoretical core of the new institutionalism', *Politics and Society* 26(1): 5.
Immergut, E.M. and Anderson, K.M. (2008) 'Historical institutionalism and West European politics', *West European Politics* 31(1–2): 345–69.
Krasner, S.D. (1984) 'Approaches to the State: Alternative conceptions and historical dynamics', *Comparative Politics* 16(2): 223.
Lecours, A. (2000) 'Theorizing cultural identities: Historical institutionalism as a challenge to the culturalists', *Canadian Journal of Political Science* 33(3): 499–522.
Ma, S. (2007) 'Political science at the edge of chaos? The paradigmatic implications of historical institutionalism', *International Political Science Review* 28(1): 57–78.
Mahoney, J. (2000) 'Path dependence in historical sociology', *Theory and Society* 29(4): 507.
Peters, B.G. (1999) *Institutional Theory in Political Science*, London: Pinter.
Peters, B.G., Pierre, J. and King, D.S. (2005) 'The politics of path dependency: Political conflict in historical institutionalism', *The Journal of Politics* 67(4): 1275–300.
Pierson, P. (1994) *Dismantling the Welfare State? Reagan, Thatcher, and the Politics of Retrenchment*, Cambridge: Cambridge University Press.
——(1996) 'The path to European integration: A historical institutionalist analysis', *Comparative Political Studies* 29(2): 123–63.
Pierson, P. and Skocpol, T. (2000) *Historical Institutionalism in Contemporary Political Science*, Paper prepared for presentation at the American Political Science Association Meetings, Washington, DC, August.
Radaelli, C.M. (1999) 'Taxation as politics', in M. Lamb and A. Lymer (eds) *Interdisciplinary Research in Taxation: Research approaches and bibliographic survey*, research report sponsored by the Institute of Chartered Accountants in England and Wales, Centre for Business Performance.
Rothstein, B. (1996) 'Political institutions: An overview', in R. Goodin and H.-D. Klingemann (eds), *A New Handbook of Political Science,* Oxford: Oxford University Press.
Skocpol, T. (1992) *Protecting Soldiers and Mothers: The political origins of social policy in the United States*, Cambridge: Harvard University Press.
Steinmo, S. (1993) *Taxation and Democracy: Swedish, British and American approaches to financing the modern state*, New Haven, CT: Yale University Press.

——(2001) 'The new institutionalism', in B. Clark and J. Foweraker (eds), *The Encyclopaedia of Democratic Thought,* London: Routledge.

——(2008a) 'What is historical institutionalism?' in D. Porta and M. Keating (eds), *Approaches in the Social Sciences,* Cambridge: Cambridge University Press.

——(2008b) 'What should the state do? A political economy of ideas and institutions', in J. Campbell and P. Naargard (eds) *Institutions and Politic,* Copenhagen: DJOF Press.

Steinmo, S. and Tolbert, C.J. (1998) 'Do institutions really matter? Taxation in industrialized democracies', *Comparative Political Studies* 31(2): 165.

Thelen, K. (2002) 'The explanatory power of historical institutionalism', in R. Mayntz (ed.), *Akteure-Mechanismen-Modelle: Zur Theoriefahigkeit makro-sozialer Analysen,* Frankfurt: Campus Verlag.

Thelen, K. and Steinmo, S. (1992) 'Historical institutionalism in comparative politics', in S. Steinmo, K. Thelen and F. Longstreth (eds) *Structuring Politics: Historical Institutionalism in Comparative Analysis*, Cambridge: Cambridge University Press.

12

COMMUNITIES OF EXPERTS

Lynne Oats and Helen Rogers

The tax system in any country is a complex endeavour that relies heavily on the expertise of those involved in making it work, administrators, taxpayers, practitioners acting on behalf of taxpayers, lawyers and judges called upon to adjudicate uncertainties.

This chapter outlines two quite different, but nonetheless compatible conceptual frameworks that mobilise the concept of knowledge expertise. The first of these, communities of practice, was used by Oats and Tuck (2008), as described in Chapter 20.[1] There has been limited use of the conceptual framework of communities of practice in tax scholarship. The second is a framework that has been used more often, most notably by Braithwaite and Drahos (2000), but also by Helen Rogers, who details her research into transfer pricing, although not this framework, in Chapter 22.

Communities of practice

This concept has popular appeal: having originated as part of a critique of cognitive theories of learning it has subsequently been used in a wide range of research sites, morphing along the way as such intuitive concepts often do. There has recently been some criticism about the direction of this strand of theorising, with its originators, Jean Lave and Etienne Wenger, apparently unable to be sure who first came up with the idea (Wenger 1998: xiii). The concept emerged in their joint 1991 work entitled *Situated Learning: Legitimate Peripheral Participation*, which attempted to move beyond seeing learning as an essentially cognitive process, but a contextual process, i.e. knowledge is seen as being produced within an active situational context rather than being passively received. Wenger subsequently (in 1998) published a book entitled *Communities of Practice: Learning Meaning and Identity*. There, he notes that 'practices are … the property of a kind of community created over time by the sustained pursuit of a shared enterprise. It makes sense, therefore, to call these kinds of communities "*communities of practice*"' (Wenger 1998: 45).

The concept of communities of practice is relational, as described by Lave and Wenger:

> In using the term community, we do not imply some primordial culture-sharing entity. We assume that members have different interests, make diverse contributions to activity, and hold varied viewpoints. In our view, participation at multiple levels is entailed in membership in a community of practice. Nor does the term community imply necessarily co-presence, a well-defined, identifiable group, or socially visible boundaries. It does imply participation in an activity system about which participants share understandings concerning what they are doing and what that means in their lives and for their communities … A community of practice is a set of relations among persons, activity, and world, over time and in relation with other tangential and overlapping communities of practice.
>
> *(Lave and Wenger 1991: 98)*

Wenger (1998) describes three dimensions of communities of practice, as follows:

1 Mutual engagement of participants – 'people are engaged in actions whose meanings whose meanings they negotiate with one another' (ibid.: 72).
2 Joint enterprise – 'not in that everybody believes the same thing or agrees with everything, but in that it is communally negotiated' (ibid.: 78).
3 Shared repertoire – 'over time, the joint pursuit of enterprise creates resources for negotiating meaning … They gain their coherence not in and of themselves as specific activities, symbols or artefacts, but from the fact that they belong to the practice of the community pursuing the enterprise' (ibid.: 82).

Communities of practice produce their practice, but that is not to say that they cannot be influenced or manipulated. Rather, 'the power – benevolent or malevolent – that institutional prescriptions or individuals have over the practice of a community is always mediated by the community's production of practice' (ibid.: 80). Their existence is viewed by Wenger as neither intrinsically beneficial nor harmful, but he acknowledges the capacity for communities of practice to be instrumental in effecting organisational transformation (ibid.: 85). Indeed, the Australian Taxation Office recognises this as discussed in a recent Organisation for Economic Co-operation and Development (OECD) (2011) report on Tax Administration. 'They're groups of people informally bound together by shared expertise and passion for a joint enterprise – engineers engaged in deep-water drilling, for example … people in communities of practice share their experiences and knowledge in free-flowing, creative ways that foster new approaches to problems' (Wenger and Snyder 2000: 139–40).

Communities of practice are not static, but have constantly changing membership. Lave and Wenger discuss how newcomers to a community of practice are introduced in the following terms:

> From a broadly peripheral perspective, apprentices gradually assemble a general idea of what constitutes the practice of the community. This uneven

> sketch of the enterprise (available if there is legitimate access) might include who is involved; what they do; what everyday life is like; how masters talk, walk, work, and generally conduct their lives; how people who are not part of the community of practice interact with it; what other learners are doing; and what learners need to learn to become full practitioners.
>
> *(Lave and Wenger 1991: 95)*

Communities of practice do not exist in isolation; rather they are connected to other communities and the wider environment in complex ways. Connections to other practices arise, for example, through reification: artefacts can become boundary objects that have meaning for and serve multiple constituencies (Wenger 1998: 117). Connections to other practices also arise through brokers, who are agents able to make connections across different communities. The boundaries of communities of practice do not necessarily correlate with institutional boundaries, and it is the community that decides who belongs, how the boundaries will be defined and to what extent the peripheries of the community are open (ibid.: 119).

The concept of communities of practice has been used quite extensively in management studies, in particular organisation studies, as an aid to understand organisational behaviour and development. The link between communities of practice and organisational learning has been developed by Brown and Duguid (1991, 2000), among others. It is concerned with meaning creation and has been adapted to the knowledge management and transfer environment, for example by Swan *et al.*, who suggest that communities of practice can overcome limitations of cognitive approaches:

> Cognitive, IT-led approaches to [knowledge management] typically fail to take into account the preexisting organizational structures, norms and cultural values that lead different groups to have divergent, possibly even irreconcilable, interpretations of what needs to be done and how best to do it. They unrealistically assume that building networks that provide structural links between these different groups will somehow automatically produce knowledge creation and sharing. The community view recognises that knowledge has to be continuously negotiated through interactive social networking processes.
>
> *(Swan* et al. *1999: 273)*

There is some overlap between the concepts of communities of practice and Bourdieu's notion of habitus (see Chapter 13). According to Gherardi (2000), Bourdieu's concept of *sens pratique* (practical direction) provides a way of understanding the relationship between tacit and explicit knowledge; *sens pratique* is pre-reflexive and, through it, participants in a practice learn the logic of that practice. Moreover, 'the sens pratique of organizing is inscribed in the bodies and in the habitus of practices' and cannot be transcribed into standard operating procedures (Gherardi 2000: 216). Gherardi *et al.* (1998) argue that the way knowledge is retained in a community of practice is best understood as a habitus (Bourdieu 1977) that is sustained collectively by the community. See also Roberts (2006) in relation to the link between Bourdieusian habitus and knowledge management.

There is also some overlap, particularly with Wenger's extended notion of 'constellations' of interconnected communities of practice, with social network theory. As an analytical concept, Wenger describes communities of practice as a mid-level category. 'It is neither a specific, narrowly defined activity or interaction, nor a broadly defined aggregate that is absolutely historical and social' (Wenger 1998: 126–7). Its appropriateness as an analytical tool in terms of tax research would seem to be linked to research that considers tax practice in the real world. Oats and Tuck (2008), for example (see Chapter 20), found the concept useful in helping to understand developments occurring within Her Majesty's Revenue & Customs (HMRC), whereby financial reporting experts were being employed to augment the tax expertise within the Large Business Service. This interview-based empirical investigation revealed the emergence community of practice of accountants that interacted with, but remained separate from, the community of tax specialists (without accounting expertise). The glossy annual report of the corporate taxpayers which come within the purview of the Large Business Service is an example of a boundary object, or reified artefact that connects the two communities, being an object that both communities share, but understand differently.

While communities of practice as a conceptual category has mainly been used in studies of specific organisational practices, the second analytical tool explored in this chapter is much broader in scope, frequently deployed to help to explain global phenomena. For those readers interested in pursuing this strand of theory, Gajda and Koliba (2009) is recommended. There, in addition to canvassing the use of the construct across a range of literature, the authors argue that it is largely normative and under-operationalised, and offer suggestions as to how its theoretical development could be moved forward.

Epistemic communities

The origin of the phrase 'epistemic community' is usually attributed to Haas (1992: 27), who used it to conceptualise 'a concrete collection of individuals who share the same world view or episteme', in a study of international policy coordination, which remains the field of enquiry in which the concept is most prevalent. The concept goes beyond merely shared world views, however, and embraces an element of knowledge expertise of professionals. Braithwaite and Drahos (2000: 24) used the concept in their sweeping analysis of global business regulation where they defined epistemic communities as being 'large audiences of state, business and NGO [non-governmental organisation] actors who meet sporadically and share a common regulatory discourse based on shared knowledge, sometimes technical knowledge, requiring professional training'.

Dezalay and Garth (1995), while primarily adopting Bourdieusian concepts of the legal field and the struggle for capital therein (see Chapter 20), also used the notion of epistemic community in their analysis of the role of lawyers in international commercial arbitration.

Adler and Haas (1992: 367) set out a vision for the analytical purchase of the concept of epistemic communities in the field of international relations more broadly. In their conception it is an approach that is 'methodologically pluralistic … [seeking] to bridge the gap between positivist-empirical and relativist-interpretive phenomenological approaches'. They set the concept up as a corrective to neorealist approaches in international relations scholarship that are unable to disentangle international structures and domestic concerns. They claim to 'relate institutions to the dynamic interaction between domestic and international political games, and we describe these games not only in terms of material interests but also as part of the bargaining and negotiation that take place among different epistemic understandings and practices "carried" by epistemic communities and later by policymakers as well' (ibid.: 369). Epistemic communities, they state, exert influence on policy innovation by framing the range of political controversy surrounding an issue, defining state interests, and setting standards. In the special issue of *International Organization* (1992), from which these comments are drawn, a number of studies demonstrate the range and extent of influence of epistemic communities across such diverse fields as environmental pollution, trade in services, telecommunications and banking regulation.

The construct of epistemic communities provides a way of understanding the way in which convergence occurs in various policy and regulatory environments. Van Waarden and Drahos (2002: 923), for example, explore epistemic communities as part of their attempt to understand the convergence in Europe of competition policies. They draw on three approaches in their attempt to understand developments: 'a) institutionalism, emphasising the role of central European integration; b) neo-functionalism, perceiving integration as the result of pressure from international business; and c) the epistemic community approach, highlighting the importance of transnational expert communities'. The authors observe that the epistemic community of lawyers they identify differs from scientific or engineering communities which were the focus of the original application of the concept, identifying five features of difference:

1. Law is innately normative, and particularly in relation to *procedural* norms, this leads to path dependency;
2. Their concern is *social and political issues* rather than natural science;
3. 'They are strongly *institutionalised* and at the forefront of policy making';
4. 'Their epistemic community is, unlike others, *hierarchically* structured, along the lines of the legal institutions'; and
5. They 'not only generate interpretations and ideas, but also have *interests*, which are derived from their institutional task: to defend their clients' interests'.

(Van Waarden and Drahos 2002: 930, italics in original)

This study demonstrates the benefits to be gained from combining theoretical perspectives where one alone appears to be inadequate to explain the phenomena under study. In this way, Van Waarden and Drahos (2002) are undertaking a form of metatriangulation suggested by Lewis and Grimes (1999) (see Chapter 2).

In tax scholarship, Ring's (2007) case study analysis of double tax relief identified an epistemic community that encompassed official representatives of supranational organisations such as the OECD and the United Nations (UN), although Rogers (2009) suggests that Ring's conception of epistemic community is too narrow in its focus on official representatives and the failure to explicitly include the broader community of professionals. Rogers (ibid.) develops Ring's approach through application to transfer pricing, where she identifies an elite group of professionals from a number of different organisations and disciplinary backgrounds working together to legitimise and authorise their activities.

A more recent study by Ring (2010: 131) applies the concept of epistemic communities to a broader analysis of international tax policy-making. She asks 'who are these experts [to whom states turn for advice] (or epistemic communities), how do they function and how might they exert influence on decision-making?' And further, '[g]iven the highly technical nature of many tax questions, the degree to which one can identify likely networks and groups of tax experts working in concert, the stories of international tax organizations and tax policy are likely intertwined with the story of knowledge and expertise' (ibid.).

Conclusion

These two theoretical frameworks were developed from within quite different disciplinary settings, communities of practice within learning theory and subsequently adopted in management studies and epistemic communities within international relations. They each have the potential to help us to better understand different aspects of the way tax systems operate in practice, as well as the way in which tax policy is developed and diffused more broadly.

Notes

1 The discussion of communities of practice here draws on the report that flowed from the research project described in Chapter 20, and for which the research assistance of Dianne Skinner is gratefully acknowledged, as is the financial support of the Institute of Chartered Accountants in England and Wales.

References

Adler, E. and Haas, P.M. (1992) 'Conclusion: Epistemic communities, world order, and the creation of a reflective research program', *International Organization* 46: 367–90.

Bourdieu, P. (1977) *Outline of a Theory of Practice*, Cambridge: Cambridge University Press.

Braithwaite, J. and Drahos, P. (2000) *Global Business Regulation*, Cambridge: Cambridge University Press.

Brown, J.S. and Duguid, P. (1991) 'Organizational learning and communities-of-practice: Toward a unified view of working, learning and innovation', *Organization Science* 2: 40–57.

——(2000) *The social life of information*, Boston, MA: Harvard Business Press.

Dezalay, Y. and Garth, B. (1995) 'Merchants of law as moral entrepreneurs: Constructing international justice from the competition for transnational business disputes', *Law and Society Review* 29(1): 27–64.

Gajda, R. and Koliba, C. (2009) '"Communities of Practice" as an analytical construct: implications for theory and practice', *International Journal of Public Administration* 32: 97–135.
Gherardi, S. (2000) 'Practice-based theorizing on learning and knowing in organizations: An introduction', *Organization* 7(2): 211–23.
Gherardi, S., Nicolini, D. and Odella, F. (1998) 'Toward a social understanding of how people learn in organizations', *Management Learning* 29(3): 273–97.
Haas, P.M. (1992) 'Epistemic communities and international policy coordination', *International Organization* 46: 1–35.
Lave, J. and Wenger, E. (1991) *Situated Learning: Legitimate Peripheral Participation*, New York: Cambridge University Press.
Lewis, M.W. and Grimes, A.J. (1999) 'Metatriangulation: Building theory from multiple paradigms', *Academy of Management Review* 24(4): 672–90.
Oats, L. and Tuck, P. (2008) *The Relationship between HMRC and Large Corporate Taxpayers: The Changing Role of Accountants*, ICAEW Centre for Business Performance, London.
OECD (2011) *Forum on Tax Administration: Tax Administration in OECD and Selected Non-OECD Countries: Comparative Information Series*, Paris: OECD.
Ring, D. (2007) 'International tax relations: Theory and implications', *Tax Law Review* 60: 83–155.
——(2010) 'Who is making international tax policy? International organizations as power players in a high stakes world', *Fordham International Law Journal* 33(3): 648–722.
Roberts, J. (2006) *Limits to Communities of Practice, Journal of Management* 43(3): 623–39.
Rogers, H. (2009) *Uncertainty in Transfer Pricing Rules: the Role of APAs*, unpublished PhD thesis, University of Warwick.
Swan, J., Newell, S., Scarbrough, H. and Hislop, D. (1999) 'Knowledge management and innovation: Networks and networking', *Journal of Knowledge Management* 3(4): 262–75.
Swan, J., Scarborough, H. and Roberston, M. (2002) 'The construction of communities of practice in the management of innovation', *Management Learning* 33(4): 477–96.
Van Waarden, F. and Drahos, M. (2002) 'Courts and (epistemic) communities in the convergence of competition policies', *Journal of European Public Policy* 9(6): 913–34.
Wenger, E. (1998) *Communities of Practice: Learning, Meaning and Identity*, Cambridge: Cambridge University Press.
Wenger, E.C. and Snyder, W.M. (2000) 'Communities of practice: The organizational frontier', *Harvard Business Review* 78(1): 139.

13

INSIGHTS FROM BOURDIEU

Lynne Oats and Louise Gracia

The purpose of this chapter is to introduce the work of Pierre Bourdieu, which has rarely, if at all, been drawn on in tax scholarship, by explaining the key concepts that he develops and speculating as to their usefulness in informing tax scholarship, broadly conceived. Although labelled as a sociologist, Pierre Bourdieu initially trained in philosophy and his early ethnographic work was anthropological in orientation, so his work is difficult to classify, which arguably is one of the reasons for the apparent neglect of his work in a number of disciplines and geographical locations.

One of the main strengths of Bourdieu's work is that he 'attempts to go beyond both subjectivist theories of action in terms of the intentions or rational calculations of individual subjects and objectivist theories ... which explain practices in terms of rules grounded in collective symbolic structures' (Cronin 1996: 64). As Madsen and Dezalay (2002: 191) observe, this allows for 'an analysis that is informed by both the objective structures and the way actors perceive, think about and construct the structures in a more complete way'.

Although not widely used in legal scholarship (but see Bourdieu 1987), Madsen and Dezalay (2002: 191) suggest that Bourdieu provides a conceptual toolbox or 'inter-related and open-ended concepts enabling a complex assessment of the different dimensions of law such as the state, the legal profession and legal language'. We can easily substitute 'tax' for 'law' here, and in order to see the potential of Bourdieu's work in our field of scholarship, we need to understand the building blocks of the various concepts he develops. Like many influential thinkers, such as Foucault who is discussed in Chapter 14, Bourdieu was prolific in his writing and for a newcomer to his work it can be difficult to know where to start. The corpus of Bourdieu's writings also spans a long period of time, during which he developed and altered some of his concepts, which makes the task of understanding them even more difficult. The aim here, then, is to try to explain some key concepts, but we strongly urge those who see merit in a Bourdieusian approach to spend time becoming more familiar with his ideas and the way they have been used in other areas of scholarship.

Bourdieu is fundamentally concerned with social practices (1990, 1998). One of Bourdieu's key works is *Distinction* (1979), in which he develops a formulation for understanding practice as comprising a relationship (although not clearly specified) between three other concepts – habitus, capital and field. As Swartz (2008: 48) notes, '[p]ractices flow from the intersection of habitus with capital and field positions'.

Bourdieu defines habitus as a 'durably inculcated system of structured, structuring dispositions' (1990: 52), a definition that raises more questions than it answers. Taking this definition apart then, 'dispositions' refers to our way of being. These dispositions are durable, in that they stay with us over time largely, but not completely, unchanging. They are inculcated in that they are internalised, becoming part of the way we are, by processes of training, upbringing and social interactions, i.e. are structured. Our dispositions are also structuring, however, in that collectively they shape social practices and become 'objectified in material culture' (Cronin 1996: 65). According to Hoy (2005: 108), 'habitus is acquired from early experience and then forgotten; it becomes a "second nature" that is "the basis of the perception and appreciation of all subsequent experiences"' (Bourdieu 1990b: 54). Rey gives the following example:

> what an agent from, say the urban American working class expects from life, and how he or she perceives of and reacts to any life experience or social condition, will be similar to the expectations, perceptions and reactions of other urban working class Americans because their respective habitus is always and inevitably class-ed habitus, which predisposes her or him to perceive, appreciate and act in ways reflective of the material conditions of the class existence that contribute to her or his habitus' formation. Therefore class identity is the key formative influence on habitus.
>
> *(Rey 2007: 50)*

Madsen and Dezalay (2002: 93) suggest that habitus is 'the internalised scheme which guides the player's behaviour. This internalisation, in turn, takes place in a dialectical process. The habitus both produces and is produced by the social world'. Note here the use of the word 'player'. This is in keeping with Bourdieu's conception of the social world comprising fields and subfields, which he loosely explains by reference to the metaphor of a 'game'. Habitus can therefore also be thought of as a 'feel for the game'.

The second key concept is capital, but before examining that more closely we'll clarify the third concept, which is that of field. A field is a domain or space of social practice which has a degree of autonomy from other fields that together comprise the wider social field in which we all interact. It has boundaries, and defined membership, although both of these attributes are fluid rather than permanent features of the field. Fields each have their own logics and properties (i.e. are homologous) and are interdependent. They are not only occupied by individuals, but also groups of individuals, organisations and institutions.

Bourdieu (1986) sees social or cultural fields as interrelated and overlapping. An overarching field, in Bourdieu's conception of social space, is the field of power. As Madsen and Dezalay (2002: 194) note, a field is 'an open fluid space constituted by a mixture of loosely connected symbolic practices occupying different positions within the particular social space but with a reference to a larger field of power as well as other fields'.

Rey (2007: 154) defines a field as 'any sub-space of society in which individuals occupy positions in relation to one another in a struggle over the production, control and consumption of forms of capital specific to the sub-space; alternatively conceivable as a market'. So capital is a component of social fields and is something over which field members struggle.

Capital in Bourdieu's thought is not only material as in an economic sense, but refers to a wide variety of resources, including financial, legal and technical, 'that can become both the objects and instruments of struggle in fields within and across organisations (Swartz 2008: 48). Capital is a field attribute over which field members struggle for control. It is in this conception of 'capital' that Bourdieu distinguishes his work from Marxism; he extends 'the notion of economic interests to ostensibly non-economic goods and services' (Swartz 1997: 66). There are numerous forms of capital, of which Bourdieu concentrates on four generic forms.

The first is economic capital, which is largely conceived of as material resources such as money and property. This is the most obvious form of capital, but one important aspect of Bourdieu's work is his extension of this 'economic' concept of capital to non-economic forms, as seen in the remaining three forms of capital.

The second generic form of capital in Bourdieu's thinking is cultural capital, which 'covers a wide variety of resources including such things as verbal facility, general cultural awareness, aesthetic preferences, information about the school system, and educational credentials' (Swartz 1997: 75). In empirical research, for example, Bourdieu found that success in school was better explained by cultural capital than by intellect or individual achievement. Cultural capital exists in both objectified form, in objects such as books and works of art, and also in institutionalised form, in educational credential systems. It is 'the unequal distribution of cultural capital across social classes' that Bourdieu sees as 'one of the key dimensions of social inequality in modern societies' (ibid.: 77).

The third generic form of capital is social capital, which consists of connections such as social acquaintances and networks. Social capital has become a problematic concept because of its appropriation in non-Bourdieusian scholarship that has led to it taking on a life of its own (confusingly), and so care must be taken when seeing the use of the term 'social capital' not to assume that it is being used in the Bourdieusian sense, in particular in the context of its relationship to other forms of capital as well as its relationship to other concepts such as habitus and field. Detached from the wider corpus of Bourdieu's thinking, social capital has been popularised, for example, in behavioural economics in a way that is completely contrary to Bourdieu's usage (see Fine 2010 for a detailed explanation of the use and misuse of this concept).

Finally, the fourth form of capital is symbolic capital, which refers to legitimation: for Bourdieu it is 'a way of talking about the legitimation of power relations through symbolic forms' (Swartz 1997: 92). It arises from successfully using the other forms of capital.

These and other more specific forms of capital are power resources for field actors. Different social fields will place different values on each of these forms of capital, which to some extent are capable of being exchanged for one another.

Bourdieu does, however, consider that economic capital tends to predominate and is at the root of other forms of capital and is also more stable than, say, cultural capital, which may be subject to fads and fashions. Later scholars have taken these generic forms of capital and sought to refine them, and we now find a variety of forms of capital identified in Bourdieu-inspired scholarship: religious, political, professional and linguistic capitals, for example.

As an example of the relationship between forms of capital, Rey (2007: 45) uses a Master of Business Administration degree (MBA) from a prestigious university, which as a form of symbolic capital will endow its holder with greater potential to increase his or her economic capital, which could then, for example be used to invest in the political field to perhaps secure political favours. Importantly, 'the MBA … is a piece of symbolic capital that contributes to the naturalisation of the notion that the people who hold such a degree are "smart", "hardworking", "entrepreneurial" and have high incomes, that's just the way it is; meanwhile, issues of access to quality higher education, like inheritance or racial inequality, are thereby effectively masked'.

Going back to the idea of the field being a form of game, the idea of the field presumes rules of the game and interested players who all believe in the value of the game. Bourdieu refers to this as the field 'illusio'. As Rey says, it is 'the belief of any individual or status group that selected fields have value and that the forms of capital 'at stake' in the fields are worthy of pursuit, or, the belief that the games that comprise society are worth playing' (2007: 155).

In terms of Bourdieu's conceptualisation of power, symbolic power is seen to be as important, if not more so, than economic power: another way in which Bourdieu distinguishes his ideas from those of Marxism. According to Swartz (1997: 83), Bourdieu combines constructionist and structuralist perspectives, offering 'a theory of symbolic power that tightly couples the cognitive, communicative and political dimensions of all symbolic systems'. The cognitive function of symbolic systems refers to the different ways of apprehending the world such as language, myth and religion. Symbolic systems are also 'codes that channel deep structural meanings shared by all members of a culture' and so perform a communicative function. Finally, symbolic systems serve as 'instruments of domination', providing distinctions and hierarchies and thereby fulfilling a political function (ibid.). Symbolic power is closely associated with another key concept of Bourdieu's: symbolic violence. This is 'the power to construct and impose mental structures, categories of perception and thought, which become institutionalised in social and mental structures, and so present themselves as matter of fact, or even natural' (Madsen and Dezalay 2002: 194).

By way of example of some of Bourdieu's concepts, a study by Everett (2007) explores ethics education within accounting programmes using Bourdieusian framing. He conducted a series of in-depth, qualitative interviews with accounting academics who had completed PhD programmes in the same departments as editors of the four (allegedly) most influential accounting academic journals. In the academic field, cultural capital is institutionalised in the form of doctoral degrees, and objectified in the form of research papers and books. Social capital is derived from being a member of, say, academic associations or editorial boards. Economic capital is obviously the monetary benefits flowing from producing top-class research. Symbolic capital in the form of a long list of research publications enables actors to 'set the prices in the field's symbolic market, by naming that which counts as valuable' (Everett 2007: 255).

Everett (2007: 256) suggests that social actors exist within two fields: a restricted field of production, nested within a larger, widespread field of practice. In the first of these, 'the production of cultural capital is primarily for other producers (… science for science's sake), while in the latter the production is primarily for consumers (… science for commercial purposes) … and social actors almost always misrecognise or deny the importance of their embeddedness in the wider field'.

Misrecognition is an important concept in Bourdieusian theorising. Everett suggests that 'on account of the nature of the habitus', the academic market, which is both materially and symbolically based, is 'difficult for even academics – holders of the objective viewpoint par excellence – to fully appreciate' (2007: 265). One implication for Everett's study of the academic field is that 'academic researchers may be unaware of the degree to which their epistemological and sociological presuppositions are influencing their research' (ibid.: 256). He suggests, for example, that researchers who adhere to rational actor theory as in neoclassical economics 'have difficulty recognising any form of action other than rational action or mechanical reaction' (ibid.).

The most enthusiastic use of Bourdieu's work is probably within education research. Other disciplines have been much slower to embrace and make use of his ideas. In law, Bourdieu is used most frequently in the context of studies of the legal profession, for example Dezalay and Sugarman (1996) and Madsen and Dezalay (2002). For a paper that explains the use of Bourdieu in accounting research, see Malsch *et al.* (2011). Swartz (2006) speculates why Bourdieu appears to be neglected by North American political sociologists and scientists and suggests that his broad reach is difficult to place in the tightly specialised US discipline environment. He argues that 'Bourdieu's sociology makes no distinction between the sociological approach to the study of the social world and the study of political power … [indeed he] sees *all* of sociology as fundamentally dealing with power … not as an independent domain that can be separated from culture or economics but a force that pervades all human relations' (ibid.: 87).

There is some commonality between Bourdieu's ideas, particularly that of social fields, and the new institutional sociology, which was discussed in Chapter 10, although the links are not always explicit. In terms of tax research, recent work by Gracia and Oats (2011) has begun to map the tax world against Bourdieusian concepts. There we conceive of the tax field as being overlaid by and intertwined with a number of other social and professional fields, including the accounting, political, bureaucratic, economic and juridical fields. The struggles within the field are not only for economic capital in the form of monetary reward, but also for symbolic capital in the power to name and define the boundaries within the field, for example the boundary between compliance and non-compliance. Within this broad conception of the tax field there are numerous ways in which the insights from Bourdieu can be brought into play to improve our understanding of tax as a social and institutional practice.

References

Bourdieu, P. (1979) *Distinction: A Social Critique of the Judgment of Taste*, trans. R. Nice, 1984, Cambridge, MA: Harvard University Press.

——(1986) 'The Forms of Capital', in J.G. Richardson (ed.), *Handbook of Theory and Research for the Sociology of Education,* New York: Greenwood, pp. 241–58.

——(1987) 'The force of law: Toward a sociology of the juridical field', *Hastings Law Journal* 38: 805.

——(1990a) *The Logic of Practice*, Cambridge: Polity Press.

——(1990b) *In Other Words: Essays Towards a Reflexive Sociology*, Stanford, CA: Stanford University Press.

——(1998) *Practical Reason*, Cambridge: Polity Press.

Cronin, C. (1996) 'Bourdieu and Foucault on power and modernity', *Philosophy & Social Criticism* 22(6): 55–85.

Dezalay, Y. and Sugarman, D. (1996) *Professional Conduct and Professional Power: Lawyers, Accountants and the Social Construction of Markets*, London: Routledge.

Everett, J. (2007) 'Ethics education and the role of the symbolic market', *Journal of Business Ethics* 76: 253–67.

Fine, B. (2010) *Theories of Social Capital: Researchers Behaving Badly*, London: Pluto Press.

Gracia, L. and Oats, L. (2011) *Boundary Work and Tax Regulation: A Bourdieusian View*, unpublished working paper (on file with the authors).

Hoy, D.C. (2005) *Critical Resistance: From Poststructuralism to Post-Critique*, Cambridge, MA: MIT Press.

Madsen, M.R. and Dezalay, Y. (2002) 'The Power of the Legal Field: Pierre Bourdieu and the Law', in R. Banakar and M. Travers (eds), *An Introduction to Law and Social Theory*, Oxford and Portland, OR: Hart Publishing.

Malsch, B., Gendren, Y. and Grazzini, F. (2011) 'Investigating Interdisciplinary Translations: The Influence of Pierre Bourdieu on accounting literature', *Accounting, Auditing and Accountability* 24(2): 194–228.

Rey, T. (2007) *Bourdieu on Religion: Imposing Faith and Legitimacy*, London: Equinox.

Swartz, D. (1997) *Culture and Power: The Sociology of Pierre Bourdieu*, David Swartz.

——(2006) 'Pierre Bourdieu and North American political sociology: Why he doesn't fit in but should', *French Politics* 4: 84–99.

——(2008) 'Bringing Bourdieu's master concepts into organizational analysis', *Theory and Society* 37: 45–52.

14
GOVERNMENTALITY

Lynne Oats

Michel Foucault was a French thinker whose work is difficult to classify, yet had a profound, and continuing, effect on social theory. Governmentality is a neologism devised by Foucault to denote governmental rationality (Gordon 1991: 1). Before examining the concept of governmentality as a potential analytical framework for tax research, this chapter will first outline some of Foucault's other ideas and concepts by way of background.

Foucauldian-inspired analyses often take the form of 'histories of the present', which aim to expose different ways of asking questions and by 'inventing new rules for the game of truth in relation to which we conduct ourselves individually and collectively' (Burchell 1996: 32). This is in large part the appeal for critical scholars, including feminist scholars, who see in Foucault's ideas inspiration to challenge the status quo, expose inequities and inconsistencies and bring about new ways of thinking. Philipps (1996), for example, draws, albeit elliptically, in part on Foucault's disciplinary society and the rise of technical expertise which frames issues as capable of resolution in neutral terms through privileging 'scientific' discourse.

Foucault's overriding concern was with relations of power, which he conceived of not as coercive or negative, but rather in close connection with knowledge, 'the myriad ways people are constrained to act together within a particular, ultimately arbitrary system of power/knowledge' (Bishop 2007: 66). Foucault saw culture and social institutions as evolving 'in contingent ways, so there is no necessity or direction to these evolutions' (ibid.). The social sciences, according to Foucault, are deeply implicated in the emergence of new power/knowledge regimes that shape us and how we live our lives.

Foucault's own work can be divided into three broad periods or phases: archaeology, genealogy and care of the self. His early, archaeological, work was 'concerned with understanding the tacit knowledge which constitutes the conditions of possibility, without the mechanics of how they are fought for or resisted' (Haugaard 2002: 181). These tacit knowledge systems are described as 'epistemes', which

Foucault sees as self-contained and layered, hence the notion of archaeology used to describe their discovery.

Foucault's genealogical work contained more explicit attention to power and in this work he 'supplements archaeological descriptions of system of thought with an account of how they are constituted by and in turn constitute, relations of power' (Haugaard 2002: 182). In this phase of Foucault's work 'episteme' was supplanted by 'discourse' to describe the 'tacit knowledge which informs particular ways of making sense of the world' (ibid.: 185). The most popularised concept arising from this work, from *Discipline and Punish*, is that of the panopticon, adapted from Jeremy Bentham, which is used to show how 'truth is used to pacify others by privileging certain ways of interpreting the world, particular discourses, and disqualifying others' (ibid.). Power here is the 'imposition of particular knowledge as truth' (ibid.). Subsequent work drawing on Foucault's panopticon finds the principles it espouses not only in formal institutions of confinement, such as prisons, but also in other settings: schools, open-plan workspaces. Work that draws on this strand of Foucault's thinking often refer to the 'disciplinary society'.

Likhovski (2007: 670) draws on Foucault in his study of tax compliance in Israel during the 1950s, to uncover the darker side of compliance, telling a compelling story of the creation of normalised, individualised, self-policing, model citizens. In particular, Likhovski identifies in the devices used by the Israeli Revenue traces of 'constant surveillance by the gaze of disciplinary power' (ibid.: 683). Preston (1989) also drew on the construct of disciplinary technologies in his case study of the relationship between the UK Inland Revenue (as it then was) and a UK record company.

The final phase of Foucault's work turned to the question of the formation of the ethical self, which he explored, inter alia, through a history of ancient sexuality. Governmentality is a concept that draws various threads of his work together, defined as an 'encounter between the technologies of domination of others and those of the self' (Foucault 2000: 225).

Governmentality

According to Dean (1994: 174), the notion of governmentality defines a novel thought space across domains of ethics and politics, of what might be called 'practices of the self' and 'practices of government' that weaves them together without a reduction of one to the other. It can be thought of as 'conduct of conduct', that is, directing (as in conducting an orchestra) behaviour, comportment, etc. (see also Dean 1999). At the time of his death in 1984, Foucault's ideas about governmentality had not been fully articulated and have therefore been the subject of some speculation and controversy. Progressive posthumous publication in English of various work, including lecture series, have kept Foucauldian scholars and their critics busy in acts of interpretation, application, and disputes over meaning and significance.

McKee (2009) notes that governmentality originally emerged from a lecture series from the 1970s concerned with the shift in thinking to the management of populations rather than the management of territories. As a phenomenon, governmentality studies took off in the 1990s with increasing attention to the objectives and tactics of authorities.

Governmentality, according to Dean (1994: 177), is therefore a pivotal concept, providing continuity between Foucault's early concerns with micro-physics of power and concerns with government on a much wider scale, of nations and societies. It is not a theory of state, but rather an invitation to analyse the operation of governmental power. Lemke (2001) suggests that the linking of governing with modes of thought in the notion of governmentality requires us to study both technologies of power and the political rationality that underpins them. It should be noted that Foucault's use of the word 'government' is not in the narrow modern sense of 'the government', but rather refers to an older, much wider meaning of the term.

Governmentality as a concept has allowed scholars across various disciplines and interdisciplinary endeavours to challenge and critique neoliberalism. Lemke (2001) reminds us that the neoliberal forms of government that have emerged in the latter part of the twentieth century feature not only direct intervention but also indirect techniques of control that lead individuals in their behaviour (conduct their conduct) without assuming responsibility for them. The rise of economic efficiency has spread into many formerly non-economic domains of social life. For Lemke (2001: 203) the theoretical strength of governmentality lies in its ability to conceive of neoliberalism not as mere ideological rhetoric, but 'above all as a political project that endeavours to create a social reality that it suggests already exists'.

McKee (2009) identifies three key contributions of governmentality:

1 It is not restricted to analyses of institutions or political power of the state; as Dean (1999: 467) observes, 'the word play on conduct encompasses any calculated attempt to direct human behaviour towards particular ends'. Governmentality 'traces' multiple sites of government beyond traditional sites.
2 '[B]y emphasising the connections between thought and modes of governing … attention is directed to what authorities wanted to happen, in pursuit of what objectives and by what means.'
3 Governmentality is 'underpinned by a perspective on power that is fundamentally productive, facilitative and creative, which operates by shaping and mobilising particular subjectivities' (ways of being).

Rose *et al.* (2009: 2) trace Foucault's thinking in relation to governmentality and observe that his concern was to 'understand the birth of liberalism … not as a theory or ideology, but as a political rationality, a way of doing things'. O'Malley *et al.* (1997: 504) observe that 'the concept of governmentality was designed to form a mid-range explanatory level between the history of political philosophy and the empirical study of social relations'. They are critical, however, of governmentality studies that focus on political rationalities and technologies but disregard the 'messy actualities of social relations' (ibid.), claiming that this weakens their diagnostic potential.

Certainly the version of governmentality promulgated by Miller and Rose and others, who have been referred to as the 'London governmentalists' (McKinlay and Pezet 2010), has concentrated on the 'mentalities of rule as evidenced primarily in texts of government' (O'Malley *et al.* 1997: 509). O'Malley *et al.* (1997) argue that this strand of research obscures both resistance and the multivocality of government programmes, and further that we need to reconnect governmentality with critical theorising and accord theoretical prominence to occurrences of resistance as well as actual implementation.

Miller and Rose have recently published a compendium of their governmentality work in a volume entitled *Governing the Present*, and this forms an excellent introduction to this particular strand of governmentality work. In their 'Introduction', they state: '[w]e have found the insistence on analysing power and politics without necessary recourse to the state as locus, origin or outcome to be incredibly fruitful' (Miller and Rose 2008). This is where the strength of governmentality as a conceptual framework lies: in focusing attention on the dispersion of governmentality beyond the state apparatus and to probe the underlying rationalities of the intricate and subtle technologies that pervade modern social life.

It is the London school of governmentality that has arguably been influential in the adoption of governmentality as a conceptual framing by critical accounting scholars, including critical accounting historians. Oats and Sadler (2008) draw on this work in their analysis of the stamp act crisis which preceded the American Revolution. Another influential strand of work emanating from accounting scholarship is that of Hoskin and Macve. Lamb (2001) analyses income tax practices in mid-nineteenth-century Britain, using Foucauldian concepts, in particular the transition from sovereign power to disciplinary power, seeking to trace social and institutional connections between tax and accounting. '"Discipline" in this context implies both a coercive power to control as well as a creative power to shape knowledge and subjects' (ibid.: 278). Lamb is influenced by the work of Hoskin and Macve (1986, 1994). Tuck (2010, and also Chapter 19) uses a Foucauldian approach to analyse changing practices within the UK tax authority. She demonstrates 'the interplay between expert knowledge formation ... wider organisational context ... role and identity formation'(2010: 594).

In the US Foucault is mostly associated with discourse analysis, whereby the 'internal organisation of discourse directly forms and shapes reality and subjectivities' (Rose *et al.* 2009: 9). Governmentality studies do not in general follow this constructionist path, but rather view 'language and other signifying systems as one element among many for rendering a reality governable' (ibid.).

Meanwhile, across one of the disciplinary divides, substantial work in legal scholarship has also drawn on Foucault in general and governmentality in particular. A growing group of legal scholars have embraced governmentality. Hunt and Wickham's *Foucault and Law: Towards a Sociology of Law as Governance* is an important contribution here, and is a good starting point for legal scholars seeking an introduction to Foucault's concepts and their application in law. Wickam and Pavlich's (2002) *Rethinking Law, Society and Governance: Foucault's Bequest*, contains a series of studies using Foucauldian (and post-Foucauldian) concepts to analyse aspects of the law. More recently, Golder and Fitzpatrick have published *Foucault and Law*, a collection of previously published pieces that draw together the various strands of Foucauldian concepts.

Wickham (2006) speculates on why Foucault has been so influential in the legal field, when actually he said little about it, indeed, many have argued that Foucault at best misunderstood and at worst neglected the role of law. He goes on to suggest that in fact Foucault's power-knowledge approach to law is less compelling since the terrorist attacks of 11 September 2001.

Miller and Rose (2008) warn against 'cookie cutter typology or explanation' to explain and account for existence of phenomena by subsuming it under a heading such as 'neoliberal', and suggest that we need to pay attention to how rationalities are constantly changing as new problems and solutions are identified. They further state:

> Thirty years on from the initial formulation, the language and approach of governmentality has dispersed, hybridised with other approaches, and gone in many different ways … what remains salient and challenging about this approach is its insistence that to understand how we are governed in the present, individually and collectively … requires us to turn away from grand theory … [and] instead investigate the role of the grey sciences, the minor professions … In the mundane business of governing everyday economic and social life. Every practice for the conduct of conduct involves authorities, aspirations, programmatic thinking, the invention or redeployment of techniques and technologies.
>
> *(Miller and Rose 2008: 24)*

Foucault's ideas, and the subsequent developments by scholars who have moved these ideas in different directions, give us a powerful set of concepts with which to reappraise aspects of tax practice. As with any body of theory, including those considered in previous chapters, it is important to take time to become familiar with the idiosyncratic ways of presenting concepts and ideas, and be careful to avoid unintentional misuse of special phrases and terminology. In Chapter 15 Rebecca Boden draws on Foucauldian concepts in her wider discussion of power in the context of tax.

References

Bishop, R.C. (2007) *The Philosophy of the Social Sciences*, London: Continuum.

Burchell, G. (1996) 'Liberal government and techniques of the self', in A. Barry, T. Osborne and N. Rose (eds), *Foucault and Political Reason*, London: UCL Press.

Burchell, G., Gordon, C. and Miller, P. (1991) *The Foucault Effect: Studies in Governmentality*, Chicago, IL: University of Chicago Press.

Dean, M. (1994) *Critical and Effective Histories: Foucault's Methods and Historical Sociology*, London: Routledge.

——(1999) *Governmentality: Power and Rule in Modern Society* London: Sage.

Foucault, M. (2000) 'Technologies of the Self', in P. Rabinow (ed.), *Michel Foucault: Essential Works of Foucault 1954–1984, Ethics*, London: Penguin, pp. 223–51.

Golder, B. and Fitzpatrick, P. (2010) *Foucault and Law*, London: Ashgate.

Gordon, C. (1991) 'Governmental rationality: An introduction', in G. Burchell, C. Gordon and P. Miller (eds), *The Foucault Effect: Studies in Governmentality*, Chicago, IL: University of Chicago Press, pp.1–51.

Haugaard, M. (2002) *Power: A Reader*, Manchester: Manchester University Press.

Hoskin, K. and Macve, R. (1986) 'Accounting and the examination: A genealogy of disciplinary power', *Accounting Organizations and Society* 11: 105–36.

——(1994) 'Writing, examining, disciplining: the genesis of accounting's modern power', in A.G. Hopwood and P. Miller (eds), *Accounting as a Social and Institutional Practice*, Cambridge: Cambridge University Press, pp. 67–97.

Hunt, A. and Wickham, G. (1994) *Foucault and Law: Towards a Sociology of Law as Governance*, London and Chicago, IL: Pluto Press.

Lamb, M. (2001) 'Horrid appealing: accounting for taxable profits in mid-nineteenth century England', *Accounting Organizations and Society* 26: 271–98.

Lemke, T. (2001) '"The birth of bio politics": Michel Foucault's Lecture at the College de France on Neo Liberal Governmentality, *Economy and Society* 30(2): 190–207.

Likhovski, A. (2007) 'Training in citizenship: Tax compliance and modernity', *Law & Social Inquiry* 32(3): 665–700.

McKee, K. (2009) 'Post Foucauldian Governmentality: What does it offer critical social policy analysis?' *Critical Social Policy* 29(3): 465–86.

McKinlay, A. and Pezet, E. (2010) 'Accounting for Foucault', *Critical Perspectives on Accounting* 21: 486–95.

Miller, P. and Rose, N. (2008) *Governing the Present*, Cambridge: Polity Press.

Oats, L. and Sadler, P. (2008) 'Accounting for the stamp act crisis', *Accounting Historians Journal* 35(2): 101–43.

O'Malley, P., Weir, L. and Shearing, C. (1997) 'Governmentality, criticism, politics', *Economy and Society* 26: 501–17.

Philipps, L. (1996) 'Discursive deficits: A feminist perspective on the power of technical knowledge in fiscal law and policy', *Canadian Journal of Law and Society* 11: 141–62.

Preston, A.M. (1989) 'The taxman cometh: Some observations on the interrelationship between accounting and Inland Revenue practice', *Accounting Organizations and Society* 14: 389–413.

Rose, N., O'Malley, P. and Valverde, M. (2009) *Governmentality*, Sydney Law School Legal Studies Research Paper No. 09/94.

Tuck, P. (2010) 'The emergence of the tax official into a T-shaped knowledge expert', *Critical Perspectives on Accounting* 21: 584–96.

Wickham, G. (2006) 'Foucault, law and power: A reassessment', *Journal of Law and Society* 33 (4): 596–614.

Wickham, G. and Pavlich, G. (2002) *Rethinking Law, Society and Governance: Foucault's Bequest*, Oxford: Hart Publishing.

15
TEA PARTIES, TAX AND POWER

Rebecca Boden

There is a renewed interest in tea parties of late – but only of the kind that is concerned with tax. In 2011 the US political movement that takes its name from the riotous events in Boston harbour in 1773 openly challenged the taxing and spending plans of US President Barack Obama. Tea parties, old and new, can be seen as querying the rights of states to tax human or corporate citizens. Such disputes highlight the operation of, and challenge to, power that lies at the heart of taxation as a socio-economic activity.

In England, taxes have their origin in feudal obligation; under the systems of *scutage* knights could buy their way out of fighting for the king – the payments allowed the monarch to use mercenaries instead. Taxation became more a matter of law after Magna Carta in 1215, when King John agreed not to levy new taxes without the barons' agreement. This effectively enshrined in law the principle that taxation should be by consent (Frecknall Hughes and Oats 2007). It became the bedrock of the notion of democratic rule in England, effectively circumscribing the ultimate power of the sovereign authority because no ruler can act without the necessary cash. Indeed, in 1773 the tea plunged to its fate because of a constitutional argument about whether the British government had the right to tax the American colonists without their consent – part of a long-running battle over tax (see, for example, Oats and Sadler 2008).

History therefore points to a long-standing power relationship between rulers and those whom they rule that is articulated through tax regimes. States, whether feudal or modern, need money to operate, to pursue their various programmes, from war to welfare. As citizens may be unwilling to relinquish their money voluntarily, the state must have powers to require payment, with sanctions for non-compliance. By the same token, this power is held in balance in democracies by the principle of consent, exercised through representation. Ultimately, taxpayers give their consent to be dominated and have their money taken away from them.

This contingent nature of the state's power in taxation – taxation 'by consent' – chimes with Foucault's notion that power can never be absolute (Foucault 1977). Nor, Foucault argues, is power only hierarchical or structural, rather it works in a capillary fashion. As such, the analysis of such power relationships is central to the critical tax project – only by viewing tax structures, policies and practice through the prism of the power relationships that shape them can we understand how and why they are constituted and what their effects are likely to be.

In this chapter I first offer a conceptual framework for interrogating the operation of power in taxation on two axes. The first axis considers and then problematises the conceptualisation of authorities with tax-raising powers. The second axis addresses taxed subjects, and reflects how the exercise of power over them by tax authorities may constitute and discipline them. Having done this, I discuss in particular how the work of Stephen Lukes (1974, 2005) might be useful in analysing issues of power in this field of study.

Taxing authority?

Legally, taxes are the prerogative of state authorities, be they local, regional or national. When I was commissioned as an inspector of taxes my official warrant was signed by the Queen. Indeed, the UK tax authority is still called Her Majesty's Revenue & Customs (HMRC). At first blush the exercise of power is simple: the state sets and collects tax to finance public expenditure, the state being generally directed by the democratic choices of the electorate. In a strictly legal sense, this is exactly what happens. However, such a conceptualisation of how tax authorities are constituted does not take us very far towards understanding *why* the tax regime is as it is – suggesting that a more nuanced notion of who is doing the governing of taxes is needed.

Foucault (see, for example, Foucault 1977, 1982) thoroughly disrupted our notion of government in the modern era. Rather than seeing it as the simple and observable exercise of power vested in a widely recognised body – 'the government' – he conceptualised government as a discursively framed mentality – sets of practices, knowledge, beliefs and understandings that constitute how we come to govern ourselves – 'govern-mentality'. This governmentality is constituted by a set of scripts, norms, expert knowledge, bodies and authorities that coalesce into powerful assemblages of 'government'. Government therefore consists of far more than the institutions and bodies that are formally named as such. Indeed, government is about the myriad ways in which we rule ourselves – the 'conduct of conduct' (Foucault 1977).

So, government is not so much a *thing* – a set of buildings with staff in a capital – but a way of doing things, a way of interacting, of disciplining, of behaving. This means that what government is in the context of taxation is much more complex and nuanced than simply a legal power to set policies and raise revenues exercised by a 'sovereign body'. Rather, it is the expression of a complex web of relationships, assumptions, subjective choices, beliefs and expert knowledge, etc. Only by getting to the bottom of these can we really understand how tax works and why.

In feudal times in England, rulers such as King John derived their temporal power from spiritual authority – kings had an absolute right to rule derived from God. Of course, what really gave King John power was a consensus that he did have divinely mandated temporal authority. Once this belief was fractured by his repeated demands for taxes, the barons revolted (Frecknall Hughes and Oats 2007). In more modern times, the discursive constitution of the power to govern is somewhat more complex and nuanced, driven by the accelerating development of first agrarian and then industrial capitalist activity. By the late eighteenth century government relied on more liberal, enlightened ideologies as a source of power and authority. Thus, the quest for appropriate government meant finding:

> a form of association which will defend and protect with the whole common force the person and goods of each associate, and in which each, while uniting himself with all, may still obey himself alone, and remain as free as before.
>
> *(Rousseau 1973: Part 1, Chapter 6)*

Taxation had a part to play in this new schema for government too, and by 1776 Adam Smith was setting out his ideal tax system (Moran 2009). This was grounded in his now famous canons: taxes should embody equality and certainty whilst at the same time being convenient for the taxpayer to pay and economical to collect (Smith 1776). Of course, not everything went neatly to plan, and even eighteenth-century governments were assemblages of powerful social and economic actors, notwithstanding Enlightenment theorising. Thus, the Tea Tax, which led ultimately to the Boston Tea Party, was levied to support and sustain the monopolistic position of the East India Company, the directors of which were powerful social and economic actors. The Tea Tax was, therefore, the product of a powerful assemblage of economic actors, enacted through Parliament.

In much more modern times, and especially since the 1980s, governmentality is characterised as 'neoliberal' – a much-used and rarely defined term. Broadly speaking, unlike early liberal ones, *neo*liberal regimes exist not to be as minimal as possible, congruent with providing a suitable framework for the development of capitalism. Rather, neoliberalism's role for the state in the governance assemblage is to purposively mould individuals and organisations into activity that shapes and sustains economic development and profitability (Miller and Rose 2008). In particular, the state must harness the human resources of the population – *biopower* – towards economic ends (Dean 1999). It does this via a complex network of rational and techno-rational sets of routines and practices, the performance of which not only causes 'government' to happen, but which also creates a hegemonic social, cultural and economic paradigm, shaping the way we think (Boden 2005). In essence, the state and its apparatus are only part of what government is.

Taxation can be seen as one of the techno-rational knowledges that form part of governmentality, not only raising the revenue that provides cash for government, but also privileging some at the expense of others and, indeed, shaping and forming who we are, what we do and what we believe. An extreme example of this is the scandals engulfing Caribbean tax havens since 2007. A number of these small states have been unable to perform basic public services because of insufficient government revenues and, problematically, have been unwilling to raise taxes for fear of offending the super-wealthy who frequent their shores (Peel 2011).

Taxing subjects?

The power to determine tax policies, pass laws and collect revenues is therefore formally vested in identifiable legal authorities, but those bodies are simply part of greater assemblages of powerful social, economic and cultural actors, all of which bring influence to bear on what the tax system ultimately looks like. Tax systems are rational categorical devices, the starting point of which is the definition of who or what is to be taxed (and by how much).

The definition of the incidence of tax involves subjective choice by the assemblages of powerful actors that constitute the tax system. This process of the creation of taxable categories of persons (human or corporate) is not rational or absolute, but subjective. For instance, the legal recognition of same-sex relationships via civil partnerships in the UK from 2004 created a new category of taxable subject in the same-sex couple. The definitions can have significant impact on human subjectivity – for instance, UK tax laws used to accord married women a very particular (and adverse) socio-economic position (Boden *et al.* 1995). In counterpoint, the much-contested UK laws that favour those with non-domiciliary status may represent the exercise of power to advantage particular categories of people. Thus, the exercise of the power to define taxable subjects has the effect of creating categories of people which in turn shapes their lives and identities (see, for example, Infanti and Crawford 2009). Indeed, some tax policies avowedly take the stance that their aim is to affect human social and economic behaviour – for instance, by giving tax breaks to people who stay married, or those who save for old age rather than spend. Such policies help to define us as individuals – encouraging us to become family-centred savers, for instance. Whilst such behaviour might or might not be 'good' for us, it does relieve the state of the cost of supporting children and the elderly, and helps to provide capital for the economy via pension funds. The state might therefore be seen as having a vested interest in encouraging us to behave in certain ways.

Theorising power

From the above it is clear that an analysis of power in tax policy can play a valuable, indeed central, part in critical tax research. This begs the question, however, as to how power can be theorised or conceptualised and, from that, how we can tackle the resulting methodological issues. A slim book, little more than an extended essay, first published in 1974 by Steven Lukes, has proved to be of enduring use to many scholars here. Lukes has now published a considerably expanded second edition of *Power: A Radical View* (2005), which engages with the extensive debates in this area over the 30 years since the first publication of his book.

Lukes' original work was very much a product of its time – a critique of existing approaches to the understanding of power in US politics – which needs to be read in that context. The book approaches the definition and study of the operation of power by conceptualising it as having three dimensions. Lukes, using an Aunt Sally technique, sets up the one- and two-dimensional views in order to knock them down as unsatisfactory, paving the way for his three-dimensional view. This is a technique he rehearses again in the new edition, perhaps unfairly, in discussing Foucault.

Lukes explores the one-dimensional view of power by engaging with the work of Robert Dahl (1961). Dahl was a positivistic behaviouralist who asserted that power could only be understood by observing its operation via the actual outcomes of decision-making processes. This led to an understanding of US politics as a democratic marketplace to which issues were brought and dealt with openly by explicit rules, with those seen to be prevailing having consequently legitimate 'power'. Because different groups prevailed in different decisions, Dahl concluded that US politics was pluralist, thereby denying (conveniently, perhaps, given the era) the possibility of the existence of what Marxists might call a ruling elite. Thus, everything in the American political garden was robustly and fairly democratic, in a classical sense.

Lukes concluded that this one-dimensional view of power:

> involves a focus on *behaviour* in the making of *decisions* on *issues* over which there is an observable *conflict* of (subjective) *interests*, seen as express policy preferences, revealed by political participation.
>
> (Lukes 1974: 15)

His critique of this approach is classically anti-positivist: it is methodologically unsound to conclude that, in any given situation, where no conflict (and therefore operation of power) is observable, there is no exercise of power. Lukes tackles this point by drawing on the work of Bachrach and Baratz (1962) to refute Dahl's one-dimensional view of power, arguing that it has two dimensions, the second involving the making of 'non-decisions'. Non-decisions occur where decisions are made, overtly or covertly, to do nothing, thereby thwarting challenge or moves for change. In Schattschneider's (1960) famous phrase, 'organisation is the mobilisation of bias'. Thus, Bachrach and Baratz's most famous work concerned why a steel city in the USA took no steps to control a serious problem with environmental pollution.

However, Lukes remains dissatisfied with this second-dimensional view too, bemoaning that Bachrach and Baratz rely methodologically on the observation of conflict (whether overt or covert) and evidence of (non-)decision-making. This means that, ultimately, the second-dimensional view of power is still basically behaviouralist in its approach, with all of the positivistic flaws inherent to that. That said, it can also be seen as an advance on Dahl's (1961) one-dimensional work.

This begs the question of what power is if it is not simply overt or even covert conflict leading to decisions or non-decisions that favour particular groups. Lukes (1974) utilises the work of Talcott Parsons and Hannah Arendt to argue that, outside of rule by sheer physical force and terror, power is the institutionalisation of authority and that the capacity to exercise power represents a consensus of collective will. That is, we allow others to have power over us. For the sociologist, this begs the question of how that will is formed if, like Lukes, we reject the notion that consensus is reached by the observable conflicts in politics. In Lukes' three-dimensional view of power, then, the concern is with the ways in which the very consciousness and critical awareness of people and organisations are shaped – how our 'will' is formed and why we comply with domination.

Lukes in his later edition (2005) turns his attention to Foucault, much of whose leading work postdates the original publication of *Power: A Radical View*. Whilst acknowledging the contribution that Foucault makes to our thinking about power, he declines to support the notion that power is what forms us and our identities. Confusingly, perhaps, he then goes on to utilise a great deal of poststructuralist and postmodern work, such as that of Bourdieu, to argue that the three-dimensional view of power is the only one that can give us a sufficiently nuanced insight into how power works. Therein lies the methodological attraction of Lukes' work: the important thing about the three-dimensional view of power is that we acknowledge that we should be concerned with the way in which the dominant, the hegemonic, is held in place – and our methodological and theoretical approaches need to be fit for that purpose. Lukes acknowledges the difficulty of investigating the ways in which will is formed, what he calls the 'hidden operation' of power, but argues that it can be achieved. Dean (1999) argues cogently, for instance, that researchers can use critical incidents which offer a dangling thread that can be pulled, revealing an entire picture (Boden 2005).

Where does this leave critical tax research? In 1995, together with Mary Childs and Wendy Wild, I wrote my first paper on tax (Boden *et al.* 1995). Our concern was with the way in which tax policy in the UK was gendered, seriously discriminating against women. A one-dimensional view of sexist tax policies would perhaps have concluded that women have the vote in roughly equal numbers to men and that the laws had been determined by Parliament in a democratic fashion. Perhaps Dahl would have argued that there was no exercise of power over women in these laws – there had been no observable conflict and therefore the treatment of women was entirely consensual. Bachrach and Baratz might have pointed to various commissions and suchlike and found overt or covert non-decision-making on the subject, with male bias being mobilised to organise the issue off of any agenda. Our perspective was different – in the history of tax law-making we found the persistence of gendered systems of governmentality that consistently militated against women's interests. We also found arguments that the tax system was active in constituting a disadvantaged identity for women. Thus the UK Equal Opportunities Commission (the governmental body then charged with equity issues) said that:

> Taxation is not only a method of raising revenue; it is also an instrument of social policy. Governments customarily use changes in taxation as a way of encouraging or discouraging a very wide range of social behaviour ... the structure of personal taxation can, either deliberately or, more often,

> unwittingly, contribute to, or hinder progress towards equal opportunities for men and women.
>
> *(Equal Opportunities Commission 1978: 3)*

In conclusion

This short chapter draws attention to the need for critical tax research to be mindful of the issue of power. The operation of power affects not just the constitution of taxing authorities and the policies that they develop and implement, but can also be constitutive of their taxed subjects. Lukes' (1974, 2005) analyses argue cogently that largely positivistic, behaviouralist approaches will fail to give a sufficiently nuanced understanding of how the hegemonic is held in place – how it is that we give our consent to domination and to be taxed. Rather, and perhaps in a heterogeneous theoretical manner, we need to explore what holds the dominant in place, and therefore why we are compliant with taxes and are shaped accordingly. This, in turn, opens the door to the possibility of resistance and change (a central part of the critical studies agenda). The methodological issues of identifying such power are not inconsiderable, but this need not prevent us from finding ways around the challenges.

References

Bachrach, P. and Baratz, M.S. (1962) 'The two faces of power', *American Political Science Review* 56: 941–52.

Boden, R. (2005) '*Sed Quis Custodiet Ipsos Custodes?* The role of government in corporate governance and ethics', *Advances in Public Interest Accounting* 11: 71–94.

Boden, R., Childs, M. and Wild, W. (1995) 'Pride and Prejudice: Women, Tax and Citizenship', *Critical Perspectives in Accounting* 6(2): 125–48.

Dahl, R.A. (1961) *Who Governs? Democracy and power in an American City*, New Haven, CT: Yale University Press.

Dean, M. (1999) *Governmentality: Power and Rule in Modern Society*, London: Sage.

Equal Opportunities Commission (1978) *Income Tax and Sex Discrimination*, Manchester: EOC.

Foucault, M. (1977) *Discipline and Punish: The Birth of the Prison*, Harmondsworth: Penguin.

——(1982) 'The subject and power', in H.L. Dreyfus and P. Rabinow (eds) *Michel Foucault: beyond structuralism and hermeneutics*, Brighton: Harvester.

Frecknall Hughes, J. and Oats, L. (2007) 'King John's tax innovations: Extortion, resistance, and the establishment of the principle of taxation by consent', *Accounting Historian Journal* 34 (2): 75–107.

Infanti, A.C. and Crawford, B.J. (eds) (2009) *Critical tax Theory: An Introduction*, New York: Cambridge University Press.

Lukes, S. (1974) *Power: A Radical View*, London and Basingstoke: MacMillan Press.

——(2005) *Power: A Radical View*, Basingstoke and New York: Palgrave MacMillan.

Miller, P. and Rose, N. (2008) *Governing the Present*, Cambridge: Polity Press.

Moran, B. (2009) 'Adam Smith and the search for an ideal tax system', in I.W. Martin, A.K. Merotra and M. Prasad (eds) *The New Fiscal Sociology*, New York: Cambridge University Press.

Oats, L. and Sadler, P. (2008) 'Accounting for the stamp act crisis', *Accounting Historian Journal* 35(2): 101–43.

Peel, M. (2011) 'Tax havens: In a sea of troubles', *Financial Times*, 12 January, available at: www.ft.com/cms/s/0/63e415ac-1e87-11e0-87d2-00144feab49a.html#axzz1TO7Cz2Mo (accessed 29 July 2011).
Rousseau, J.J. ([1762] 1973) *The Social Contract and Discourses*, London: J.M. Dent and Sons.
Schattschneider, E.E. (1960) *The Semi-Sovereign People: A Realist's View of Democracy in America*, New York: Holt, Rhinehart and Winston.
Smith, A. (1776) *An Enquiry into the Nature and Causes of the Wealth of Nations*, www.econlib.org/LIBRARY/Smith/smWN21.html (accessed 24 April 2006).

16

ACTOR-NETWORK THEORY AND TAX COMPLIANCE

Karen Boll

Actor-Network Theory (ANT) is a distinct social theory primarily developed by Bruno Latour, John Law and Michel Callon. It originated in the field of science studies in the 1980s. However, it is now used to analyse a broad spectrum of phenomena which in this chapter includes tax compliance practices. It is interesting at the outset to analyse tax compliance ANT as this approach provides a lens that reveals new aspects of tax compliance practices. Particularly, the approach focuses on the human and non-human elements of tax compliance and how tax compliance should not be seen as primarily affected by personal values and social norms. Instead, the ANT approach suggests that it is useful to understand tax compliance as 'heterogeneously engineered'. This will be elaborated in this chapter. In the broad picture, ANT is probably best known for its alternative view on agency as the approach insists that both human and non-human actors have agency. Further to this, ANT is known for its rejection of 'social explanations', which is a way of explaining phenomena that characterise much contemporary social theory. These characteristics of ANT are central to this chapter's argument that ANT can be used as an analytical lens that generates new insights into the field of tax compliance.

The chapter is divided into two parts. The first part gives an introduction to ANT by explaining ANT's position within the wider theoretical landscape, how ANT has a controversial view on agency (and on other matters), and how ANT is a response to many taken for granted assumptions within social science. The second part exemplifies how ANT can be used to analyse tax compliance practices. This analysis illustrates how using ANT to analyse tax compliance generates specific new insights about tax compliance. It is argued that these insights are of interest to academics in the tax compliance field and to tax practitioners working to regulate tax compliance.[1]

Part I: introducing ANT

ANT's position within the wider theoretical landscape

Tax researcher Margaret McKerchar (2008) highlights the need for reflection upon the philosophical paradigms within tax research. In this section I will use McKerchar's reflections to introduce the philosophical paradigm of ANT and I will introduce some 'guiding labels' whereby ANT is placed within the broader landscape of social science research.

McKerchar (2008: 6) explains that two broad philosophical research paradigms exist: positivism and interpretivism. These exhibit different characteristics and produce different kinds of research and knowledge. In this distinction between research paradigms ANT is placed in the interpretive paradigm. Furthermore, McKerchar suggests that interpretive research often uses a qualitative methodology (ibid.: 13). This is also true for ANT, as the approach often relies on ethnographic studies or interview-based material. For instance, when ANT started in the 1980s it was a novel idea that social science researchers went into science laboratories and made ethnographic studies of how the scientists produced scientific facts (Knorr-Cetina and Mulkay 1983; Latour 1987; Latour and Woolgar 1986). This way of doing ethnographic studies in diverse places has since been an aspiration of almost all ANT-inspired research. As a final reference to McKerchar, it should be mentioned that she suggests that within the interpretive/qualitative research paradigm there is a variety of theoretical frameworks. These cover such approaches as narrative research, phenomenology and grounded research (McKerchar 2008: 14). ANT is not mentioned in McKerchar's listing of approaches, but the approach is clearly a member of this family of theoretical frameworks.

What more specifically characterises ANT is 'constructivism' and 'heterogeneous engineering'. The label 'constructivism' refers to a belief that phenomena do not have an essential core and they do not mysteriously pop up out of nowhere (Latour 2005: 88). On the contrary, all phenomena have construction sites. Just as houses and buildings are fabricated at a construction site by architects, city planners, homeowners, etc., so too are all phenomena constructed somewhere by somebody or something (ibid.). When ANT states that phenomena are constructed, this means that ANT researchers are interested in accounting for how phenomena as coherence assemblages have been made. Here it is important to note that ANT is not 'social constructivism', where the focus is only on the social and human beings' role in the construction. Instead, ANT builds on 'socio-material constructivism' where both human and non-human actors are always seen as participating in the construction.

Because of this focus, 'heterogeneous engineering' has become another key term in ANT (Law 1987). 'Heterogeneous engineering' means that both human and non-human actors are engaged in building up the phenomena that we study. Concerning 'heterogeneous engineering', Law writes: 'the stability and form of artifacts should be seen as a function of the interaction of heterogeneous elements as these are shaped and assimilated into a network' (1987: 113). In line with this focus, much

ANT research aims at gaining insights precisely into the heterogeneous elements that shape and stabilise phenomena. This point will be further illustrated when the chapter later introduces how 'tax compliance practices' are also 'heterogeneously engineered'.

ANT's view on actor and network

Now, where does this leave us with respect to the actor and the network in Actor-Network Theory? Basically, an actor is a human or non-human that does something, that is, that makes things happen. The network is the name for the assemblage of heterogeneous actors that holds together or makes up the actor. In ANT's understanding of the world, all phenomena are actor-networks. This means that sometimes a phenomenon will appear as a single stabilised actor, while at other times the same phenomenon will appear as a network showing the heterogeneous actors that make up the phenomenon. As an example of this two-sided quality of phenomena let us look at what Latour terms a:

> tiny innovation commonly found in European hotels: attaching large cumbersome weights to room keys in order to remind customers that they should leave their key at the front desk every time they leave the hotel instead of taking it along on a tour of the city.
>
> *(Latour 1991: 104)*

If our object of study were to understand the phenomenon of leaving a hotel key at a reception desk, ANT suggests two readings of the situation. The practice of leaving the key can be understood as a stabilised practice whereby the hotel guests naturally do exactly the same thing whenever leaving the hotel. However, the practice can also be seen as a network wherein a lot of 'heterogeneous engineering' has been set in place to create this specific way of acting. In this case the heterogeneous network consists of an oral statement from the hotel manager asking the guests to leave their keys; it consists of a sign saying: 'Please leave your room key at the front desk before you go out'; and it consists of a large metal weight on the key. Together these diverse elements make the hotel guests more than happy to 'rid themselves of this annoying object which makes their pockets bulge and weighs down their handbags' (ibid.) and it prevents hotel keys from disappearing into thin air. Thus, there is a network of human and non-human actors which participates in shaping the apparent mundane practice of leaving the hotel key at the desk.

ANT as a response

The development of a theory is nearly always a response to either an empirical puzzle or in response to other theories that are seen as inadequate. This is also true of ANT. In the broader picture ANT can be seen as a theory that through close attention to the empirical reality questions many of the taken for granted assumptions within social science and especially within sociology. To sum up, ANT challenges what conventionally is seen as characterising an actor. It does this by stressing that agency stems from a network of human and non-human actors. When ANT is described as having a 'controversial insistence on the agency of non-humans', it is thus this definition of the actor being constituted as an actor-network and being constituted by both human and non-human actors which is referred to. Furthermore, ANT challenges the assumptions that given phenomena exist per se by drawing attention to the 'heterogeneous engineering' that constructs phenomena. Finally, ANT suggests that there is no such thing as the purely social. ANT will always point to the phenomena's socio-material construction. There are always materials, techniques and devices involved in constructing phenomena.

To these theoretical aspects of ANT there should also be added a methodological comment. Since the early science studies, ethnographic fieldwork has been closely linked to ANT. To 'follow the actor' has been a mantra within ANT and Latour describes doing ANT as tracing the different controversies, actors and networks that constitute a phenomenon (Latour 1987). Such a work of tracing which actors make up phenomena cannot be done 'theoretically'. It implies that the object under study is being closely followed and investigated. Thus, nearly all ANT-inspired studies involve a combination of in-depth interviews, observations, participant observation and study of written material, archives and so forth (Chapter 7).

In introducing relevant ANT literature it is useful to distinguish between 'classic' ANT literature and 'after-ANT' literature. The classic ANT literature was written in the 1980–90s and presents many of the basic assumptions in ANT (such as Callon 1986; Latour 1981, 1983, 1987, 1988, 1991, 1992; and Law 1994). This chapter builds primarily on this literature. The after-ANT literature was written from the late 1990s onwards. The term 'after-ANT' literature derives from the book *Actor-Network Theory and After* (Law and Hassard 1999). In this book a number of the authors behind ANT reflect on the approach's status and on some of the critiques of the theory (such as Gad and Jensen 2010; Latour 1999a, 1999b, 2005; Law 2004; Law and Hassard 1999; Mol 2002; Star 1991; and Vikkelsoe 2007).

Part II: using ANT to analyse tax compliance

Moral as an effect

The aim of this second part of the chapter is to illustrate how an ANT analysis of tax compliance could look. To do this, Latour's (1992) text 'Where are the Missing Masses? The Sociology of a Few Mundane Artefacts' is introduced. The aim is to use Latour's thoughts on how compliant seat belt users are constructed to gain insights into how tax compliance practices are constructed. In the article Latour discusses how 'driving with a seat belt' is accomplished. Latour says:

> Early this morning, I was in a bad mood and decided to break a law and start my car without buckling my seat belt. My car usually does not want to start before I buckle the belt. It first flashes a red light 'FASTEN

> YOUR SEAT BELT!', then an alarm sounds; it is so high pitched, so relentless, so repetitive, that I cannot stand it. After ten seconds I swear and put the belt on.
>
> *(Latour 1992: 225)*

This incident causes Latour to reflect upon his morality of driving with the seat belt buckled. He asks whether it is *him* who is acting morally, being influenced by the power of artefacts, or if the moral is in the *artefacts*, which force him to obey the law. Latour concludes that it is neither him nor the artefacts alone that make him buckle the seat belt. Instead, his morality is made as an effect of him, plus the car, plus dozens of patented engineers (the seat belt technology, the red light, the alarm, etc.), plus the police (ibid.: 226). Following the presentation of ANT in the first part of the chapter, it could be said that 'Latour as a compliant driver' has been 'heterogeneously engineered' and that both human and non-human actors have participated in constructing him as such. What is important to note is that in this example Latour tries to illustrate that his morality is neither purely humanly made – that is entirely individualistic – nor is his morality purely technologically or structurally determined. More appropriately, his morality might be characterised as a 'hybrid' composed of several different elements that operate at the same practical level instead of being derived either from external structures or internal motivations.

Looking at the same situation with traditional sociological lenses would probably provide a 'social' explanation of the fact that more people today use seat belts. Such an explanation would say that the use of seat belts is due to a general change in morals influenced by the police and laws. What was before the law perceived as normal – driving yourself and with your kids without safety belts – is now morally unacceptable. The morals have changed and this is the cause for more people using seat belts. Latour and ANT oppose such an explanation, as the point in ANT is that 'a new moral concerning the use of seat belts' is not the cause of the change, but the outcome of this 'heterogeneous engineering' process. As an effect of this new constellation of human and non-human actors people have adopted a new attitude to using seat belts.

Tax compliance as 'heterogeneously engineered'

Latour's seat belt story is illustrative if we switch from looking at compliance in traffic to being compliant in relation to tax regulation. Now, the question is how tax compliance practices are being constructed. A traditional 'social' explanation within tax compliance research emphasises how personal values and social norms influence tax compliance. Such a view is, for instance, advanced by the tax researcher Marjorie Kornhauser. She writes:

> Recent literature reveals ... that the decision to comply is not purely rational. Rather, personal values, social norms, and non-rational cognitive processes also strongly affect the decision ... Research shows that tax compliance is affected by (social and personal) norms such as those

regarding procedural justice, trust, belief in the legitimacy of the government, reciprocity, altruism, and identification with the group.

(Kornhauser 2007: 138)[2]

Taking Latour's hotel key and seat belt examples into consideration, it is reasonable to say that Latour would probably disagree with Kornhauser in her emphasis on personal values and social norms as strongly affecting decisions to comply. Instead, Latour would say that these are not the causes, but the effects of a specific network of heterogeneous actors that construct specific attitudes and practices of tax compliance. Following this line of thought the next question is how to gain access to this network of heterogeneous actors.

As discussed at the beginning of the chapter, the early ANT researchers went into laboratories to undertake ethnographic studies of how the scientists produced facts. In this way they started seeing the 'heterogeneous engineering' of the facts. Similarly, I went into business offices, typically sitting beside the desk of a bookkeeper, to study ethnographically how tax compliance was being enacted in the office. During the fieldwork I talked to numerous bookkeepers, business owners and auditors, and I observed their work of being compliant with the tax regulations. These people showed me the offices wherein tax compliance takes place and I heard stories about actors that play a role in constructing tax compliance. I was shown how cash registers in restaurants were used, how warning registers are set in action towards bad payers, how bookkeepers use different coloured pens to make notes in the accounts, how plastic pockets were kept with questions to ask the tax officials, how reminder notices were sent to businesses with small angry men drawn on them, how different IT systems were used for filing and registring, and how phones displaying money transfers were used to monitor businesses payments, etc. (see also Chapter 7 on ethnography and tax compliance).

Through the fieldwork I began to see the 'hybrid' character of tax compliance practices by seeing the different actors that shape tax compliance. Looking at the situation where pens, computers, forms, memos, telephone conversations, stomach pains and the like were at play to construct tax compliance, it makes little sense to reduce tax compliance to being primarily affected by personal values and social norms. If we do so, all the practicalities, artefacts, exciting small details and expression disappear. Tax compliance in practice is not just about the bookkeeper's or the business owner's personal values, it is about a complex network of various very different elements that have to be coordinated in the office. What is fascinating is that an ethnographic study opens up these practicalities of actually doing tax compliance; practicalities that are erased in much of the present qualitative research, and all of the quantitative research, on tax compliance.

The ANT approach permits the researcher to see which actors participate in the networks constituting tax compliance. A point is that the networks constituting tax compliance vary from business to business. Having an auditor and a minimum of cash in the network help to create a compliance practice, whereas the absence of auditor and cash economy enhance non-compliance. Paraphrasing Law, it can be said that 'the stability and form of *tax compliance* should be seen as a function of the interaction of heterogeneous elements as these are shaped and assimilated into a network'. This issue is especially relevant for tax authorities. If an element such as 'cash economy' is assimilated into the network shaping tax compliance in a business, this consequently alters the stability and form of the business's tax compliance. If problematic elements are removed from the network, it might help to enhance compliance. This way of understanding the elements that shape tax compliance practices opens up the possibility of quite direct intervention from tax authorities towards businesses. In having knowledge about the elements constituting the network, the regulating authorities can work at excluding or assimilating elements into the network.

In this ANT-inspired analysis tax compliance is understood as a practice that includes the activities of numerous actors. Contrary to Kornhauser's view, the analysis does not see 'personal values' and 'social norms' as causes of tax compliance. Instead, personal values and social norms are the outcome of how the network of actors is put together. The central point is that the ANT approach does not acknowledge personal values and social norms as explanations of tax compliance as it is exactly such phenomena and their construction that need to be explained by the analysis. The tricky thing about an ANT analysis is thus to understand how all those elements that social scientists tend to use as explanations are now what need to be explained. In addition, the methodological challenge is that the explanations are sought by meticulously focusing on how practices are enacted, shaped and changed in the everyday life of hotel guests, safe drivers, bookkeepers or whatever the ANT researcher wishes to analyse.

Summing up: ANT and tax compliance research

This chapter has introduced ANT and it has given a preview of how ANT can be used to analyse tax compliance practices. Summing up the chapter, it is relevant to pay attention to how the ANT approach can contribute to the field of tax compliance research. First, it should be emphasised that using ANT opposes a 'social' explanation of tax compliance, where focus is on personal values and social norms. Second, using ANT as an analytical frame includes non-humans in understanding how tax compliance is constructed. Third, ANT draws attention to the 'heterogeneous engineering' of tax compliance. Taken together, the ANT approach helps to produce insights into the daily practices of complying with the letter of the tax law. This is interesting for academics as it shows how using a theory within the interpretive and qualitative paradigm can be applied to the tax field. In addition, the analysis is of interest for tax authorities as it provides a detailed analysis of the elements constituting tax compliance. This can provide a background for intervention to enhance tax compliance. By highlighting these features and the usability of an ANT-inspired analysis, this chapter has aimed to show that new insights into tax compliance can be produced by using an ANT approach. Such new insights can complement the vast majority of tax compliance research which is based in the positivist and quantitative research paradigm and which emphasises the role of social factors such as morals, values and norms in relation to tax compliance.

Notes

1 The chapter refers to theoretical ideas developed within the author's PhD project. The PhD focuses on how ethnography and ideas within Actor-Network Theory can be used to analyse tax compliance.

2 For more researchers who regards tax compliance as determined by 'social' factors, see for instance Alm and Gomez (2008); Alm *et al.* (2010); Murphy (2004, 2008); and Wenzel (2007).

References

Alm, J. and Gomez, J.L. (2008) 'Social capital and tax morale in Spain', *Economic Analysis and Policy* 38(1): 73–87.

Alm, J., Martinez-Vazquez, J. and Torgler, B. (2010) *Developing Alternative Frameworks for Explaining Tax Compliance*, New York: Routledge.

Callon, M. (1986) 'Some elements of a sociology of translation: Domestication of the scallops and the fishermen of St Brieuc Bay', in J. Law (ed.), *Power, Action and Belief: A New Sociology of Knowledge?* London: Routledge, pp. 196–223.

Gad, C. and Jensen, C.B. (2010) 'On the consequences of post-ANT', *Science, Technology & Human Values* 35(1): 55–80.

Knorr-Cetina, K.D. and Mulkay, M. (eds) (1983) *Science Observed. Perspectives in the Social Study of Science*, London: Sage Publications.

Kornhauser, M.E. (2007) 'Normative and cognitive aspects of tax compliance: Literature review and recommendations for the IRS regarding individual taxpayers', in N.E. Olson (ed.), *National Taxpayer Advocate – 2007 Annual Report to Congress*, Taxpayer Advocate Service. Research Studies and Reports 2, pp.138–80.

Latour, B. (1981) 'Unscrewing the big Leviathan: how actors macro-structure reality and how sociologists help them to do so', in K.D. Knorr-Cetina and A. Cicourel (eds), *Advances in Social Theory and Methodology*, Routledge.

——(1983) 'Give me a laboratory and I will raise the world', in K.D. Knorr-Cetina and M. Mulkay (eds), *Science Observed. Perspectives on the Social Study of Science*, London: Sage, pp.141–70.

——(1987) *Science in Action. How to Follow Scientists and Engineers Through Society*, Cambridge, Mass: Harvard University Press.

——(1988) 'The politics of explanation', in S. Woolgar (ed.) *Knowledge and Reflexivity*, London: Sage, pp. 155–77.

——(1991) 'Technology is society made durable', in J. Law (ed.) *A Sociology of Monsters: Essays on Power, Technology and Domination*, London: Routledge, p. 240.

——(1992) 'Where are the missing masses? The sociology of a few mundane artifacts', in W. Bijker and J. Law (eds), *Shaping Technology-Building Society. Studies in Sociotechnical Change*, Cambridge: MIT Press, pp. 225–59.

——(1999a) 'On recalling ANT', in J. Law and J. Hassard (eds) *Actor Network Theory and After. Sociological Review Monographs*, Oxford: Blackwell, p. 256

——(1999b) *Pandora's Hope: Essays on the Reality of Science Studies*, Cambridge: Harvard University Press.

——(2005) *Reassembling the Social. An Introduction to Actor-Network-Theory*, Oxford: Oxford University Press.

Latour, B. and Woolgar, S. (1986) *Laboratory Life*, Princeton, NJ: Princeton University Press.

Law, J. (1987) 'Technology and Heterogeneous Engineering: The Case of Portuguese Expansion', in W.E. Bijker, T.P. Hughes and T. Pinch (eds) *The Social Construction of Technological Systems. New Directions in the Sociology and History of Technology*, Cambridge, MA and London: The MIT Press.

——(1994) *Organizing modernity*, Oxford: Blackwell.

——(2004) *After Method Mess in Social Science Research*, London: Taylor & Francis.
Law, J. and Hassard, J. (1999) *Actor Network Theory and After*, Oxford: Blackwell Publishers.
McKerchar, M.A. (2008) 'Philosophical paradigms, inquiry strategies and knowledge claims: Applying the principles of research design and conduct to taxation', *eJournal of Tax Research* 6(1): 5–22.
Mol, A. (2002) *The Body Multiple. Ontology in Medical Practice*, Durham, NC: Duke University Press.
Murphy, K. (2004) 'The role of trust in nurturing compliance: A study of accused tax avoiders', *Law and Human Behavior* 28(2): 187–209.
——(2008) 'Enforcing tax compliance: To punish or persuade?' *Economic Analysis and Policy* 38(1): 113–35.
Star, S.L. (1991) 'Power, technologies and the phenomenology of conventions: On being allergic to onions', in J. Law (ed.), *A Sociology of Monsters: Essays on Power, Technology and Domination*, London: Routledge, pp. 26–56.
Vikkelsoe, S. (2007) 'Description as intervention: Engagement and resistance in actor-network analyses', *Science as Culture* 16(3): 297.
Wenzel, M. (2007) 'The multiplicity of taxpayer identities and their implications for tax ethics', *Law & Policy* 29(1): 31–50.

PART III
Tales from the field

The aim of Part III is to bring the research process to life by providing glimpses into real research projects. All of the contributors to this part have very generously agreed to share with readers some insights into how they went about their research projects. In so doing, they have not been tied to any particular format or narrative style but rather have been allowed to choose how best to present their work. Therefore, readers will see a number of different ways of describing research, which tend to vary from discipline to discipline. Within law, for example, it is usual to see a more formal approach with use of the third person. In some other disciplines, for example accounting, there is increasingly a more personal tone, particularly for interpretive studies, in acknowledgement of the role of the researcher (see Chapter 2). The contributors were specifically asked to keep their chapters short, which is a difficult thing to ask of any researcher. The chapters should not, therefore, be read as complete explanations of the underlying research and readers should refer to the original studies for fuller coverage.

All of the chapters contained in this part deal with aspects of tax practice in some shape or form. Current issues in tax administration from the perspective of the administrator, for example, are dealt with by Oats and Tuck (Chapter 20), and Tuck (Chapter 19). Tax practice from a practitioner view is the focus of Hasseldine, Holland and van der Rijt (Chapter 17), Doyle, Frecknall Hughes and Glaister (Chapter 18), and Freedman, Loomer and Vella (Chapter 21). International corporate tax is the subject of Mulligan (Chapter 24), who focuses on the taxpayer perspective, and Rogers (Chapter 22), who considers both the taxpayer and tax authority views. Broader issues of tax policy are the subject of Marriott (Chapter 25), Heij (Chapter 23), and Evans and Collier (Chapter 26).

Hasseldine, Holland and van der Rijt, in Chapter 17, describe their approach to a research project funded by a professional body. The project described by Oats and Tuck (Chapter 20) was similarly funded by a professional body. Funding from such bodies carries with it a responsibility to deliver a research report that is accessible to a practitioner audience, which at one level can inhibit the depth of analysis. These two examples of funded research projects both make use of theoretical framings from other disciplines to analyse their findings. Hasseldine, Holland and van der Rijt draw on the knowledge management literature, while Oats and Tuck look to communities of practice (see Chapter 13).

Obtaining access to an organisation or individual interviewees is one of the most problematic aspects of qualitative fieldwork research, and a number of contributors describe their experiences in this regard. Rogers (Chapter 22), Mulligan (Chapter 24), and Oats and Tuck (Chapter 20) all leveraged their professional qualifications and background in order to secure access, but then also during the course of interviews to achieve greater depth. Oats and Tuck (Chapter 20) had to enter into a formal confidentiality agreement with Her Majesty's Revenue & Customs (HMRC) as part of their access arrangements.

A number of contributors used preliminary or pilot interviews and found them helpful in preparing for the main interviews in terms of identifying and clarifying the issues, for example Rogers (Chapter 22) and Mulligan (Chapter 24).

Some of the contributions deal with the difficult issue of comparative taxation, studying similar phenomena in two or more jurisdictions. Heij (Chapter 23) researches Vietnam and Indonesia, Marriott (Chapter 25) Australia and New Zealand, and Rogers (Chapter 22), although less overtly comparative, the UK and USA.

Finally, most of the contributions draw on theoretical frameworks to understand their findings, but two contributions in particular describe the actual process of developing an analytical framework by combining concepts from two sets of literature. Mulligan (Chapter 24) brings together the tax planning literature and new institutional sociology, as extended by work on endogeneity of law. Heij (Chapter 23) brings together different versions of institutional theory from politics and sociology.

It is hoped that readers will benefit from a behind-the-scenes glimpse of some specific research projects and draw inspiration from them in pursuing their own research agendas.

17

THE MANAGEMENT OF TAX KNOWLEDGE

John Hasseldine, Kevin Holland and Pernill G.A. van der Rijt

This chapter outlines a funded research project undertaken in 2007. Funded by the Association of Chartered Certified Accountants (ACCA), the project adopted a multi-method approach that entailed a series of face-to-face and telephone interviews as well as a written questionnaire. To the best of our knowledge, this project is the first to focus on the management of tax knowledge within UK corporate taxpayers. We also examine corporate taxpayers, Her Majesty's Revenue & Customs (HMRC) and accounting firms as tax advisers in the wider setting of a market for tax knowledge. Our aim was to determine how corporate taxpayers develop and use tax knowledge, and in particular the processes by which externally derived tax legislation is incorporated into corporate taxpayers' tax knowledge along with internally generated knowledge based on experience. We were particularly interested in:

- What determines the categories of tax knowledge within a corporate taxpayer, and what is the role of HMRC and external advisers in this respect?
- What information sources do corporate taxpayers use to construct tax knowledge?
- How is tax knowledge retained and its relevance ensured?
- How do various parties with corporate taxpayers access tax knowledge?

The design of the project and the analysis of the findings were informed by the literature on knowledge management. Knowledge management is a multidisciplinary profession that has established a relatively strong position in various disciplines, such as economics, organisation studies, business and management, communication science, and information technology. Two of the authors had previously identified (Hasseldine and Holland 2005) four characteristics of the UK's corporate income tax system that impose significant compliance and related tax-planning costs on companies. These characteristics have knowledge management consequences as they must all be managed within the tax function of corporate taxpayers, and are: 1 the complexity of legislation; 2 uncertainty over the nature of the administrative requirements; 3 awareness and interpretation of changes in legislation and administrative procedures; and 4 the administrative effort required to satisfy a particular item of legislation.

Little attention has been given to knowledge management in accounting and finance research, and in addition other research disciplines rarely pay specific attention to knowledge management issues in the taxation profession. Furthermore, current research on knowledge management is largely aimed at explaining and facilitating intra-organisational processes of knowledge-sharing (e.g. Hansen *et al.* 1999; O'Dell and Grayson 1998; Riege 2005; Szulanski 1995; and Tsai 2002). Studies that are conducted in the field of inter-organisational knowledge-sharing primarily focus on cooperation processes between competitors (e.g. Bengtsson and Kock 2000; Foti 2004; Loebbecke and Angehrn 2003; Loebbecke *et al.* 1999; Sjogren and Fay 2002), and in strategic alliances (e.g. Kale *et al.* 2000; Phan and Peridis 2000). A specific area in research on inter-organisational knowledge-sharing that has been underexposed so far concerns the relationship between potentially non-competitive organisations. Additionally, there are limited publications about the link between inter- and intra-organisational processes of knowledge-sharing.

Our study sought to contribute to filling these gaps. The central aim of our study is to seek insights into how developments in tax legislation in the UK are captured by corporate taxpayers and are incorporated into their tax knowledge. The institutions that play a crucial role in the implementation of tax knowledge are the government – more specifically HMRC – accounting firms, and corporate taxpayers. There is a limit to the extent to which these organisations can be competitive towards each other. They have a mutual dependency in enabling the successful implementation of new legislation, and are considered to be willing to share knowledge for this purpose. The study focuses on exploring both processes of knowledge-sharing between organisations, and on the implementation and utilisation of knowledge within each of these organisations. Relevant themes that are addressed are the mutual understanding between these organisations, the way they share and incorporate tax knowledge, and under which conditions they do so. Besides the theoretical considerations mentioned above, the study has practical relevance too. We argue that our study could well benefit HMRC, accounting firms and corporate taxpayers. For example, more insight into the implementation of changes in tax legislation by accounting firms and corporate taxpayers could result in more successful applications of the legislation, particularly when the legislation has a desired behavioural objective. In terms of cost effectiveness this may imply a benefit to HMRC due to lower administrative costs and a higher efficacy in making accounting firms and corporate taxpayers comply with regulations. Similarly, accounting firms and corporate taxpayers may experience fewer compliance costs and more appropriate tax burdens.

Knowledge markets

The relationship between the three organisations in our study that are involved in communicating, implementing and utilising changes in tax legislation – HMRC, accounting firms and corporate taxpayers – can be placed in a knowledge management context by using Davenport and Prusak's (2000) view on knowledge markets. In these markets, the authors argue, knowledge is regarded as an economic asset. In the transaction of this asset, several players are active. These players are described as knowledge buyers, sellers and brokers. Davenport and Prusak mention that 'an individual can perform all three roles in a single day and sometimes play more than one role simultaneously' (ibid.: 27). Knowledge buyers are people who actively seek knowledge. People who share knowledge with others, in return for (financial) compensation, are defined as knowledge sellers. Finally, knowledge brokers are people who connect buyers and sellers. All three types of players aim to benefit from exchanging knowledge. Possible motivations for sharing knowledge that are mentioned by Davenport and Prusak are reciprocity, repute and altruism.

Davenport and Prusak (2000) define knowledge markets on an organisational level and their players on an individual level. However, we believe that knowledge markets may also operate on an inter-organisational level, with organisational instead of individual players. In this respect the relationships between the three major parties that are involved in our study can be perceived as a knowledge market in tax legislation. HMRC, which develops and communicates new tax legislation and experiences, can be regarded as a knowledge seller. Both corporate taxpayers and accounting firms are organisations that are likely to seek knowledge about new tax legislation. In this respect they can be defined as knowledge buyers. Accounting firms, however, may also have the role of knowledge brokers. They are considered to function as intermediaries between corporate taxpayers (knowledge buyers) and HMRC (knowledge seller), a role that can also be described as 'gate keeping' or 'boundary spanning' (Choo 1998).

Qualitative interviews

The goal of our study was to gain more insight into inter- and intra-organisational processes of knowledge-sharing about new tax legislation. For this purpose, a total of 19 in-depth interviews were conducted with employees from HMRC, accounting firms and corporate taxpayers throughout the UK.

Three employees from HMRC were interviewed: one was involved with 'general guidance' and two were involved with providing guidance on a specific corporate tax area. We used the 'Top 50 accountancy firms' published by *Accountancy Age* to select four accounting firms (and seven interviewees) for participation in the study. These included three interviewees from the 'big four'[1] and two with mid-tier firms. In addition, we obtained access to a single office partnership and a sole proprietor. Of the seven interviewees, two worked in the area of 'formal' knowledge management systems while the remaining five were involved with practical aspects of corporate tax. All interviewees held senior positions within their respective firms.

To obtain a reasonable coverage of likely issues faced by corporate taxpayers, we identified several key factors and screening requirements prior to selecting for interview. Factors that were used in selecting potential corporate taxpayers to interview are the degree of regulation, the degree of capital intensity, increases in research and development (R&D) expenditure, incurring a tax loss, size and foreign presence. Also, in securing a minimum level of regulatory responsibility, corporate taxpayers were required to be quoted on the London Stock Exchange. Corporate taxpayers were identified in the following industries: manufacturing; wholesale, retail, trade; transport and communication; government; and electricity, gas and water. The Thompson Financials *Datastream* and Bureau Van Dijk *FAME* databases were used to select corporate taxpayers for participation in the project by reference to the characteristics identified above. The corporate taxpayers were contacted by telephone and email. Ultimately, nine corporate taxpayers in several fields agreed to participate. The interviewees were all occupied in the field of taxation and/or knowledge management. Eleven interviews were conducted face to face, and eight interviews were conducted by telephone. Most face-to-face interviews were conducted by two interviewers, and the telephone interviews by one interviewer.

In total, three different interview guides were designed for conducting the interviews: one for HMRC, one for the accounting firms, and one for the corporate taxpayers. An interview guide is different from an interview questionnaire in the sense that there is no strict order in the questions that are asked by the interviewers. In addition, the precise formulation of questions can vary with each interview. Interviews conducted with an interview guide have a relatively open character and the course of the interview is largely determined by the information that is provided by the interviewee. The guide lists several topics and focal points that enable the interviewers to steer the interview. In the interview guides that were used in the present study, a variety of subjects was covered, among which communication flows about new tax legislation between HMRC, accounting firms and corporate taxpayers, communication flows about new tax legislation within HMRC, accounting firms and corporate taxpayers' firms, and barriers to and facilitators of sharing knowledge within and between organisations. All interviews were recorded and transcribed. Subsequently the transcripts were coded and analysed with the help of NVivo software.

In our literature review we elaborated on potential relationships between the parties involved in our study by referring to a knowledge market (Davenport and Prusak 2000). In line with the common players on such a knowledge market, HMRC was identified as a knowledge seller, accounting firms were defined as knowledge brokers, and corporate taxpayers as knowledge buyers. Besides the focus on the knowledge flows between these organisations, we also pointed out the significance of knowledge flows that take place within each of these organisations.

Our interview findings confirm Davenport and Prusak's (2000) original definition of knowledge markets. We found knowledge sellers, brokers and buyers both within the organisations that participated in the study and also between the organisations. Inter-organisational knowledge flows appear to be crucial for the creation of intra-organisational knowledge and vice versa. For instance, HMRC interviewees mentioned the importance of contributions of accounting firms in internal training sessions. They also reported the appreciation of receiving feedback from accounting firms and corporate taxpayers, as this feedback provides opportunities to improve tax legislation and tax administration, in which case issues of timing become relevant. Some of the other findings are as follows:

- Identification of target audiences and timing of the knowledge flow are important considerations for HMRC in their external communication. HMRC use knowledge brokers such as accounting firms to distribute knowledge amongst their (potential) clients and will also in some cases seek to make contact with knowledge buyers (corporate taxpayers) directly.
- Corporate taxpayer interviewees also use external sources for acquiring and developing internal tax knowledge. In turn, the interviews show that intra-organisational knowledge flows are essential for successful inter-organisational flows of knowledge. Only with the appropriate knowledge are corporate taxpayers able to utilise this knowledge to their benefit. In this respect, several interviewees mentioned that their company is often dependent on non-tax professionals in making successful tax claims. Consequently, internal knowledge buyers and sellers can be identified. Dependent on the direction of intra-organisational knowledge flows, the identity of internal knowledge buyers and sellers can be reversible.
- If the tax professionals within the corporate taxpayer are not fully informed of the context, and alternative or competing non-tax professionals exist with differing incentives, conflicts can arise. The avoidance of these conflicts requires a certain level of knowledge and has implications for the appropriate level of decision-making delegation.
- Successful transfer of knowledge can be improved by the appropriate motivation and use of subject experts, both internally and externally. For instance, a particular seller can add credibility to a particular transfer.
- The dynamic relationship and interdependence between inter- and intra-organisational knowledge flows can also be found in the interviews that were conducted with employees of accounting firms. An important issue mentioned here focuses on knowledge capture, level of detail and concerns over information overload.

In line with the literature review, the interviews indicate that the intermediate role of accounting firms is acknowledged by all players in the knowledge market. Both HMRC as a knowledge seller and corporate taxpayers as knowledge buyers perceive accounting firms as knowledge brokers. Accounting firms seem to vigorously conquer and defend this position. HMRC interviewees seem to have a relatively positive attitude towards the mediating role of accounting firms in communicating with corporate taxpayers. In addition, corporate taxpayer interviewees mentioned benefits from having accounting firms as intermediates in knowledge flows from and to HMRC.

Nevertheless, the interviews do show that knowledge sellers and buyers also experience hesitation towards the role of knowledge brokers. In particular the commercialisation of knowledge by accounting firms is criticised. For instance, HMRC interviewees expressed concerns about the possibility of accounting firms having a different interpretation of tax legislation and administrative procedures. Corporate taxpayers appear to experience doubts about the reliability of the accounting firms, especially when accounting firms formally contracted as a knowledge seller simultaneously act as a knowledge buyer (or 'knowledge rustler'). Aside from quality and reliance issues, the choice of knowledge supplier can be influenced by the ability to retain or capture the knowledge created. There are potential limitations to retain both internally and externally generated knowledge.

Interviewees did provide examples of competitive and non-complementary behaviour, particularly when accounting firms, formally contracted as knowledge brokers, change their focus to knowledge 'buyers' (or knowledge rustlers), and where HMRC and corporate taxpayers transacted directly without the knowledge or 'approval' of accountancy firms. Although these tensions do inhibit effective knowledge-sharing, their underlying causes are a necessary aspect of the market. In one respect this has a beneficial effect, as the high fixed cost involved in acquiring knowledge and skills to the necessary degree of competence would prohibit the majority of corporate taxpayers from gaining access to appropriate advice.

Mail survey

The second strand of this research project consisted of two surveys, one of accounting firms as tax advisers and the second of corporate taxpayers. Prior to being hosted on an independent website, the two surveys were piloted among a group of academic researchers, who, in addition to their current involvement in tax-based research, had varying degrees of practical tax experience. Minor modifications were made to the surveys following this process.

An invitation to participate, along with details of the research project, was contained in ACCA's electronic journal *Accounting and Business*. This was followed up by sector-targeted emails sent by ACCA to sections of its membership. In total, 445 responses were received, split almost equally between the two groups: 223 corporate taxpayers and 222 advisers.

The results from the mail surveys fed into our policy recommendations. The surveys provided further support for the findings of the interviews that the initial characterisation of the tax knowledge market is generally non-competitive. A recurring theme from the interviews with accountancy firms and HMRC was confirmed by the mail surveys, which showed a low level of dealings with operational decision-makers within corporate taxpayers, e.g. the staff of human resources departments, production or R&D-related responsibilities. Accountancy firms also indicated that the information they require from operational decision-makers is not generally delivered either in an appropriate format or on a timely basis. This is consistent with low-level awareness among operational decision-makers within corporate taxpayers, often as a consequence of a lack of any formal requirement to consider taxation when making operational decisions. Paradoxically, a lack of tax awareness amongst corporate taxpayers may not be in the interests of HMRC as it can adversely impact both the success of tax incentives and tax management in general.

Increasing tax awareness amongst corporate taxpayers is one of a number of policy implications that follow from the project. The full set of implications is set out in a report prepared for ACCA (Hasseldine *et al.* 2009). The report also contains full details of the project, including details of the interview schedules and mail survey questionnaires. In addition, further analysis of our findings in the context of the critical accounting literature was undertaken in Hasseldine *et al.* 2011.

Note

1 These are Deloitte Touche Tohmatsu, Ernst & Young, KPMG and Pricewaterhouse-Coopers.

References

Bengtsson, M. and Kock, S. (2000) '"Coopetition" in business networks: To cooperate and compete simultaneously', *Industrial Marketing Management* 29: 411–26.

Choo, C.W. (1998) *The Knowing Organization: How Organizations Use Information to Construct Meaning, Create Knowledge, and Make Decisions*, New York: Oxford University Press.

Davenport, T.H. and Prusak, L. (2000) *Working Knowledge: How Organizations Manage What They Know*, Boston, MA: Harvard Business School Press.

Foti, R. (2004) 'A novel approach', *PM Network*, June: 24–30.

Hansen, M.T., Nohria, N. and Tierney, T. (1999) 'What's your strategy for managing knowledge?' *Harvard Business Review* 77(2): 106–16.

Hasseldine, J. and Holland, K.M. (2005) 'The compliance costs and burdens associated with businesses meeting their Corporation Tax obligations. A consultancy report for the National Audit Office', in *Corporation Tax: companies managed by HM Revenue and Customs' Areas Office,* National Audit Office HC 678 Session 2005–06.

Hasseldine, J., Holland, K.M. and van der Rijt, P. (2009) *The Management of Tax Knowledge*, Research report 112, London: Association of Chartered Certified Accountants.

——(2011) 'The Market for Corporate Tax Knowledge', *Critical Perspectives on Accounting* 22: 39–52.

Kale, P., Singh, H. and Perlmutter, H. (2000) 'Learning and protection of proprietary assets in strategic alliances: Building relational capital', *Strategic Management Journal* 21: 217–37.

Loebbecke, C. and Angehrn, A.A. (2003) 'Open source platforms under co-opetition: A comparative analysis of SourceForge and "CodeX" (Xerox) as two "co-opetitive learning and knowledge exchange networks" (CoLKENs)', Proceedings of the 11th European Conference on Information Systems, ECIS 2003, Naples, Italy, 16–21 June 2003, is2.lse.ac.uk/asp/aspecis/20030088.pdf (accessed 29 November 2006).

Loebbecke, C., Van Fenema, P.C. and Powell, P. (1999) 'Co-opetition and knowledge transfer', *The DATA BASE for Advances in Information Systems* 30(2): 14–25.

O'Dell, C. and Grayson, C.J. (1998) 'If only we knew what we know: Identification and transfer of internal best practices', *California Management Review* 40(3): 154–74.

Phan, P.H. and Peridis, T. (2000) 'Knowledge creation in strategic alliances: Another look at organizational learning', *Asia Pacific Journal of Management* 17: 201–22.

Riege, A. (2005) 'Three-dozen knowledge-sharing barriers managers must consider', *Journal of Knowledge Management* 9(3): 18–35.

Sjogren, J. and Fay, J. (2002) 'Cost issues in online learning: Using "co-opetition" to advantage', *Change* May/June: 53–57.

Szulanski, G. (1995) 'Unpacking stickiness: An empirical investigation of the barriers to transfer best practice inside the firm', *Academy of Management Proceedings* 437–41.

Tsai, W. (2002) 'Social structure of "coopetition" within a multiunit organization: Coordination, competition, and intraorganizational knowledge sharing', *Organization Science* 13(2): 179–90.

18

ETHICS IN TAX PRACTICE

An exploratory analysis

Elaine Doyle, Jane Frecknall Hughes and Keith W. Glaister

Introduction

Tax, once the remit of the 'general practitioner' accountant or lawyer, has grown in complexity and importance and has become a distinct and highly specialised profession in itself. The combination of self-assessment systems, complex tax codes, increased penalties for non-compliance with tax legislation and higher levels of cross-border activity has resulted in an increased reliance on tax practitioners' advice. As significant players in the tax compliance process, tax practitioners are in a position to influence the level of tax that their clients pay through their reporting recommendations, thus making them worthy of focused research.

However, there is a growing concern regarding the ethical behaviour of tax practitioners (Shafer and Simmons 2008). Many firms in the USA have been investigated in recent years for facilitating aggressive tax avoidance through the marketing of questionable tax shelters (Herman 2004; Johnston 2004; Scannell 2005), and companies are often accused of using 'tax havens' for the primary purpose of avoiding, or indeed evading, their tax obligations (Godar *et al.* 2005). Shafer and Simmons (2008) suggest that some tax advisers have abandoned concern for the public interest or social welfare in favour of commercialism and client advocacy. They go so far as to suggest that tax practitioners do not believe strongly in the value of ethical or socially responsible corporate behaviour. Nevertheless, while many studies in recent years have focused on ethics in accounting, it is acknowledged that the nature and dimension of ethical issues in tax practice have been largely unexplored (Erard 1993; Marshall *et al.* 1998; Frecknall Hughes 2002).

The aim of the research project described in this chapter was to contribute to the debate on ethics in tax practice by carrying out interviews with tax practitioners concerning their perceptions of ethics, and by exploring the process and links by which ethics seems to be increasingly equated or linked with risk management. This chapter describes the research process that was undertaken and reports the primary research findings. The emphasis of the chapter is on the research process undertaken rather than the findings, which are consequently presented in summary form rather than discussed comprehensively.[1]

The literature

A review of several strands of literature on tax practitioners relating to tax compliance, ethics and risk management was undertaken with a view to exploring the context within which tax practitioners operate. The literature review highlighted the increasingly important role of tax practitioners in the tax compliance process (see, for example, Collins *et al.* 1990; Erard 1993; Andreoni *et al.* 1998; Marshall *et al.* 1998). It provided evidence of the increased recognition that there is an ethical dimension to tax work (e.g. Boucher 1993; Stainer *et al.* 1997; Marshall *et al.* 1998; Hume *et al.* 1999; Bobek and Radtke 2007). Both the endogenous variables particular to tax practitioners, which have been recognised as influencing ethical behaviour, and the exogenous variables, which the literature has identified as making tax practice environments particularly susceptible to ethical pressures, are identified in the literature (see, e.g. Kaplan and Reckers 1985; Jackson and Milliron 1986; Mason 1987; Kaplan *et al.* 1988; McGill 1988; Milliron 1988; Ayres *et al.* 1989; Duncan *et al.* 1989; Helleloid 1989; LaRue and Reckers 1989; Sanders and Wyndelts 1989; Hite and McGill 1992; Pei *et al.* 1992; Roberts and Cargile 1993; Cuccia 1994; Carnes *et al.* 1996; Jeffrey and Weatherholt 1996; Yetmar *et al.* 1998; Hume *et al.* 1999; Cruz *et al.* 2000; Yetmar and Eastman 2000). The literature also describes the particular ethical issues that present problems for tax practitioners (e.g. Marshall *et al.* 1998; Bobek and Radtke 2007).

In addition to examining the literature on tax practitioners and ethics, the risk-management literature concerning tax practice was also reviewed as part of this research project (see, e.g. Fisher 1994; Yancey 1996; Schaefer and Zimmer 1998; Eckstein 2004; Beasley *et al.* 2006). This was undertaken in the context of the link between ethics and risk management – a link discovered during the course of the study. Consequently, the review of the literature on risk management was undertaken after the interviews had been carried out and the importance of risk management as an issue in tax practice had become clear, providing a good example of how the research process often consists of inductive loops rather than following a linear path.

Research question, methodology and methods

The review undertaken at the outset of the research project revealed several gaps in the relevant literature. As mentioned, the objective of the research was to probe the role that ethics play in tax practice, as perceived by tax practitioners themselves. The gaps in the literature gave rise to the following research question. What are tax practitioners' perceptions regarding the role of ethics in contemporary tax practice?

The research question emerging from the literature was exploratory in nature and an inductive approach to the research was therefore appropriate. The data gathered were qualitative and were collected by conducting semi-structured interviews with tax practitioners. The purpose was to map the landscape of how ethics in tax practice are perceived by tax practitioners, that is, to get an overview of what participants felt was 'going on'. Given the sensitive nature of the subject matter, face-to-face interviews were considered appropriate in order to make interviewees feel comfortable with, and trusting of, the interviewer. Semi-structured interviews allowed the interviewer to prompt the interviewee to consider different types of dilemma, but then also allowed the interviewee to proceed, unprompted, to discuss the ethical issues that he/she had experienced and the role of ethics in tax practice as perceived by him/her.

This research was carried out in Ireland and in the UK, where the researchers are based, and had access to a network of tax practitioners. Both Ireland and the UK are common-law jurisdictions and there is no reason to believe that tax practitioners working in Ireland and the UK would not be essentially similar to practitioners in other common-law jurisdictions. The regulatory frameworks governing the tax professions in Ireland and the UK are comparable and the issues that emerged from the interviews would be relevant in both contexts.

Ethics approval for the research was applied for and granted by both the University of Sheffield in the UK and the University of Limerick in Ireland, where the authors were employed at the time the research was being carried out.

Ireland

Using purposeful sampling, potential interviewees were identified by prior personal knowledge, professional contact or recommendation. According to Patton:

> The logic and power of purposeful sampling lies in selecting *information-rich* cases for study in depth. Information-rich cases are those from which one can learn a great deal about issues of central importance to the purpose of the research, thus the term *purposeful* sampling.
>
> *(Patton 1990: 169, emphasis added by the authors)*

Tax partners were particularly targeted for interview on the basis that their range of experience would be likely to yield richer data than tax practitioners at more junior levels, and they would be more likely to have encountered ethical dilemmas. Bobek and Radtke's (2007) study found that tax partners reported encountering significantly more ethical dilemmas than participants at all other levels of the firm. It was also important to gather views from tax practitioners working in different contexts so that the views expressed were representative of the tax practitioner community at large. Consequently, ten potential interviewees representing practitioners from a wide range of business categories were contacted by email. Each was given information on the broad nature of the research, assured as to the confidentiality of names and firm/organisation, and asked if he/she would contribute his/her time on a voluntary basis. All ten agreed to be interviewed.

The ten interviewees comprised practitioners from three of the 'big four' firms (n = 4), a middle-tier firm (n = 1), a small accounting practice (n = 1), a legal practice (n = 1), a large multinational company (n = 1), a sole practitioner (n = 1) and a director within a relevant professional institute (n = 1). Three of the interviewees were women and seven were men. Interviewee title, firm or organisation profile and region are set out in Table 18.1.

Open-ended questions and probes were used to elicit each participant's views. All ten interviews were carried out in Dublin and Limerick. Most were carried out at the interviewees' place of work, with three being conducted more informally in social settings. The interviews lasted between 45 and 90 minutes. All participants consented to interviews being tape-recorded and the interviews were transcribed verbatim at a later date. The Microsoft Word files containing the transcripts of the interviews do not refer to the interviewees by name. The only electronic file containing interviewees' names is password protected. These procedures are consistent with recommendations in the research methods literature for conducting this type of research (see, for example, Robson 2002; Saunders *et al.* 2007).

The UK

To obtain the interview data, a search was carried out on a number of the FTSE top 100 companies, across different industry sectors, to determine appropriate organisations, that is, those involved in overseas transactions. Again, this was a cross between purposive and convenience sampling. It was felt that interviewing firms with international involvement would provide richer data because of their necessary wider involvement in complex tax issues. As a determinant of international involvement, the most recent financial statements and other information were examined to establish if the organisation owned overseas subsidiary companies, and if so, how many and where they were located. A short list was made of 18 UK-based public limited companies. A letter requesting an interview and briefly outlining the nature of the project was sent to either the named Finance Directors or Company Secretaries of the

Table 18.1 Profiles of the Irish interviewees

Title	*Firm/organisation profile*	*Region*
Tax Partner 1	Big Four	Dublin
Tax Partner 2	Big Four	Dublin
Tax Partner 3	Big Four	Limerick
Risk Management Partner	Big Four	Dublin
Tax Partner 4	Middle-tier firm (international practice, non-Big Four)	Limerick
Managing Partner	Small accounting practice	Limerick
Tax Consultant	Sole practitioner	Dublin
Law Partner	Small legal practice	Wexford
Senior Staff Official	Relevant professional institute	Dublin
Tax Director	Multinational company	Dublin

companies. The letter asked that the request be forwarded to senior tax personnel if this was more appropriate. This approach to obtaining interviews was adopted on the grounds of pragmatism, to establish primarily if there were public limited companies willing to discuss issues likely to be considered confidential in nature.

Managers from seven companies agreed to interviews, which were undertaken with one of the authors. It was felt that seven organisations comprised a number sufficient to provide the range of case study data that was sought. In approaching companies the sensitive nature of the topic was acknowledged and assurances of anonymity and confidentiality were given.

An open-ended, semi-structured questionnaire was used for the interviews, covering ethics as well as other areas. Issues for discussion were derived primarily from the literature reviewed at the outset of the project. Interview questionnaires were sent in advance of the interviews to six of the seven interviewees at their request. Interviews were undertaken in the respondents' offices, lasted from 60 to 90 minutes, were tape-recorded (with the interviewees' permission) and subsequently professionally transcribed verbatim. The transcriptions were sent to the interviewees to ensure that the transcribed version reflected accurately their comments. Some changes to transcriptions were requested and made. These were chiefly for the sake of clarity and to maintain confidentiality.

The characteristics of the interview-sample firms are shown in Table 18.2.

In total the number of interviews undertaken in Ireland and the UK was 17. Given the inherently sensitive nature of taxation, which practitioners are often reluctant to discuss, this represents a significant number of interviews.

The narrative data (audio-tapes) were converted into partly processed data (verbatim transcripts) before coding and analysis. The semi-structured nature of the interviews facilitated coding during the analysis stage of the study. The transcripts of the interviews were read and re-read in order to develop a full understanding of the responses. Data were coded using typical template analysis procedures (see, e.g. Cassell and Symon 2004: 256–70; Lincoln and Guba 1985; Taylor and Bogdan 1984). Although themes for analysis were established a priori, it transpired that many other themes were evident also in the data. In the interests of space constraints, only the primary themes that emerged from the semi-structured interviews carried out with tax practitioners are discussed below and in summary form. Extensive quotes from the interviewees were used when reporting the interview findings 'to allow the reader to hear the interviewees' voices … [and to] … allow the richness of the data to shine through' (O'Dwyer 2004: 403). However, these quotes have been omitted from the summarised discussion below in the interests of brevity.

Research findings

Many interesting themes emerged from the semi-structured interviews, including: the importance of reputation; the impact of firm size on ethical issues; the ethicality of contingent fees; the prevailing ethical culture within particular firms; and the impact of group decision-making on ethical decisions. The role of risk management and its interaction with ethics, as perceived by tax practitioners, was a significant and

Table 18.2 Characteristics of interview-respondent firms in the UK

	Firm A	*Firm B*	*Firm C*	*Firm D*	*Firm E*	*Firm F*	*Firm G*
Size of tax department	50	7	29	30	50	10	200 worldwide; 6 in head office
Use external tax advisers	Yes	Yes	Yes	Yes	Yes	Yes	Yes
International presence	Operates in over 80 countries	Subsidiaries in about 30 countries	Worldwide operations: 40% Europe, 40% USA, 20% Asia	Most European countries and the USA	1,000 companies worldwide	Majority of the business is in the USA	Operates in 76 countries.

unexpected issue that was raised.

Focusing on the main findings, interviewees did not have a clear sense of the role of ethics in tax practice and often contradicted themselves as to whether ethics were relevant in this context at all. Many boldly stated that ethics have no place in tax practice – or indeed, business. Others admitted that there must be some role for ethics in tax practice but they were unable to identify exactly what that role was. The entire concept appeared vague and intangible to them. The general dearth of any real understanding of the involvement of ethics in the day-to-day activities of a tax practitioner is a worrying phenomenon, especially in the context of the importance of ethics in tax practice as identified in the literature. It may suggest that tax practitioners have a problem recognising ethical dilemmas. A failure to recognise that a decision may have ethical implications may result in a failure to behave ethically (Rest 1983: 569).

Interviewees were unanimous in their view that any tax advice given to a client that complies with the letter of the law is considered ethical and that advice breaching the rule of law is unethical. They considered that tax practitioners' only duty is to their clients, their firm and themselves. There was agreement that individual practitioners may 'bend' the law to varying degrees where the legislation is ambiguous, depending on their personal risk profile and the culture of the firm for which they work. They were unanimous in their agreement that tax practitioners have no broader responsibility to society to ensure that the government coffers are filled.

Once interviewees progressed from talking specifically about tax work and focused on client-relationship issues, it was clear that thorny problems can sometimes arise in this sphere of tax work. However, in addressing client-relationship dilemmas, it was risk-management principles and procedures that were evoked, rather than a consideration of these problems as ethical dilemmas. However, interviewees also recognised that there was a need to manage risk appropriately and, therefore, to observe risk management-procedures.

Indeed, risk management was identified as crucial by all interviewees, but how risk management interacts with ethics was unclear to them. Some saw ethics and risk management as separate concepts while others regarded them as one and the same. Interviewees were very comfortable discussing risk procedures for themselves, their firm and their clients. There was no question of not being extremely well versed in risk-management principles and, whereas the concept of ethics was nebulous, risk management was tangible and actionable. All interviewees commented on the vast amounts of resources that were being expended on risk management in terms of money, time and documentation. There was an acceptance among interviewees that having rigid risk-management procedures in place to cover every eventuality might desensitise the ethical antennae of tax practitioners. Risk management 'kicked in' and directed behaviour before an ethical decision was taken.

The analyses of interviewees' perceptions of ethics in tax practice, when considered in the context of their views on risk management, led to the conclusion that in most cases risk management seems to have replaced the role of ethics in tax practice. The central tenet of risk management identified by the interviewees was the avoidance of expensive litigation and the preservation of their reputations and the reputation of the firm, often in the context of uncertainty as to how transactions would be perceived.

The suggestion that the existence of strict risk-management policies in tax practice may be serving to desensitise the ethical antennae of tax practitioners is very much in line with Power's (2004) expressed concern about a risk-management approach that is heavily focused on organisational processes. He argues that an intensified concern for organisational process may incubate risks of its own, not least the failure to see, imagine or act on the 'bigger picture' (ibid.: 44). The more positive conclusion put forward is that risk-management procedures are an attempt by firms to operationalise broad ethical principles. In other words, the underlying theoretical construct is that of ethics, but risk management is its linguistic expression and operational form.

Conclusion

The interviews carried out with tax practitioners provided a rich source of information about how ethics are perceived in tax practice. The apparent confusion as to the role of ethics is interesting given that there is such an emphasis being placed on ethics in the larger firms, with the establishment of firm-specific ethical codes of conduct and the creation of roles, and even departments, the remit of which appears to be centred around ethics and values. One is led to question whether the focus on increasing ethical profile is simply a public-relations exercise and an attempt to manage risk to prevent litigation rather than being motivated by a genuine will to increase ethical standards among practitioners.

There appears to be a dearth of research into the impact of the relatively new phenomenon of integrating strictly controlled risk-management procedures into accounting and tax practices and an analysis of this was carried out as part of the research project described in this chapter. It is suggested that the existence of tightly controlled risk-management policies in tax practice may be serving to desensitise the ethical antennae of tax practitioners. However, it is possible that risk-management procedures are an attempt by firms to operationalise broad ethical principles.

The project described in this chapter provides a good example of exploratory research into a sensitive issue. The research method chosen was appropriate in terms of both the overall subject matter and in terms of the specific research question that emerged from the review of the relevant literature.

Note

1 For a comprehensive report of the research findings from this project see Doyle *et al.* (2009).

References

Andreoni, J., Erard, B. and Feinstein, J. (1998) 'Tax Compliance', *Journal of Economic Literature* 36(2): 818–60.

Ayres, F., Jackson, B. and Hite, P. (1989) 'The economic benefits of regulation: Evidence from professional tax preparers', *Accounting Review* 65(2): 300–12.

Beasley, M., Jenkins, J. and Sawyers, R. (2006) 'Brainstorming to identify and manage tax risks', *The Tax Advisor* 37(3): 158–62.

Bobek, D.D. and Radtke, R.R. (2007) 'An experimental investigation of tax professionals' ethical environments', *Journal of the American Taxation Association* 29(2): 63–84.

Boucher, T.P. (1993) 'Paying tax: Simply the right thing to do', *The CCH Journal of Australian Taxation* (October/November): 50–6.

Carnes, G.A., Harwood, G.B. and Sawyers, R.B. (1996) 'The determinants of tax professionals' aggressiveness in ambiguous situations', *Advances in Taxation* 8: 1–26.

Cassell, C. and Symon, G. (eds) (2004) *Essential Guide to Qualitative Methods in Organizational Research*, Sage.

Collins, J.H., Milliron, V.C. and Toy, D.R. (1990) 'Determinants of tax compliance: A contingency approach', *Journal of the American Taxation Association* 12(1): 9–25.

Cruz, C.A., Shafer, W.E. and Strawser, J.R. (2000) 'A multidimensional analysis of tax Practitioners' ethical judgments', *Journal of Business Ethics* 24(3): 223–44.

Cuccia, A. (1994) 'The effects of increased sanctions on paid tax preparers: Integrating economic and psychological factors', *Journal of the American Taxation Association* 16(1): 41–66.

Doyle, E., Frecknall Hughes, J. and Glaister, K. (2009) 'Linking ethics and risk management in taxation: Evidence from an exploratory study in Ireland and the UK', *Journal of Business Ethics* 86(2): 177–98.

Duncan, W., LaRue, D. and Reckers, P. (1989) 'An empirical examination of the influence of selected economic and noneconomic variables on decisions making by tax professionals', *Advances in Taxation* 2: 91–106.

Eckstein, K. (2004) 'Negligence claims against tax advisors', *Irish Tax Review* 17(3): 241–44.

Erard, B. (1993) 'Taxation with representation: An analysis of the role of tax practitioners in tax compliance', *Journal of Public Economics* 52(2): 163–97.

Fisher, A. (1994) 'Finding the right tax advisor', *Fortune* 129(6): 77–80.

Frecknall Hughes, J. (2002) *An Empirical Investigation of the Share Valuation Work of Taxation Practitioners*, unpublished PhD thesis, University of Leeds.

Godar, S.H., O'Connor, P.J. and Taylor, V.A. (2005) 'Evaluating the ethics of inversion', *Journal of Business Ethics* 61(1): 1–6.

Helleloid, R. (1989) 'Ambiguity and the evaluation of client documentation by tax professionals, *Journal of the American Taxation Association* 11(2): 22–26.

Herman, T. (2004) 'IRS to issue rules on tax shelters: Ethical guidelines target "opinion letters" often used to justify questionable transactions, *Wall Street Journal* 8 December: D1.

Hite, P.A. and McGill, G.A. (1992) 'An examination of taxpayer preference for aggressive tax advice', *National Tax Journal* 65(4): 389–403.

Hume, E.C., Larkins, E.R. and Iyer, G. (1999) 'On compliance with ethical standards in tax return preparation', *Journal of Business Ethics* 18(2): 229–38.

Jackson, B.R. and Milliron, V.C. (1986) 'Tax compliance research: Fndings, problems and prospects, *Journal of Accounting Literature* 5: 125–65.

Jeffrey, C. and Weatherholt, N. (1996) 'Ethical development, professional commitment, and rule observance attitudes: A study of CPAs and corporate accountants', *Behavioral Research in Accounting* 8: 8–31.

Johnston, D.C. (2004) 'Changes at KPMG after criticism of its tax shelters', *New York Times* 13 January: C1.

Kaplan, S.E. and Reckers, P.M.J. (1985) 'A study of tax evasion judgments', *National Tax Journal* 38(1): 97–102.

Kaplan, S.E., Reckers, P.M.J., West, S.G. and Boyd, J.C. (1988) 'An examination of tax reporting recommendations of professional tax preparers', *Journal of Economic Psychology* 9(4): 427–43.

LaRue, D. and Reckers, P. (1989) 'An empirical examination of the influence of selected factors on professional tax preparers' decision processes', *Advances in Accounting* 7(1): 37–50.

Lincoln, Y.S. and Guba, E.G. (1985) *Naturalistic Inquiry*, Beverly Hills, CA: Sage.

McGill, G.A. (1988) *The CPA's Role in Income Tax Compliance: An Empirical Study of Variability in Recommending Aggressive Tax Positions*, unpublished PhD dissertation, Texas Tech University.

Marshall, R.L., Armstrong, R.W. and Smith, M. (1998) 'The ethical environment of tax practitioners: Western Australian evidence', *Journal of Business Ethics* 17(12): 1265–79.

Mason, R. (1987) 'A communication model of taxpayer honesty', *Law & Policy* 9(3): 246.

Milliron, V.C. (1988) 'A conceptual model of factors influencing tax preparers' aggressiveness', in S. Moriarity and J. Collins (eds), *Contemporary Tax Research*, Oklahoma: University of Oklahoma, pp.1–15.

O'Dwyer, B. (2004) 'Qualitative data analysis: Exposing a process for transforming a "messy" but "attractive" nuisance', in C. Humphrey and B. Lee (eds), *A Real Life Guide to Accounting Research: A Behind the Scenes View of Using Qualitative Research Methods*, Amsterdam: Elsevier, pp. 389–405.

Patton, M.Q. (1990) *Qualitative Evaluation and Research Methods*, Newbury Park, CA: Sage.

Pei, B.K.W., Reckers, P.M.J. and Wyndelts, R.W. (1992) 'Tax professionals' belief revision: The effects of information presentation sequence, client preference and domain experience', *Decision Sciences* 23(1): 175–99.

Power, M. (2004) *The Risk Management of Everything: Rethinking the Politics of Uncertainty*, London: Demos.

Rest, J. (1983) 'Morality', in J. Flavell and E. Markman (eds) *Manual of Child Psychology, Vol. 3: Cognitive Development*, New York: John Wiley and Sons, pp. 556–629.

Roberts, M. and Cargile, B. (1993) *CPAs' Response to Conflict in Auditing and Tax Situations*, unpublished working paper, University of Alabama.

Robson, C. (2002) *Real World Research*, 2nd edn, Oxford: Blackwell.

Sanders, D.L. and Wyndelts, R.W. (1989) 'An examination of tax practitioners' decisions under uncertainty', *Advances in Taxation* 2: 41–72.

Saunders, M., Lewis, P. and Thornhill, A. (2007) *Research Methods for Business Students*, 4th edn, Harlow: Pearson Education.

Scannell, K. (2005) 'KPMG apologises to avert charges: Firm takes responsibility for improper tax shelters', US Debates Indictment, *Wall Street Journal* 17 June: A3.

Schaefer, J. and Zimmer, M. (1998) 'Limiting insurance decisions and premium charges among CPA firms: An empirical analysis', *Journal of Applied Business Research* 14(1): 69–84.

Shafer, W.E. and Simmons, R.S. (2008) 'Social responsibility, Machiavellianism and tax avoidance', *Accounting, Auditing and Accountability Journal* 21(5): 695–720.

Stainer, A., Stainer, L. and Segal, A. (1997) 'The ethics of tax planning', *Business Ethics: A European Review* 6(4): 213–19.

Taylor, S.J. and Bogdan, R. (1984) *Introduction to Qualitative Research Methods*, 2nd edn, New York: Wiley.

Yancey, W. (1996) 'Managing a tax practice to avoid malpractice claims', *CPA Journal* 66(2): 12–18.

Yetmar, S., Cooper, R. and Frank, G. (1998) 'Ethical issues facing CPA tax practitioners', *CPA Journal* 68(10): 28–33.

Yetmar, S. and Eastman, K. (2000) 'Tax practitioners' ethical sensitivity: A model and empirical examination', *Journal of Business Ethics* 26(4): 271–88.

19

A STUDY OF THE CHANGING RELATIONSHIP BETWEEN LARGE CORPORATES AND THE INLAND REVENUE

Penelope Tuck

Corporation Tax is an extremely important part of the UK taxation system. Given the complexity and rapid development of modern business the tax legislation cannot cover every eventuality and therefore, particularly for larger and more complex companies, the Corporation Tax liability is often determined, at least partially, by negotiation between Her Majesty's Revenue & Customs (HMRC) and the taxpayer.

This chapter outlines my doctoral research thesis, which was funded by the Chartered Accountants' Trust for Education and Research of the Institute of Chartered Accountants in England and Wales. The study (Tuck 2007) addressed the following research questions:

- How is the process of corporate tax compliance changing for groups of large companies?
- How is this process being managed by the Inland Revenue (IR)?[1]

The empirical evidence consisted of 33 semi-structured elite interviews conducted in 2002–04 with elite interviewees comprising senior IR officials, tax directors and tax managers of large corporates (mainly FTSE 100 companies), and tax partners from a 'big four' accounting firm. The study also drew upon archival data including state papers and documentary data from the IR. At the time my study took place few researchers had examined the practices of UK tax administration (PricewaterhouseCoopers 2000, 2002, 2005; Porter 1999), in particular the IR, or indeed had access to senior officials in the IR.

Theoretically the study drew from the new public management, tax administration and tax compliance literatures. However, I argued that an approach grounded purely in these literatures did not adequately explain the changing tax compliance environment for large groups. So I utilised other literatures, which drew on Foucault's work on multiple expertise constructing subjects engaging with disciplinary knowledge and power, to assist in filling this gap (Roberts *et al.* 2006; Bush and Maltby 2004; Anderson-Gough 2002; Hodgson 2002; Neu 2000; Hoskin and Macve, 1986, 1988).

The study theorised the impact of these changes and the tensions arising from securing corporate tax compliance in a changing environment within both the IR and the corporates. One focus was on the IR becoming a strategic and managerial organisation (Tuck *et al.* 2011). It was also arguably recontextualising traditional bureaucratic practice so that doing 'the same' work as before does not necessarily carry the same significance and importance. The second focus was on the knowledge expertise inside the taxpaying entities, and within the inter-relations between the IR and the taxpayer. Tax officials and tax managers dealing with large corporates are mostly elite professionals who have specialised in the taxation of large corporates for at least ten years.

Drawing on a governmentality framework, as articulated by Foucault and his latter works (Foucault 1977, 1986, 1994), I argued that the nature of the corporate tax compliance game resembles a truth game between two kinds of subject generated in this transdisciplinary world: the new shape tax official and the visible customer (the taxpayer). The IR official – the HM Inspector of Taxes – has been remoulded from one type of knowledge expert to another, which is a three-dimensional transdisciplinary T-shaped tax official (Tuck 2010). This is a tax official who both has the detailed, deep technical knowledge as a knowledge expert but also has to relate, in a broader sense, to the new way of operating in a strategic and marketing organisation. The emergence of the corporate taxpayer as a visible customer has changed the process of corporate tax compliance for large corporates whereby they exercise certain power in the relationship by virtue of this visibility.

The theoretical contribution of the research was that this research tracked a new kind of interaction of the interplay between subjectivisation[2] and objectivisation[3], which seemed to have become established and developed a theoretically informed way of looking at emergent governmental and more wide-ranging forms of application. In addition, the empirical contribution was significant in that at the time the research site was novel and, I would argue, still is.

Research context

The process of corporate tax compliance has an historical or 'diachronic' dimension that has to be understood in its historical and cultural context, which includes the internal evolution of the IR as part of the UK governmental apparatus and as an entity in its own right. This evolution includes not only internal reorganisations, culminating most recently (though outside the terms of my fieldwork) in the merging of the IR with Customs and Excise to form HMRC, but also the increasing incorporation across UK government of what has been called the New Public Management[4] (NPM) as a means of revitalising or moving beyond old-style bureaucracy.

It is also a process with a here and now or 'synchronic' dimension. This includes the doing or enacting of the process in 'real time', involving such practical and material aspects as paying the agreed amount of tax at the right time, whatever is defined as the agreed amount of tax, or the mechanics of the way that the process of compliance operates (Braithwaite 2003a, 2003b; McBarnet 1991, 2003) or how these issues interrelate. It also includes the way in which doing or enacting the process is lived and experienced by its participants, who are for the most part highly qualified, skilled and reflective professionals, on both sides of the fence.

The object of the analysis undertaken here is therefore this process taken as a whole, with a particular focus on the way changes within the past decade (to 2003) have played out and arguably transformed the nature of the process of corporate tax compliance in significant ways, whose effects can be expected to have reverberations as the compliance process evolves in the future. It is a process which has had to evolve because of the growing economic power of major transnational corporations and their ability to engage in tax avoidance, whether on a global scale or by exploiting differences within the European Union (EU) between national tax regimes and EU practice. Revenue authorities are therefore not in a position simply to impose tax demands and expect them to be met. There is necessarily a game involving negotiation and the seeking of mutually optimal outcomes (Picciotto 2007). Precisely because of the globalisation of tax activity and the attendant evolution in approaches and attitudes, corporate tax has become a more high-profile and strategic issue for many large corporates, causing them to seek to manage their taxation affairs more actively than previously, when the focus was largely on compliance with national-level legislation.[5]

Part of the motivation for this research is that the focus on the IR as a research site is relatively new[6] and the research shows that is a key site/vehicle for NPM practices. Tomkins *et al.* (2001) have highlighted the under-researched area of tax management.

A crucial aspect of this study is the high-level access obtained to key players within the IR and the corporates. Evidence has been obtained from 33 semi-structured interviews with informants involved in the process. These informants from within the IR include those who have initiated, directed and led the process; those who have implemented the process; those who are significant players in the process; and those who have the ability to alter future processes. This has enabled significant insights to be obtained into the process from different perspectives. Fourteen interviews were carried out with senior IR officials, 14 with tax directors or tax managers of FTSE 100 companies and five with tax partners of a 'big four' accountancy firm. Each interview lasted for at least 60 minutes, with the longest being 120 minutes. Where possible interviews were taped and transcribed. This was not possible on two occasions where consent to being recorded was not given. In these cases notes were written up immediately after the interview, to supplement notes taken during the interview. The transcripts were then coded using a software package so that dominant themes emerged from the data.

Research findings

New practices of government have developed and altered the relationship between the tax authority and taxpayer. Complex power relations exist between the IR and the large corporate taxpayer. On one level the IR is the regulator of the tax compliance process and it has recourse to law and ultimately to the Courts by virtue of its position as a regulator. There are strengths and weaknesses on each side. The IR is employing new practices such as open questioning and new discourses such as the construct of the customer for taxpayer, such that the taxpayer is referred to by the IR as a 'customer' (Tuck *et al.* 2011). However, the large corporates have a range of practices available to them – 'a whole series of specific governmental apparatuses' – with which they can also deploy and exert power in the relationship. For instance, there is potentially greater expertise to be employed and/or deployed on the private-sector side, which potentially results in an unstable balance of power between the two sides in the relationship.

No robust theorising on these practices had been previously undertaken. I considered an appropriate approach was to utilise a Foucauldian framework based on a governmentality and disciplinarity approach (Anderson-Gough 2002; Neu 2000; Preston 1989; Hoskin and Macve 1986, 1988). The disciplinary model tells us that we need to understand and factor in the constitutive role of knowledge in the operation of power relations. Subjects are embedded in a net of expertise where they have to engage actively with knowledge and being knowledgeable. Therefore they are never purely passive objects of some external rule-based disciplining but also become self-disciplining and self-regulating. People at the top of organisations and bureaucracies, and outside experts are all exponents of disciplinary expertise. A key aspect of this research was tracing how these knowledge experts are taking on new kinds of expertise and how they interact both inside the bureaucracy and externally as expert 'subjects'.

The study argued that modern apparatuses of government are being developed in terms of their external relations to taxpaying subjects through the adoption of a customer-focused approach, and in respect of the large corporate taxpayer an added-value approach. At a more specific level the corporate tax compliance process is undertaken by representatives both of the IR and of the corporate taxpayer. These elite professionals are being made into expert knowledge subjects both by discourse and the practices of the Corporate Tax Compliance process. During the event that forms part of the process of compliance, these expert knowledge subjects undertake 'truth games' whereby the detail of the tax computation is investigated by the IR to ensure that the appropriate amount of tax is assessed.

The corporate tax compliance process must be viewed against the background of a bureaucratic organisation that itself is changing as a consequence of NPM. The changes to the IR have not just been limited to the range of its activities being expanded. In addition, the new approach has been demonstrated by a wider appreciation of managerial activities such as strategic policy-making; reconceptualising the taxpayer as a customer; new IT approaches; the use of performance targets; and the introduction of the Resource Accounting and Budgeting system.

All of these factors have caused significant changes to the way in which the IR deals with large corporate taxpayers and the relationships it has with them. Part of this development is structural with the setting up of the Large Business Office (LBO), which deals with 900 of the largest UK groups of companies, including banks, building societies and insurance companies. There are approximately 850 employees[7] of the LBO. Another development is the change in the practices and discourse used when dealing with large corporates. These include different practices internally within the LBO such as remaking employees to be outwardly facing, and externally by the LBO to clients in general (customers) and large corporates.

The great majority of the interviews were carried out with tax directors and tax managers of FTSE 100 groups. These groups have complex structures and tax affairs and are able to structure their activities to take advantage of tax planning opportunities. The in-house tax departments have direct experience of dealing directly with the IR rather than through an intermediary and some of the IR changing practices such as the New Compliance Process (NCP) have been directed at those groups that have an in-house tax department.

The impact of the change in the Corporation Tax compliance process has given rise to changes in the way each party operates and therefore would seem to alter the traditional balance of power between the IR and large corporates, raising new opportunities and threats for each party. Correspondingly the IR is engaging in a different game with these large corporates. Traditionally enquiries into the tax return have been commenced by written correspondence with recourse to meetings if an impasse in the negotiations has occurred. There is a move towards meetings held before the submission of tax computations and commencement of enquiries by letter. With the introduction of Corporation Tax Self-Assessment (CTSA), areas of concern now have to be disclosed by corporates to the IR rather than waiting for the IR to raise questions (e.g. transfer pricing issues). Additionally the IR now assumes that the information shown on the return is correct unless it is found to be otherwise following IR enquiries, and this has altered the audit methods employed in the examination of the tax return.

The impact of the phenomenon of NPM on tax administrations can be seen. Tax administrations have incorporated new-style working practices, frequently using practices first developed in the private sector (Total Quality Management (TQM), key performance indicators, etc.), which have changed both the organisational structure and the processes and practices of tax administration. The IR operations have developed from a localised nature with individual authority, in that the focus was on the site of the taxpayer's business or residence not on the taxpayer itself, to one where IR operations focused on the large corporate taxpayer as a stratified taxpayer. These can be considered the first steps towards defining the large corporate taxpayer as a subject. However, the past cannot be ignored as there are still localised origins in this style of operations within the LBO, such as the regional offices dealing with banks and insurance groups in London and Edinburgh. Within these structures, bureaucratic practices have been supplemented by entrepreneurial governance where outcomes are more important than inputs (Osborne and Gaebler 1992). This involves the reclassification of taxpayers as customers and the introduction and further refinement of performance targets. The practices of corporate tax compliance have changed as well, from a focus on activity being carried out by the IR, to one where the IR operates in a surveillance and disciplinary role. Taxpayers self-assess their tax liabilities under CTSA, and the IR audits those returns. There has been a shifting of accountability from the IR to the taxpayer. In addition, where the process was previously a long (in terms of time scale), formal and distant relationship with the IR carried out principally in writing, it has, while retaining aspects of this past, shifted towards being a mixture of the written and the oral, generating a more inclusive dialogue with the taxpayer, frequently in the form of meetings based on targeted yet potentially open-ended questioning.

At one level, even given this background of a bureaucratic entity now having a marketing and strategic focus with greater specialisation and sectorisation, the nature of the event does not change; the basic nature of tax compliance still exists. However, the corporate tax compliance game is being played by experts with different and changing expertise and under what I have conceptualised as new rules of engagement, which involve more oral interchange deploying more open-ended questions, all entailing a different kind of immediate, if still information-based, truth-telling. The representatives of the IR, the tax inspectors – knowledge expert subjects – are being made into '3D T-shaped' officials. The conceptualisation of the customer is making the taxpayer more visible. This allows new ways of investigation to develop from an 'inquisitio' approach to a practice of more examination and disclosure. The truth is being disclosed in new ways. As the corporate taxpayer becomes the visible customer, the amount of power in the relationship is increased. Both parties to the compliance process 'act as if' the taxpayer is a customer in a regulatory environment and consequently the customer becomes more customer-like.

Discussion and conclusion

This new application of the Foucauldian approach opened up the 'black box' of what goes on in the event of tax compliance. It focused on the two knowledge expert 'subjects' in the process. The subjects cannot be looked at in isolation because their subjectivisation and objectivisation are at the same time both separate and connected in that the IR official and the corporate taxpayer, each operating in different, separate organisations, are connected by the event of compliance. It has also made use of Foucault's writings on the effect of the 'truth game' within this subjectivisation and objectivisation in this research site (Foucault 1983). The saying of (true) things beyond what is usually said, or parrhesia, thus develops into a two-sided game where the questioned have a space for generating parrhesia from the inspectors as well as vice versa.

Drawing on the later work of Foucault I was able to exploit high-level access to investigate these high-level knowledge experts constituted as subjects, and how these subjects interact in high-stake, complex negotiations. This was a pioneering methodology linking governmentality, expert knowledge subjects, and subjectivisation and objectivisation. What makes this research unparalleled is that although it was carried out in a regulatory environment similar to prisons and mental hospitals,[8] large corporates, in particular FTSE 100 companies, have a choice as to where they are regulated. Within reason, they have the ability to move parts of their operations (such as head office and administrative functions, manufacturing operations and research and development) to other countries, which may offer favourable conditions such as business environment, tax concessions, availability of specialised labour, etc. Therefore, they effectively can choose at least partially whether to be regulated by the UK tax authorities or some other jurisdiction. At the same time, the IR has reconceptualised these powerful large corporates as customers.

The Foucauldian theoretical framework was applied to both the regulators and the regulatees, and so does not look purely at those who are 'disciplined' as the objects of the exercise of knowledge-based power, but also at those who exercise power as the disciplinary experts who have the relevant knowledge to occupy such positions. Arguably this is a truth game where such roles are not easily assigned, since the objects of the exercise are senior employees in the large corporates (and arguably those large corporates themselves). Additionally these regulatees (i.e. the corporates) are empowered within the playing out of the truth game through their rights to 'customer choice' and operational discretion over which state will constitute their tax jurisdiction.

In addition the interviews were carried out when the IR was undergoing a period of change. This research therefore contributes theoretically to an understanding of how change and NPM practices play out in a large, established bureaucracy. This research links governmentality to the whole of the NPM theme. The seniority of the IR employees interviewed allowed me to develop insights into how high-level officials cope and find opportunities in the new organisational reality. I was able, as well, to see how high-level tax experts engage with the IR, cope with the changing environment and find opportunities to exploit their relationship with the IR. This in essence is the new kind of truth game and it is essential for the players to understand this game to enable them to operate successfully in a globalised corporate tax and tax jurisdiction world.

Notes

1 From April 2004 IR and HM Customs & Excise were merged to form HMRC (CM 6163 2004). Given that the vast majority of the fieldwork was undertaken in the period prior to April 2004, the study limits itself to that period when the IR was a separate department of UK central government.

2 Subjectivisation refers to 'determining what the subject [individual] must be, what conditions are imposed on it, what status it is to have, and position it is to occupy in reality or in imaginary, in order to become the legitimate subject of one type of knowledge or another' (Foucault 1994: 315).

3 It is by calculation and through the 'apparatus of writing' that the individual is constituted as a 'describable, analysable object' (Foucault 1977: 190). We could refer to this as an apparatus of objectivisation.

4 The core of NPM is to remove or reduce the traditional distinction between public-sector bodies and private-sector entities and to shift 'the emphasis from process accountability towards a greater element of accountability in terms of results' (Hood 1995: 94).

5 While the merger of IR and HM Customs & Excise to form HMRC is important and some organisational change has occurred, it is unlikely to have any material effects on the underlying relationship between the taxing authority and large corporates in the context of Corporation Tax.

6 There are opportunities for further work (Lamb 2005: 70).

7 See www.inlandrevenue.gov.uk/lbo/index.html (accessed 7 April 2005).

8 Typical Foucauldian examples as used, for example, in *Discipline and Punish* (1977).

References

Anderson-Gough, F.A. (2002) *On Becoming the New Accounting Expert: Between Formal and Informal Learning*, PhD thesis, University of Leeds.

Braithwaite, J. (2003a) 'Large Business and the Compliance Model', in V. Braithwaite (ed.), *Taxing Democracy: Understanding Tax Avoidance and Evasion,* Aldershot, Hants: Ashgate, pp.229–43.

——(2003b) 'Meta risk management and responsive regulation for tax system integrity', *Law & Policy* 25(1): 1–16.

Bush, B. and Maltby, J. (2004) 'Taxation in West Africa: transforming the colonial subject into the "governable person"', *Critical Perspectives on Accounting* 15: 5–34.

CM 6163 (2004) *Financing Britain's Future: Review of the Revenue Departments*, Gus O'Donnell; Presented to Parliament by the Chancellor of the Exchequer.

Foucault, M. (1977) *Discipline and Punish*, London: Penguin.

——(1983) *Discourse and Truth: The Problematization of Parrhesia*, six lectures given by Michel Foucault at Berkeley, Oct.–Nov. 1983, foucault.info/documents/parrhesia (accessed 17 November 2004).

——(1986) *The Care of the Self: The History of Sexuality, Vol. 3*, London: Penguin.

——(as 'Florence, M.') (1994) 'Foucault, Michel, 1926–', in G. Gutting (ed.), *The Cambridge Companion to Foucault,* Cambridge: Cambridge University Press, pp. 314–19.

Hodgson, D. (2002) '"Know your customer": Marketing, governmentality and the "new customer" of financial services', *Management Decision* 40(4): 318–28.

Hood, C. (1995) 'The "New Public Management" in the 1980s: Variations on a theme', *Accounting, Organizations and Society* 20: 93–109.

Hoskin, K. and Macve, R. (1986) 'Accounting and the examination: A genealogy of disciplinary power', *Accounting, Organizations and Society* 11(2): 105–36.

——(1988) 'The genesis of accountability: The West Point connections', *Accounting, Organizations and Society* 13(1): 37–73.

Lamb, M. (2005) 'Taxation research as accounting research', in M. Lamb, A. Lymer, J. Freedman and S. James, *Taxation: An Interdisciplinary Approach to Research,* Oxford: Oxford University Press, pp. 55–84.

McBarnet, D. (1991) 'Whiter than white collar crime: tax, fraud insurance and the management of stigma', *British Journal of Sociology* 42: 323–44.

——(2003) 'When compliance is not the solution but the problem: From changes in law to changes in attitude', in V. Braithwaite (ed.), *Taxing Democracy: Understanding Tax Avoidance and Evasion,* Aldershot: Ashgate, pp. 229–43.

Montagu, N. (1999) 'Inland revenue: The future', on former Inland Revenue website, www.ir.gov.uk/about/future.htm (accessed 7 September 2001).

Neu, D. (2000) 'Presents for the Indians: Land, colonialism and accounting in Canada', *Accounting Organizations and Society* 25(2): 163–84.

Osborne, D. and Gaebler, T. (1992) *Re-inventing Government*, Reading, MA: Addison-Wesley.

Picciotto, S. (2007) 'Constructing Compliance: Game-Playing, Tax Law and the Regulatory State', *Law & Policy* 29(1): 11–30.

Porter, B. (1999) 'Survey of in-house tax departments in United Kingdom Corporates', *British Tax Review* 1: 32–51.

Preston, A. (1989) 'The Taxman Cometh: Observations on the Interrelationship between Accounting and Inland Revenue Practice', *Accounting Organizations and Society* 14: 389–413.

PricewaterhouseCoopers (1999) *Tax Function 2000*, London: PricewaterhouseCoopers.

——(2000) *Tax Function 2001: Supporting the strategic and business demands of the future*, London: PricewaterhouseCoopers.

——(2002) *The 'Best Practice' tax function*, London: PricewaterhouseCoopers.

——(2005) *Total Tax Contribution*, London: PricewaterhouseCoopers, www.pwc.com/Extweb/onsights.nsf/docid/75D58AF8B3774A3C80256F8800586AC6 (accessed 2 August 2006).

Roberts, J., Sanderson, P., Barker, R. and Hendry, J. (2006) 'In the mirror of the market: the disciplinary effects of company/fund manager meetings', *Accounting, Organizations and Society* 31(3): 277–94.

Tomkins, C., Packman, C., Russell, S. and Colville, I. (2001) 'Notes and surveys managing tax regimes: A call for research', *Public Administration* 79(3): 751–58.

Tuck, P. (2007) *A Study of the Changing Relationship between Large Corporates and the Inland Revenue*, unpublished PhD thesis, University of Warwick.

——(2010) 'The emergence of the tax official into a T shaped knowledge expert', *Critical Perspectives on Accounting* 21: 584–96.

Tuck, P., Lamb, M. and Hoskin, K. (2011) 'Customers? The Reconstruction of the "tax-payer" in Inland Revenue discourse and practice', *Accounting and Business Research* 41(4): 357–74.

20
THE CHANGING ROLE OF ACCOUNTANTS IN HMRC

Lynne Oats and Penelope Tuck

This chapter describes a joint research project undertaken in 2005 for which we received funding from the Centre for Business Performance of the Institute of Chartered Accountants in England and Wales (ICAEW). The study concerned the role of accounting professionals working within the Large Business Service (LBS) in Her Majesty's Revenue & Customs (HMRC). At the time, one of the authors was completing her PhD and the project was a spin-off. In this chapter we describe how the project was conceived and undertaken, pointing out along the way some of the difficulties we faced, which are likely to arise in any funded research project. Although we draw on the final report produced for the ICAEW (Oats and Tuck 2008), this chapter is largely a reflective piece, considering how we did the project rather than what we did.

In the UK corporation tax is a significant source of revenue for the Exchequer. A large proportion of the total corporation tax raised is generated from a relatively small number of taxpayers, the largest corporate groups, many of which have multinational operations. The way in which the relationship between the Revenue and large corporates is managed is therefore extremely important, and the project considered one specific aspect of this: the changing role of accountants. At the time, qualified accountants with significant professional financial reporting experience gained in professional practice, were being recruited by HMRC to fill an expertise gap resulting from the increasing overlap between accounting and tax profit. Our interest was in how these accounting specialists were being recruited and used by HMRC.

In the UK, computation of taxable profits for companies uses accounting profit as a starting point, with adjustments for tax-specific rules, rather than having a separate tax computation process, as in other jurisdictions. The traditional Revenue officer, while expert in the detailed application of the tax legislation and extra statutory rules, generally has little or no knowledge of the accounting rules that underpin the computation of accounting profit. One of our interests was how this knowledge gap within HMRC undermines its capacity to engage effectively with the corporate taxpayer in the tax compliance game, and further how the recruitment of financial reporting specialists could redress this potential imbalance.

There were two initial hurdles to overcome: securing funding for the project and securing access to relevant actors within HMRC in order to conduct semi-structured interviews, our preferred methodology.

We approached the ICAEW for funding to cover the costs of travel, research assistance and interview transcription, and were surprised to find some resistance to our research design based on concerns about both the methodology and the significance of the study. It soon became clear that our initial research proposal needed to be refined to allay concerns about 'value for money', but we were eventually able to produce a revised grant application (with significantly reduced cost) that met their requirements. As part of this process we had to present our proposal to a meeting of the Board and answer their questions directly. We also had to elicit support from members of the tax technical arm of the ICAEW who we needed to convince that the project would produce findings of interest to members. Fortunately we knew some of these from attendance at various tax-related conferences and found their support relatively easy to secure.

Following our meeting with the members of the tax technical team and the presentation to the Board, our revised proposal addressed the significance of the project in the following terms:

1 The incremental closing of the gap between accounting profits and tax profits has focused increasing attention on the suitability of accounting profit as a starting point for the corporation tax computation. Much of the current debate, however, is concerned with wider policy objectives, addressing questions such as whether there should be complete alignment of the two, or if not, how should the differences be defined and clarified, and what are the implications of the adoption of IFRS.
2 The increased focus of attention on accounting profits has also manifested itself in changes in the way in which HMRC approach corporate tax compliance, particularly in respect of large corporates. As part of this change, HMRC have started to recruit qualified accountants to act as financial reporting specialists to provide advice on the way in which accounting profits are calculated and presented.
3 Academic concern has to date been focused on policy, and no research has yet examined this phenomenon from the perspective of actual *practices*: how this is being played out in the process of securing corporate tax compliance. This research is therefore unique and innovative. Unprecedented access to Revenue officials will allow for new insights into the ongoing implications of the changed relationship resulting from increased focus on the accounting that underlies corporate tax computations.

The ICAEW also wanted details of who would be the beneficiaries of the project, which we identified as follows:

1 ICAEW members: The research would be of particular interest to those members engaged in corporate tax compliance of large corporates who are directly affected by the question of the closer alignment of accounting and tax profits, for example as finance directors or tax managers of large corporate taxpayers. It would also be of interest to members outside of the large corporate arena since these developments are not confined to large corporates, but are indicative of future developments across the full spectrum of corporate taxpayers. A key benefit to both groups would be a greater understanding of how the tax authority operates and the role of accounting in tax compliance. HMRC's use of Compliance Accountants is relatively new and, as yet, there is limited experience of how HMRC's increased technical accounting knowledge will impact on the negotiations with the corporate taxpayer.
2 Senior officials of HMRC: As an independent academic study and the terms of the access agreement did not bind the researchers to providing a formal report to HMRC. There was scope, however, for the research findings to be fed back to HMRC and may therefore be of assistance in formulating operational policies in the future.
3 The wider business community: The research would be of interest to the wider business community who are concerned with the way in which the Revenue approaches corporation tax compliance at an operational level. It was also suggested that the research would impact on the wider questions of tax policy relating to the alignment or otherwise of accounting and tax profits and the relationship between law and accounting.

During this process, we concurrently sought access to relevant actors within HMRC. In this, the prior experience of Penelope Tuck in securing access was important as she was known to senior Revenue officials from previous work (Tuck 2007; see also Chapter 19). We were fortunate in that the recently created Large Business Service had appointed a new head who was from the Customs and Excise arm of the organisation (our project coincided with the merger of the former Inland Revenue and Her Majesty's Customs and Excise, which had dealt with (broadly speaking) direct and indirect taxes, respectively. He was supportive of the project as a means of finding out how this particular aspect of his operations works in practice. We did not, however, undertake to produce a formal report on the project. The reason for this was that we felt it was important to be seen to be independent researchers and if interviewees thought we were conducting the research on behalf of senior management, it might inhibit their responses during interviews. As part of the access agreement, we were required to enter into a confidentiality agreement. The agreement was between HMRC and the university at which we were both employed at the time. Initially it contained a restriction on our ability to publish from our findings, but following negotiation, agreement was reached that we would be able to publish our findings subject to maintaining the anonymity of respondents.

We collected material from several sources. In addition to interviews we had access to several internal documents relating to the emerging role of the Revenue accountants which were not publicly available. While these informed our research, we were not able to refer to them directly in our final report, as they were provided to us on a confidential basis. We also examined publicly available documentation such as HMRC annual reports and material on the HMRC website.

The interviews

We conducted 28 interviews in total, by one or both of the researchers during late 2005 and 2006. Eleven of our interviewees were senior civil servants, who by virtue of their position have a large number of demands on their time, and we were conscious of this during the conduct of the interview (Odendahl and Shaw 2001). In addition, we conducted some interviews with eight HMRC accountants, two tax professionals from 'big four' accountancy practices, and one policy official from Her Majesty's Treasury.

Following the initial round of interviews in late 2005/early 2006, we felt that additional insights could be obtained from a second round of interviews, which were then arranged and conducted in late 2006. The second round of interviews captured the views of six more junior Revenue officers and, being at a later time, also allowed us to obtain information about the progress of the merger process.

Prior to the interviews we discussed the questions to be asked and formulated a broad set of questions to guide the interview without being prescriptive. Separate sets of questions were used for Revenue officials and Revenue accountants, although the core questions remained the same for both sets of interviewees, centred around career background, the appointment and deployment of financial accountants within the LBS, and the work environment (which encompassed possible future structural developments). The questions drew from our understanding of the literature as well as our own personal experience. Importantly, one of the authors has a background in tax administration and the other a background in professional tax practice, which meant that we each brought different perspectives to the research. As the interviews progressed the questions were refined and some new avenues explored:

> Each interview lasted between one and one and a half hours. At the end of each interview where both researchers were present, the researchers discussed together the key themes emerging from the interviews and notes were made. Interviewees were assured that their responses would not be attributed to them directly and would be anonymised. The credentials of the researchers were established at the start of the interview, including our prior background as tax professionals. This enabled the level of the discussion to be pitched quite high once we established our understanding of tax technical issues. During the interview, one of the researchers acted as scribe and took extensive notes. The interviews were also digitally recorded, transcribed and coded using NVivo to identify the dominant themes. Where taxpayers were referred to by name, and not all interviewees did so, the identity of the taxpayer was changed in the transcript.
>
> *(Oats and Tuck 2008: 16)*

We adopted an interpretive approach to the research, which reflects the view that actors themselves construct contexts of structure and meanings in their social interactions. In terms of our philosophical approach, we would position ourselves in the lower half of the model produced by Merkl-Davies and Brennan (2011) (see Chapter 2), as non-functionalists somewhere between the social constructionist and critical sectors.

One key feature of arranging the interviews with HMRC officials was the assistance of one particular organisational actor who had line management responsibility for the specialist accountants. Indeed, he was instrumental in arranging the interviews and it was through his direct involvement that we obtained legitimacy as outside researchers. Nonetheless, several of our respondents were highly suspicious of our interest and motivations and needed reassurance as to the confidentiality of their responses as well as the outcomes: that is, that we would not be producing a formal report for senior management.

The product of our research (apart from several conference papers) was a report produced for the ICAEW in fulfilment of a condition for receiving the grant funding. In preparing this report, a number of interesting issues arose. In particular, it was clear that the report needed to be constructed in an entirely different way given its intended audience of professional body members rather than an academic audience. We felt that it was inappropriate to infuse the report with academic theory and so deliberately presented it as a largely descriptive report, with the theoretical analysis confined to a single chapter which did not need to be read as part of the report.

In order to understand the recent developments in this key aspect of the relationship between the taxpayer and the state, specifically the payment of corporation tax by large corporate taxpayers, we utilised the concept of communities of practice (see Chapter 12).

Indeed, we found evidence of a number of interconnected communities of practice and the following extract from our report shows how we found the concept helpful, but more importantly accessible, to our practitioner audience:

> The wider community comprises the LBS as a whole, whose members share the common goal of effectively securing tax compliance from large corporate taxpayers. Within the LBS are two identifiable communities of practice; specifically that comprising the tax specialists, a long standing and well established community, and more latterly, the new community consisting of the financial reporting accountants employed to act as consultants to the tax specialists, but more than that, to participate in the wider LBS community of practice and alter its established character. Arguably both the tax specialist and the accountant communities extend beyond the LBS through their shared knowledge base with those in similar roles in local compliance.
>
> Membership of a community of practice is heterogeneous and members participate at different levels. The organisational structure of the LBS is geographically fragmented, and contains members operating on different aspects of the process; customer relationship managers (CRMs) responsible for the outward facing interactions with corporate 'customers', business

> managers responsible for allocation of resources to tasks, tax specialists at different levels with different degrees of expertise and responsibility and specialist consultants which includes the financial reporting specialist accountants.
>
> The Revenue accountants, as newcomers to the wider LBS community, need to understand 'how things work', but at the same time are compelled to seek to re-shape the community to encompass their participation. At the same time, their presence as a sub-community impacts on the sub-community comprising the tax specialists, who must learn to interact with the revenue accountants and do so at different levels and to different extents. All three communities, the wider LBS and the two sub-communities, are constantly changing and adapting to accommodate the newcomers, to some extent unwittingly.
>
> Arguably, the power struggles that can be seen between the Revenue officers and the Revenue accountants mirror those that are taking place in the wider policy arena between the definition of profits for accounting purposes and for tax purposes.
>
> Thinking of the LBS as consisting of a community of practice, within which are a number of sub-communities, two of which are most relevant to this study, the accountants and the tax specialists, allows for a better understanding of the dynamics of the changes taking place in Revenue practices which impact directly on the relationship with large corporate taxpayers.
>
> *(Oats and Tuck 2008: 41)*

We concluded that the Revenue may not be making best use of the resource that this additional accountancy expertise represents, particularly in terms of leveraging their skill sets beyond their technical accountancy expertise. We were able to recommend some potential changes and areas for future research, as well as shedding light on an important aspect of tax practice. As we have shown, research of interest to practioners and capable of feeding into policy debates can fruitfully be pursued, as Hasseldine *et al.* (Chapter 17) did, with financial backing of professional associations.

References

Denzin, N.K. and Lincoln, Y.S. (1994) *Handbook of Qualitative Research*, Thousand Oaks, CA: Sage.

Merkl-Davis, D. and Brennan, N. (2011) 'Homo economicus, homo psychologicus, homo socialis, homo fabulans and homo publicus: A theoretical framework of impression management', working paper, on file with the author.

Oats, L. and Tuck, P. (2008) *The Relationship between HMRC and Large Corporate Taxpayers: The Changing Role of Accountants*, London: ICAEW Centre for Business Performance.

Odendahl, T. and Shaw, A. (2001) 'Interviewing elites', in J. Gubrium and J. Holstein, *Handbook of Interview Research: Context and Method*, Thousand Oaks, CA: Sage.
Tuck, P.A. (2007) *Study of the Changing Relationship Between Large Corporates and the Inland Revenue*, unpublished PhD thesis, University of Warwick.

21

ANALYSING THE ENHANCED RELATIONSHIP BETWEEN CORPORATE TAXPAYERS AND REVENUE AUTHORITIES

A UK case study

Judith Freedman, Geoffrey Loomer and John Vella

The following is an abridged version of a paper presented at the 2009 Internal Revenue Service (IRS) Conference in Washington, DC, reproduced with permission from the IRS. That paper analyses in detail the results of a survey of attitudes of tax directors to the management of tax risk. The extracts below focus on the methodology used and the manner in which the study was conducted. For full details of the background to the study, and an analysis of the findings, readers are referred to the full paper, which is available from the IRS website.[1]

Revenue authorities around the world are concerned to manage the risks of reduced revenue collection resulting from various forms of taxpayer behaviour that they consider to amount to 'aggressive' or 'unacceptable' tax avoidance. At the same time, the behaviour so described may well be believed by the taxpayer in question to be within the law as it stands and with a good chance of being effective even if litigated. The law on tax avoidance is sometimes not sufficiently determinate to give a clear answer either way prior to the completion of the relevant transaction or perhaps even prior to judicial determination.[2]

There are practical management and resource allocation questions as well as rule of law issues about management of risk in this area. In recent years a number of countries have adopted innovative risk-management techniques based on fostering a trusting and co-operative relationship with taxpayers. The goals of these initiatives are to improve resource allocation by revenue authorities, to reduce compliance costs for co-operative taxpayers and to reduce incentives to participate in the behaviour described above.

The UK revenue authority, Her Majesty's Revenue & Customs (HMRC), has recently adopted a form of such enhanced co-operation within its Large Business Service (LBS), which manages the tax affairs of the largest UK businesses.[3] As part of this approach, they use a Risk Rating Approach (RRA) for taxpayers.

Between 2007 and 2008 the authors carried out a qualitative research project examining a number of issues relating to tax risk and tax risk management, avoidance and the relationship between large corporates and HMRC. They also examined examples of two new legislative approaches to avoidance in the UK, using targeted anti-avoidance rules based on the purpose of the taxpayers (TAARs) and using principles-based legislation (PBL). The research project was carried out by means of a survey of views of large businesses undertaken by the authors (referred to herein as the Main Survey).[4]

The Main Survey examined the views of tax directors obtained from in-depth interviews. In summary, the authors found that the RRA and the enhanced relationship programme have been successful in achieving some aims but not others. Thus, for example, while the RRA has led to a perceived better allocation of resources within HMRC, it seems to be less convincing as a means of moderating the tax planning of certain types of corporate taxpayer. With respect to the new legislative approach, the authors found that there was some support for the view that they could advance the simplicity and coherence of the tax system and possibly enhance competitiveness. It was clear, however, that there remain serious concerns about the certainty of application and resistance by some to modifying behaviour beyond what they perceived to be required by law; the fact that these new regimes are co-existing with the RRA approach did not necessarily moderate these concerns.

Overview of the survey

The Main Survey, which is the foundation of this chapter, took place by way of in-depth, face-to-face interviews conducted in the spring of 2008 with the tax directors of 30 corporate groups, taken from the FTSE 100, FTSE 250, and one unlisted company. The interviews focused on the workings of the LBS. The questions were designed to elicit the experiences and opinions of large business representatives with respect to the RRA, a key feature of the UK HMRC's Review of Links with Large Business (the Varney Review),[5] as well as the status of relationships between HMRC and large business more generally and the respondents' views on the practical implications of TAARs and PBL and how these approaches impact upon and are influenced by relationships between HMRC and large businesses.

Survey design

The Main Survey was designed in early 2008. Formal approval from the University of Oxford's Research Ethics Committee was obtained in March 2008 and interviews were carried out in April–June 2008. The Main Survey followed from and built upon the smaller Pilot Survey,[6] which was designed and implemented in 2007.

A key feature of both surveys was the use of detailed, hypothetical tax planning scenarios around which a series of semi-structured questions were asked by two of the present authors, bringing practical and academic experience on various aspects of tax law, corporate law and corporate governance. In addition to asking more general questions regarding firms' risk ratings, the relevant risk criteria and the perceived effectiveness of the RRA, the authors used the scenarios as a foundation for obtaining detailed, practical views on the respondents' approaches to tax planning – and, accordingly, a key element of each respondent's risk profile. The use of detailed legal scenarios distinguishes this work from the research carried out by HMRC and, indeed, from any other research of which the authors are aware, and defines the methodological approach to this qualitative survey.

In both the Pilot Survey and the Main Survey, two tax planning scenarios were sent to each interviewee a few days in advance of his or her interview. These scenarios had been designed earlier by the authors, vetted separately with tax practitioners (two tax directors and a chartered accountant specialising in tax), and subsequently revised for use in the interviews. In addition, a catalogue of standard questions was prepared and tested with the same three experts and with one tax solicitor. The two scenarios used in the Main Survey are described fully in the Main Survey Report.[7] Each scenario involved some element of tax planning, the effectiveness of which could have been affected by recent or proposed anti-avoidance legislation in the UK. Each was based on examples discussed in HMRC publications, with additional details provided in order to make the scenarios more realistic. The goal was to move beyond generalities in order to understand how businesses might assess and react to specific tax planning opportunities and to compare such assessments and reactions to the academic and policy commentary on tax avoidance and tax risk. A further goal was to draw connections between these results and the conclusions regarding firms' risk ratings and relationships with HMRC.

Sampling, implementation and analysis

Pilot Survey sample

One purpose of the Pilot Survey was to test the use of detailed legal scenarios as the basis of discussions with tax directors, and to determine whether active, in-depth interviews on these subjects would elicit responses that could reasonably be quantified or generalised. As such, a rigorous sampling methodology was not pursued in the Pilot Survey. A letter was sent to the 'Hundred Group', comprising FTSE 100 companies only, and interviews were carried out with tax directors from the nine companies that volunteered.

Main Survey sample

Although the results of the Pilot Survey were interesting, the reliability of the research was hindered by selection bias and by the small sample size. For the Main Survey the authors assembled a larger and more varied pool of survey respondents using a combination of random and 'purposeful' sampling. As observed by Patton (2002: 46), '[t]he logic and power of purposeful sampling derive from the emphasis on in-depth understanding. This leads to selecting *information-rich cases* for study in-depth'.[8]

The respondents consisted of tax directors from eight of the nine companies that participated in the Pilot Survey,[9] 21 other companies from a short list selected randomly from the FTSE 350 list,[10] and one unlisted company. The companies shortlisted randomly received a letter. Seventeen companies responded and agreed to be interviewed. Others from the random sample did not respond to the initial letter but were contacted by telephone and then agreed to be interviewed. In all, 19 companies from the FTSE 100, ten from the FTSE 250 and one unlisted company were interviewed. Twenty-seven of the companies interviewed are dealt with by the LBS.[11] Of the remaining three companies, two had been informed that they would be moved into the LBS soon. One of the 27 companies in the LBS at the time of the interview had been informed that it was being moved out. One high-level LBS official was interviewed in order to clarify some points of fact and obtain a balancing view.

The main disadvantages of using this partly purposeful sample are, first, that not all participants were randomly selected and, second, that there was a disproportionate representation of very large companies (those from the FTSE 100) compared to the population covered by the LBS. The overwhelming advantage of this sample is that most of the respondents had practical experience or general awareness of the issues that our interviews sought to explore. Although the authors cannot be absolutely certain that the Main Survey sample was representative, it is comforting that the distribution of responses regarding firms' risk ratings was in line with HMRC expectations and with official figures published in July 2008.[12] Regarding firm size, the authors found it difficult to obtain participation from *any* companies in the FTSE 250, let alone companies below this level of market capitalisation; most such companies indicated that they were not aware of or interested in HMRC's enhanced relationship model or novel approaches to anti-avoidance legislation. It is notable that research commissioned by HMRC similarly found that '[i]n practice, the extent of awareness and understanding of the Review of Links among participants prior to the research was limited' (HMRC 2007: 8). Moreover, companies having a market capitalisation below that of the FTSE 250 are unlikely to have internal tax departments[13] and therefore tend to rely on external tax advisers. The authors decided to restrict this research to the views of tax directors operating within large corporate groups, although the approach used here could be extended to external tax advisers as well.[14]

Conduct of interviews

The authors' primary goal in conducting these interviews was 'to generate data which give an authentic insight into people's experiences' (Silverman 2001: 87). It was decided that the only way to achieve this was to conduct face-to-face, semi-structured interviews with individual respondents. The other obvious options – focus group interviews and telephone or postal surveys – were discounted at an early stage. The use of focus groups almost certainly would have resulted in a lack of candour and completeness, given the sensitivity around corporate tax-risk profiles and avoidance activities.[15] Respondents would have been concerned to protect their firms' legal position vis-à-vis HMRC and competitive position vis-à-vis other participating firms. The use of telephone or postal surveys, on the other hand, would have demanded short and quantifiable answers that would have revealed none of the nuance and controversy surrounding the meaning of terms such as 'tax compliance', 'tax aggressiveness' and 'tax reputation'. As these shades of meaning were precisely what the research was designed to explore, in-depth interviews were seen as the best choice.

The survey was carried out by means of interviews lastings about one hour conducted by two of the present authors. There was an interview schedule and a catalogue of standard questions, but the interviews were not highly structured, allowing the interviewees to focus on matters of importance to their companies. This flexibility permitted the interviewers to steer the interviews away from broad generalisations to a more meaningful and concrete exchange. It also facilitated the attainment of a satisfactory depth of discussion. On the other hand, it meant that not all issues were discussed for the same length of time and in the same amount of detail with all interviewees.

One further feature of the interviews was that the questions asked, and the issues discussed, often did not lend themselves to an easy 'yes' or 'no' answer. This again led to very engaging discussions. Yet this meant that some respondents did not always provide direct answers to the questions asked. These interviewees at times responded by providing examples, recounting an anecdote, or speculating about the general view of tax directors. In the light of all this, the authors noted the difficulty encountered at times in determining the exact view of an interviewee on a particular issue. The authors have erred on the side of caution, by, for example, not attributing any specific views to the interviewees unless this was clearly stated or implied in the answers given. If a respondent's answers only provided vague support for a view, then that was made clear in the paper.

Analysis of interviews

The authors concede that it is impossible to create a 'pure' interview that would provide an exact reflection of reality in this or any other area. However, the authors were satisfied that active, in-depth interviews could and would elicit 'authentic accounts of subjective experience' regarding tax risk, tax avoidance and the other matters discussed (Miller and Glassner 2004: 125). Interviews were not electronically recorded – again to encourage candour from participants – but the two interviewers took extensive notes which they transcribed and cross-checked as soon as possible following each interview. The transcribed interviews were then coded for particular views in respect of particular themes, following typical procedures,[16] although given the highly nuanced and active nature of the interviews no attempt was made to force respondents' answers into rigid categories.[17] The authors coded the interviews independently and any discrepancies were resolved by consensus following re-examination of the original interview notes.

Therefore, while the authors attempted to put order to the answers given, to aggregate views and to draw out some main and subsidiary themes, this research remains very much of a qualitative and not a quantitative nature.

Summary of views

The respondents in the Pilot Survey agreed with the RRA in principle, but a large majority raised serious questions about its details and practical operation.[18] These reservations primarily concerned the risk rating criteria and the purported benefits of being low risk. The details of the RRA, however, had not been fully developed at the time of that survey. For the purposes of the Main Survey the authors were interested in finding out whether the uncertainties had been overcome and how the approach was translating into practice. Initial implementation of the RRA for companies within the LBS was largely complete at the time of the Main Survey interviews.[19] It should be noted that further developments and clarifications have taken place since the Main Survey was undertaken so that the responses might well be different and the conclusions might need to be modified accordingly if the research were to be repeated.[20]

The Main Survey indicated that at the time it was undertaken the respondent firms were split fairly evenly between those that were low (or lower) risk and those that were high (or higher) risk. The Main Survey revealed modest improvement in respondents' comprehension of the risk rating criteria and their relative weight, yet some confusion and scepticism remained. Most importantly, the results supported the view that the RRA should lead to a better allocation of resources within HMRC, and possibly a change in taxpayer behaviour in terms of transparency and openness, but also indicated that the RRA is unlikely to change the attitude of some types of corporate taxpayers towards tax avoidance.[21] The results also suggested that while firms have wider reputational concerns associated with public perceptions of their tax planning activities, the extent to which reputational concerns limit a given company's tax planning behaviour is far from obvious.

The literature and survey results showed that HMRC seemed to be using the RRA to induce large corporate taxpayers to stay on the right side of the acceptable/unacceptable boundary as drawn by them (rather than as drawn by the courts). One conclusion was that this mixing of the goals of resource allocation with modification of tax planning behaviour might make some large businesses consider that it was too difficult to become low risk under the RRA, even where they were willing to agree to real-time working, transparency and other risk-management requirements in terms of their systems. This might be counter-productive in terms of encouraging them to aim for low-risk status and thus in achieving the efficiency goal.

With respect to the two new legislative approaches, TAARs and PBL, the authors found that there was some support for the view that they could advance the simplicity and coherence of the tax system and possibly enhance competitiveness. It was also clear, however, that there remain serious concerns about the certainty of application and the resistance by some to the apparent scope for discretion to be used in the attempt to modify behaviour beyond what they perceived to be required by law. The fact that these new regimes are co-existing with the RRA approach did not necessarily moderate these concerns.

In sum, it was concluded that the developments examined were showing some measure of success and were well worth monitoring and considering by other jurisdictions, but this approach cannot itself define what is due under the law nor should it be relied upon to attempt to override that central question.

The methodology adopted was time-intensive and required knowledgeable and skilled interviewers, but it produced a rich seam of responses, the content of which was corroborated by other surveys and sources.

Notes

1 Available at www.irs.gov/pub/irs-soi/09resconenrelcorptaxuk.pdf (accessed 17 November 2011).

2 Further discussion by the authors of the difficult definitional issues and general analysis of tax-avoidance questions can be found in Freedman *et al.* (2009), papers.ssrn.com/sol3/papers.cfm?abstract_id = 1385042 ('Main Survey Report', accessed 17 November 2011); Freedman (2007); and Freedman (2004), papers.ssrn.com/sol3/papers.cfm?abstract_id=900043 (accessed 17 November 2011).

3 For details see www.hmrc.gov.uk/lbo/index.htm (accessed 17 November 2011).

4 Main Survey Report, Freedman *et al.* (2009).

5 HMRC (2006) *Review of Links with Large Business*, November, www.hmrc.gov.uk/large-business/review-report.pdf (accessed 17 November 2011).

6 For a summary see Freedman *et al.* 2008. For the full report see denning.law.ox.ac.uk/tax/documents/Movingbeyondavoidance.pdf (accessed 5 December 2011).

7 Main Survey Report, Freedman *et al.* (2009): Appendix II.

8 There are differing views about the importance of sample selection when a qualitative methodology is used (McKerchar 2008: 5). Whatever the sample used, it is important not to over-generalise from the results of a qualitative survey, and the authors of this paper have paid respect to this principle. Nevertheless, the authors take the view that the more representative the sample the greater its value, and that careful sample selection was therefore important.

9 One of the nine companies was unable to participate in the Main Survey.

10 The authors randomly selected 118 companies from the FTSE 350 Index as of 6 March 2008. This was done by selecting every third company on the alphabetical list. A small number of the companies that were selected following this process formed part of the sample from the Pilot Survey; in such cases that company was de-selected and the next company on the list was selected. The authors also randomly selected 20 companies from the FTSE Small Cap Index as of 6 March 2008, by selecting every 20th company on the alphabetical list, but no company contacted from the FTSE Small Cap Index was willing to participate in the research.

11 The then-current HMRC documentation indicated that the LBS was composed of 'approximately' 1,000 companies, so the authors proceeded on the assumption that most of the companies in the FTSE 350 and perhaps even the FTSE Small Cap Index would be within the LBS. That assumption was later proven to be incorrect.

12 The detailed responses from the Main Survey were as follows:

- Four companies had not had a risk rating assessment yet – all FTSE 250;
- Sixteen gave a single overall risk rating: seven of these said that they were low risk (four FTSE 100, two FTSE 250, one unlisted); two said that they were moderate risk (FTSE 250); seven said that they were high risk (FTSE 100);

- Ten did not give an overall risk rating: two of these said that they were on the lower end of the scale (one FTSE 100, one FTSE 250); eight said that they were low on some criteria and moderate or high on others. Of these eight, three were clearly on the lower end of the spectrum and could possibly be overall low risk (two FTSE 100, one FTSE 250), while the remaining five seemed to the authors to be situated somewhere on the mid–high end of the scale, possibly closer to the high end (FTSE 100).

HMRC states that 'nearly 40%' of LBS businesses were low risk (HMRC 2008b: 4). In June 2008 the actual number of businesses managed by LBS that had a low risk rating was 238 (out of around 700 possible businesses) (Hansard 2008).

13 Even some FTSE 250 companies that were contacted indicated that they do not have internal tax departments.

14 There is a small literature that analyses the views of tax accountants with respect to ethics, risk management and tax avoidance, including: Kadous and Magro (2001: 451); and Doyle *et al.* (2009: 177).

15 The authors do not dispute that focus-group interviewing can be entirely appropriate in other circumstances. See Morgan 2001: 141.

16 For example, A. Strauss and J. Corbin (1998) *Basics of Qualitative Research: Techniques and Procedures for Developing Grounded Theory*, 2nd edn, Sage Publications, pt II.

17 See Charmaz (2003: 675); Holstein and Gubrium (2004: 140).

18 Pilot Survey Full Report, see Note 6: 9.

19 In the 2008 Budget, HMRC reported that 97 percent of LBS customers had been reviewed using the new risk review template (HMRC 2008b: 10).

20 For an account of some of the changes see Freedman (2011).

21 See also Pilot Survey Full Report, see Note 6: 17–18.

References

Charmaz, K. (2003) 'Qualitative interviewing and grounded theory analysis', in J.A. Holstein and J.F. Gubrium (eds), *Inside Interviewing: New Lenses, New Concerns*, Thousand Oaks, CA: Sage, pp.311–28.

Doyle, E.M., Hughes, J.F. and Glaister, K.W. (2009) 'Linking ethics and risk management in taxation: Evidence from an exploratory study in Ireland and the UK', *Journal of Business Ethics* 86: 177.

Freedman, J. (2004) 'Defining taxpayer responsibility: In support of a general anti-avoidance principle', *British Tax Review* 332.

——(2007) 'Interpreting tax statutes: Tax avoidance and the intention of parliament', *Law Quarterly Review* 122: 52.

——(2011) 'Responsive regulation, risk and rules: applying the theory to tax practice', *UBC Law Review* 44(3): 627.

Freedman, J., Loomer, G. and Vella, J. (2008) 'Moving beyond avoidance? Tax risk and the relationship between large business and HMRC', in J. Freedman (ed.), *Beyond Boundaries: Developing Approaches to Tax Avoidance and Tax Risk Management*, Oxford: Oxford University Centre for Business Taxation, pp. 81–100.

——(2009) 'Corporate tax risk and tax avoidance: New approaches', *British Tax Review,* 74.

Hansard (2008) House of Lords, Vol. 703, col. WA70 (7 July), www.publications.parliament.uk/pa/ld200708/ldhansrd/text/80707w0003.htm (accessed 5 December 2011).

HMRC (2006) *Review of Links with Large Business*, www.hmrc.gov.uk/large-business/review-report.pdf.

——(2007) *Research to Support the Implementation of Proposals in the Review of Links with Large Business*, HMRC Research Report 58, www.hmrc.gov.uk/research/report58.pdf (accessed 17 November 2011).

——(2008a) *Update on Review of Links with Large Business: Research Summary*, www.hmrc.gov.uk/large-business/lb-summary.pdf.

——(2008b) *The Framework for a Better Relationship*, www.hmrc.gov.uk/budget2008/framework-better-relations.pdf.

Holstein, J.A. and Gubrium, J.F. (2004) *The Active Interview*, in D. Silverman (ed.), *Qualitative Research: Theory Method and Practice*, London: Sage, pp.140–61.

Kadous, K. and Magro, A.M. (2001) 'The effects of exposure to practice risk on tax professionals' judgements and recommendations', *Contemporary Accounting Research* 18: 451.

McKerchar, M. (2008) 'Philosophical paradigms, inquiry strategies and knowledge claims: Applying the principles of research design and conduct to taxation', *eJournal of Tax Research* 5.

Miller, J. and Glassner, B. (2004) 'The "inside" and the "outside": Finding realities in interviews', in D. Silverman (ed.), *Qualitative Research: Theory, Method and Practice,* 2nd edn, London: Sage Publications.

Morgan, D.L. (2001) 'Focus Group Interviewing', in J.F. Gubrium and J.A. Holstein (eds), *Handbook of Interview Research: Context and Method,* London: Sage Publications.

Patton, M.Q. (2002) *Qualitative Research and Evaluation Methods*, 3rd edn, London: Sage Publications.

Silverman, D. (2001) *Interpreting Qualitative Data: Methods for Analysing Talk, Text and Interaction*, 2nd edn, London: Sage Publications.

22
TRANSFER PRICING
Advance pricing agreements

Helen Rogers

Introduction

This chapter offers an overview of the fieldwork aspect of a qualitative research project undertaken for a PhD, that included interviews with senior tax professionals. It sets out some of the key stages: the chapter starts with a short summary of the tax topic for research and the specific research objective. The research methods used are then described, including reasons for their selection, followed by a discussion of some issues concerning access for fieldwork and carrying out interviews, ending with some brief observations on the analysis of this fieldwork data.

Transfer pricing is a topic on which there is a considerable amount of academic research, although a large part of the body of transfer pricing literature does not take tax into account. Transfer pricing relates to the prices that one part of a transnational enterprise (TNE) charges another part, in respect of transactions between them.[1] This impacts on the pre-tax profits of different individual companies within a group of companies; therefore, there is scope for TNEs to set transfer prices judiciously so that higher profits arise in low-tax jurisdictions and lower profits in higher-tax jurisdictions.

New transfer pricing tax rules were issued in the US in the mid-1990s, accompanied by active enforcement, in response to concerns that the US tax base was being eroded by the way that some TNEs were setting their transfer prices (Durst and Culbertson 2002). The Organisation for Economic Co-operation and Development (OECD) issued revised Transfer Pricing Guidelines for Multinational Enterprises and Tax Administrations in 1995 (OECD 1999) and other countries, including the UK,[2] went on to issue new transfer pricing laws, typically supported by robust penalties. These rules and guidelines required the use of the arm's length principle when determining transfer prices. This requires that the transfer price for transactions between related parties should be the arm's length price: the price that would be charged if the same transaction were taking place between unrelated third parties.

A major problem for those seeking to comply with the burgeoning transfer pricing legislation is that different countries issued different, inconsistent rules requiring the preparation of different supporting documentation. The rules for OECD member countries had an element of consistency in that they did use the arm's length principle, but the arm's length principle is very broad and open to different interpretations. Many transactions that take place within a TNE will not be replicated with a purchaser outside the TNE, so a judgement about the hypothetical arm's length price will have to be made. This gives rise to a range of different opinions as to what would be an appropriate arm's length price, rather than there being one universally accepted correct price. This uncertainty means there is considerable scope for disagreement between TNEs and tax authorities, potentially giving rise to penalties and also scope for disagreement between different tax authorities, potentially giving rise to double taxation.

Research objective and methodology

This uncertainty is not always acknowledged in the transfer pricing literature, much of which is concerned with determining the 'right' transfer price. One of the ways in which transfer pricing uncertainty is recognised and addressed by tax authorities is through the scope to agree Advance Pricing Agreements (APAs). This is a way for TNEs to agree in advance with the tax authorities appropriate transfer prices, giving the TNE certainty that those prices will not be challenged during the period of the agreement. As this was a relatively new procedure[3] and APA agreements are confidential, the research focused on the APA process. The research objective was to gain an insight into the operation of APAs in practice, in particular the extent to which they can help to deal with the uncertainty of transfer pricing rules and noting where practice might differ from the written rules.

An APA can be unilateral or bilateral (or, rarely, multilateral). Bilateral APAs were selected for attention as unilateral APAs cannot provide the same degree of certainty. I had to choose a jurisdiction to study in addition to the UK, and I decided on the US. There were many different reasons for opting for the US, not least the practical advantage of all the data being collected in English (while still recognising the potential for misunderstandings). The US has been one of the first countries to issue new transfer pricing rules and also the UK and the US are close trading partners.[4] The UK and US both have well-developed transfer pricing APA laws and administrative practices, relative to other jurisdictions; previous research had identified the UK and US as among the five nation states with the strongest level of transfer pricing enforcement (Bartelsman and Beetsma 2003). Subsequently, the closeness of links between the UK and US on many different matters was raised by interviewees during the data collection.

Although APAs were a relatively recent development there was some useful literature on APAs on which to draw. For example, there was already a comprehensive review and comparison of the UK and US APA rules (Wrappe *et al.* 2005), which highlighted the similarities and differences in approach. However, for this project, as well as these formal rules the research focus was on what happens in practice, which might not necessarily be the same as the written rules. This was subsequently recognised by interviewees: for example, one of them observed:

> it's not sufficient to read the legislation, you have to understand how it works in practice because sometimes you have a standard which is in the law which is never applied and that can be good for taxpayers. There can be tax penalties in some countries that look very harsh on paper but in real terms are never there. In some countries you have things that you don't find in the law but you find in the practices.

This proposition of a gap between written rules and what happens in practice was one of the key approaches and theories (see, for example, Lange 1999) to be explored further with reference to transfer pricing and appraised further, drawing on the fieldwork data.

Research methods

Data for this research was collected by reviewing legal texts, such as tax rules and guidelines, and by interviewing people drawn from the most senior transfer pricing tax professionals in the UK and USA. Therefore this research was based on both interview data and on legislative and policy data, the former with some of the people who helped to create and fashion the latter.

An initial, thorough examination of the written rules was considered necessary as these set out the formal requirements for taxpayers.[5] From the outset, it was envisaged that this textual analysis would be supplemented with other data, because, as well as formal procedures, the research objective was concerned with the informal ones. The importance of this is recognised in the OECD *Guidelines* which, while providing some quite lengthy guidance, acknowledge that this is supplemented by a more informal common understanding:

> Experience under the arm's length principle has become sufficiently broad and sophisticated to establish a body of common understanding among the business community and tax administrations.
>
> *(OECD 1999: paragraph 1.14)*

A key aim of this research was to gain an insight into aspects of that developing common understanding. Therefore, in terms of research method, I was looking for the most appropriate approach to best gain such an insight. I could not attend APA meetings between tax authorities and taxpayer and therefore with respect to field data I chose to pursue data derived mainly from interviews, with those working at the highest level 'among the business community and tax administrations'. The key organisations were identified as the tax authorities, the corporate taxpayers and their advisers.

The possibility of using questionnaire surveys instead of interviews, or supplementing the interview data with some form of survey was considered. Surveys have been used in transfer pricing research, although in academic transfer pricing research their use appears less prevalent in recent years. Notably there is the biennial Ernst and Young transfer pricing survey, which was a useful practitioner reference for this project and which is much referred to in academic research on transfer pricing (for example Borkowski 2008; Cools *et al.* 2008; and Elliott 2005).

This research project was concerned with looking at an emerging common understanding of relatively new concepts and procedures, as they were in the process of becoming established. Such nuances would be hard to see or unpick using survey data; surveys are typically more appropriate for clearly defined, widely understood terms, rather than emerging ones.[6] Therefore, having ruled out a survey method, it was decided that interviews would be used for data collection and that they would be semi-structured. An important advantage of using semi-structured interviews is the scope to obtain the opinions and experiences of the different interviewees 'in their own words'. This is enhanced in semi-structured rather than structured interviews because instead of a set, rigid list of questions, there is scope to follow up points made by interviewees, both to clarify what they mean and to explore it in more detail. This opportunity for further questions, to follow up issues raised by the interviewee, means that the topics and experience that are important to the interviewee can be explored further and included in the data.

Interview access

The problems in gaining access to organisations for academic research have often been raised and discussed; see, for example, Ahrens (2004). Bryman (2001: 11) quotes Van Maanen and Kolb (1983), who states that 'gaining access to most organisations is not a matter to be taken lightly but one that involves some combination of strategic planning, hard work and dumb luck'. The general difficulty of access in order to undertake academic research is exacerbated in the case of tax research; tax is a particularly confidential and sensitive topic for many professionals and TNEs. For example, Cools *et al.* (2008) acknowledge this, suggesting that only TNEs with a lack of problems with the tax authorities would agree to cooperate with such research.

In terms of securing and preserving access, Bryman (2001: 297) advises the researcher to 'play up your credentials – past work and experience'. I had experience working as a professional accountant on transfer pricing issues for some time, which I explained to potential interviewees, thus highlighting that the tone of the interview would not be elementary or basic. Nevertheless, it was also stressed when seeking out interviewees that, despite professional and commercial experience, I was now working in an academic capacity, undertaking research with the objective of writing a PhD thesis and some academic papers. I was fortunate when some senior transfer pricing experts agreed to be interviewed as it gave this stage of the research project an important impetus. Furthermore, some of them kindly and helpfully suggested other interviewees so that the project gained momentum.

All the interviewees from the different key organisations were advised that the interviews would be confidential; while some direct quotes would be used, they would not be attributed. It was also stressed that it was acknowledged that the interviewees were very busy and it was envisaged that interviews would last an hour.

Interviews – initial interviews

It had originally been planned that initial interviews would be carried out to help to clarify the direction of the research and to help to inform the main data collection, for example by providing some guidance in the framing of questions for the subsequent interviews. However, having met the challenge of obtaining access, I was very keen to get started on the main interviews; nevertheless, the pilot interview stage proved to be very valuable for a number of reasons.

Three initial interviews were undertaken, each with an interviewee from each of the identified key organisations: a tax authority, a professional advisory firm and a tax director from a large TNE. These interviews were not recorded; however, detailed notes were taken during and after each interview. These interviews canvassed general opinions on transfer pricing issues and were useful in that they helped to clarify main topical areas of attention and concern in transfer pricing and were used to inform the development of the semi-structured interview questions. All three interviewees raised APAs as an important current issue and an area in which they envisaged that activity would increase in the future.

From these initial interviews it was also identified, in the light of observations made by the interviewees, that the OECD was viewed as a key organisation. Accordingly it was accepted that representatives from the OECD could provide useful data for this research objective, if access could be obtained. I was fortunate that an interviewee suggested someone to approach and this introduction meant that I was then able to include those with OECD experience among the interviewees. Accordingly, after the initial interviews, the four key organisations identified for further research were the tax authorities, TNE taxpayers, tax advisers to TNEs, and the OECD.

Therefore, undertaking preliminary interviews ahead of the main interviews was very beneficial. As well as identifying an additional key organisation to include, they helped to frame the questions for the semi-structured interviews and provided some support as to the appropriateness of the dominant theories for the thesis. Also, these initial interviews served to provide a useful form of 'interview practice', so that I would not be going into the first main data-gathering interviews 'cold', but with some direct experience of interviewing those drawn from this group of specialists. This is an important potential benefit of initial exploratory interviews when interviewing from a group of discrete people with a common language and shared province. This would probably be particularly beneficial to a researcher with little experience of undertaking interviews or with very limited understanding of the language and culture of the respondents (Fontana and Frey 2000).

Interviews – main interviews

After the preliminary interviews, 14 main interviews were carried out. This could be held to be quite a small number but, as the interviews were all to be carried out by one person, the number needed to be manageable. Importantly, however, the main reason for the small number in this case is the topic for research itself and its focus on the elite, by definition a small number. Considerable knowledge and power in respect of transfer pricing rests with a relatively small number of people who interact with each other at the transnational level, and these were the targeted interviewees.

All but three of the interviews took place at the workplace location of the interviewee. All but one of the interviews (which was conducted by telephone) were face to face. The interviews were conducted place within the space of a five-month period at the end of 2006 (with the sole exception of one interview that took place in the following year). Therefore, the interviews took place over a relatively short period of time. As with much tax legislation, transfer pricing rules and procedures are frequently changing, so it was important to obtain interviewees' perspectives within the same time frame.

Some notes were taken during each interview and were supplemented after the interview. All but two were recorded (for those two, detailed notes were taken during and after the interview). Interview notes were read after each interview and before the next interview to help to build knowledge and understanding, and to enable reflection and to help to identify any problems.

Given the small number of interviewees and the research objective, the format of each interview was semi-structured. There was a series of questions, informed by the initial interviews and the scrutiny of the legislation and related policy documents, but there was not a set sequence or fixed time slot for these questions so that interviewees' responses could be followed up.

On the particular issue of interviewing people from an elite group, Miles and Huberman (1994: 266) refer to the possible risk of an 'elite bias' when carrying out qualitative research, recommending the inclusion of lower-status informants to temper this elite view. However, in this case the elite view was what was being sought; the focus was on the development of APA practices and a common understanding of transfer pricing at the highest level of the key organisations. The questions and subsequent data analysis focused on the views of the elite involved in this development. It was not claimed that their views and understanding would always be shared by people at different levels of the key organisations: indeed, it is readily acknowledged that this is unlikely to be the case.

Data analysis

On completion of the interviews all the interview tapes were transcribed: a very time-consuming process which gave rise to a large amount of data. The management of the data for this project was supported by NVivo software. In order to facilitate this, all interviews were analysed line by line and coded. The codes used were developed iteratively from reviewing the interview data, the tax rules and the academic literature. It has previously been observed that while the search tools in NVivo are helpful in interrogating data, they are less useful in addressing the validity of emerging themes, which requires the researcher's rigorous analysis (Welsh 2002). NVivo certainly was found to be useful for interrogating the material, particularly for swift data retrieval.

There were many different fascinating details and strands in the data, from which I had to identify the key themes on which to focus, for the analysis and writing up to be manageable; this was something with which NVivo could not assist. The volume of data meant that this was very time consuming. The theories I had previously identified were a crucial focus and filtering device for whittling down the data at this stage. My thesis drew on the literature on the gap and the links between formal law and practice and the social construction of compliance and accepted practice, and so these became useful selection criteria for helping to sift the data.

The general environment at the time of fieldwork data collection should be taken into account. It is important that the external backdrop against which interviews take place is appraised and important contemporaneous events are considered, as they form part of the context at the time of the data collection. For example, these interviews took place while a US Senate Enquiry into the APA Program was underway. This was a potentially important investigation, looking into the operation of the APA Program.[7] Also in 2006 there was publicity of the resolution of the high-profile Glaxo transfer pricing case,[8] which was also relevant to this research. It was of particular significance to this research because it was 'the biggest such payment ever' (Green 2006: 2) and because the two tax authorities involved in the dispute were the UK and US tax authorities. This was another important event in the general transfer pricing environment against which the interview data should be considered, and most interviewees mentioned it.

Conclusion

Undertaking this fieldwork was a very rewarding part of the doctoral research process. It was particularly interesting to reap the benefit of transfer pricing insights at a time when rules and practices were developing and becoming established. The contemporaneous coverage of the Glaxo case in the business press helped to raise the profile of transfer pricing generally and so it was particularly interesting to be carrying out research in the field at this time.

The interviews gave rise to some rich data, providing some wonderful, illuminating quotations that helped to draw attention to how the interviewees saw the difficulties with which they were dealing; these help to support and illustrate certain points, often vividly so. However, crucially, the fieldwork data offered the opportunity and scope for more than some nice turns of phrase and a narrative of transfer pricing and APAs in the interviewees' own words; from it came a sense of the extent of the uncertainty and the practices to address this uncertainty that were emerging and becoming accepted practice. In the context of the thesis the fieldwork data were important support in the discussion of the applicability of theories in relation to uncertainty and differences and links between formal rules and practice.

Notes

1 Much of the transfer pricing literature is concerned with the sale of goods between related parties but transfer prices might also be set in respect of other transactions such as management services and the rights to intangible assets.

2 UK tax legislation in respect of transfer pricing came into effect for accounting periods ending on or after 1 July 1999.

3 The US APA Program was formally introduced in March 1991. The UK formally introduced an APA Programme in 1999.

4 There is a significant volume of trade flows between the UK and US, 'each of which is the largest source of direct foreign investment in the other with approximately 40 percent of all US investment in the EU made in the UK' (Wrappe *et al.* 2005: 845).
5 It is not possible to examine written agreed APAs as they are confidential.
6 For example, see Borkowski (2008) for a study of the influence of the Pacific Association of Tax Administrators, which uses survey data.
7 This Enquiry has yet to publish its conclusions. The prevailing view is that a report will never be published (Nadal 2008).
8 This case was widely reported in the media, for example 'GSK faces $7bn bill for tax on US profits', *The Times*, 8 January 2004. This refers to the years going back to 1989. The US tax authorities disputed the level of Glaxo's profits in the US after taking into account intangibles developed in the UK and the level of marketing work in the US.

References

Ahrens, T. (2004) 'Refining research questions in the course of negotiating access for fieldwork', in C. Humphrey and B. Lee, *The Real Life Guide to Accounting Research*, London: Elsevier.
Ahrens, T. and Chapman, C.S. (2006) 'Doing qualitative field research in management accounting: Positioning data to contribute to theory', *Accounting, Organizations and Society* 31(8): 819–41.
Bartelsman, E.J. and Beetsma, R.M.W.J. (2003) 'Why pay more? Corporate tax avoidance through transfer pricing in OECD countries', *Journal of Public Economics* 87: 2225–52.
Borkowski, S.C. (2008) 'The history of PATA and its effect on advance pricing arrangements and mutual agreement procedures', *Journal of International Accounting, Auditing and Taxation* 17: 31–50.
Bryman, A. (2001) *Social Research Methods*, Oxford: Oxford University Press.
Cools, M., Emmanuel, C. and Jorissen, A. (2008) 'Management control in the transfer pricing tax compliant multinational enterprise', *Accounting, Organizations and Society* 33(6): 603–28.
Durst, M. and Culbertson, R. (2003) 'Clearing away the sand: Retrospective methods and prospective documentation in transfer pricing today', *Tax Law Review* 57(37): 39–136.
Elliott, J. (2005) 'International transfer pricing', in M. Lamb, A. Lymer, J. Freedman and S. James (eds), *Taxation: An Interdisciplinary Approach to Research*, Oxford: Oxford University Press.
Fontana, A. and Frey, J.H. (2000) 'The interview: From structured questions to negotiated text', in N.K. Denzin and Y.S. Lincoln (eds), *Handbook of Qualitative Research*, Sage.
Freedman, J. (2005) 'Taxation research as legal research', in M. Lamb, A. Lymer, J. Freedman and S. James (eds), *Taxation: An Interdisciplinary Approach to Research*, Oxford: Oxford University Press.
Green, G. (2006) 'The UK reaction to the Glaxo Case', *Tax Planning international Transfer Pricing* BNA 11/06: 2–5.
Lange, B. (1999) 'Compliance construction in the context of environmental regulation', *Social and Legal Studies* 8: 549–67.
Marginson, D.W. (2004) 'The case study, the interview and the issues: a personal reflection', in C. Humphrey and B. Lee, *The Real Life Guide to Accounting Research*, London: Elsevier.
Miles, M. and Huberman, A.M. (1994) *Qualitative Data Analysis*, London: Sage.
Nadal, L.M. (2008) 'Who killed the senate APA report?' *Tax Analysts* 15, January: 1–8.
OECD (1995) 'Transfer pricing guidelines for multinational enterprises and tax administrations', Report of the OECD Committee on Fiscal Affairs, Paris.
Ring, D.M. (2000) 'On the frontier of procedural innovation: APAs and the struggle to allocate income for cross border taxation', *Michigan Journal of international Law* 21: 144–234.
Rogers, H. (2009) 'Uncertainty in transfer pricing tax rules: The role of APAs', unpublished PhD thesis, Warwick University.

Silverman, D. (2005) *Doing Qualitative Research*, 2nd edn, London: Sage.
Van Maanen, J. and Kolb, D.M. (1983) 'The professional apprentice: Observations on fieldwork roles in two organizational settings', in S.B. Bacharach (ed.), *Perspectives in Organizational Sociology*, Vol. 4. Greenwich, CT: JAI Press, pp. 1–33.
Welsh, E. (2002) 'Dealing with data: Using NVivo in the qualitative data analysis process', *Forum: Qualitative Social Research* 3(2): 1–8.
Wrappe, S.C., Haigh, R. and O'Mahony, D. (2005) 'Side-by-side comparison of APA procedures: the United States and the United Kingdom', *Tax Notes International* 39, No.9 August: 845–77.

23

THEORETICAL FRAMEWORK FOR APPLIED RESEARCH ON TAX POLICIES

Gitte Heij

Introduction

The aim of this chapter is to discuss a model that describes and where possible explains who and/or what influenced the tax reforms. This chapter is based on extensive research using two case studies of tax reform in the 1980s and 1990s in Indonesia and Vietnam (see Heij 2007).

First of all, we need to accept that there is no unified definition of tax in view of the multiple taxes, levies and stamp duties that differ from country to country, and may even vary amongst states/provinces within individual countries. Many studies in this area do not give any attention to the definition of the term 'tax'. Apparently, it is assumed that everyone understands what the word 'tax' means.[1] It is important to distinguish between tax and taxation. Taxation refers to the act or practice of imposing taxes or the fact of being taxed. Taxation can also refer to the revenue gained from taxes. For this report we focus on 'tax' rather than 'taxation'. Each country will have a different interpretation of those taxes (Heij 2007).[2]

The social sciences and particularly the fiscal sociological approach were used for the two case studies. Examining the Indonesian and Vietnamese case studies requires a combination of macro- and microsocial perspectives. As Snyder (1980) argues, a microsocial perspective that focuses on local phenomena within a single country is inadequate for understanding all those aspects of legal developments it shares with many other countries.

Little sociological research focuses on law-making and particularly who and what influences law reforms; what there is mainly concerns Western democracies. The same applies *a fortiori* to research conducted in the area of fiscal sociology. The aim is to find a theoretical model that permits us to study the question of influence and can be applied to the two case studies of Asian developing nations reforming their tax systems.

Before summarising existing approaches, it is important to pay attention to the different functions of law. These different functions need to be distinguished from the theories of law-making, and may further help in analysing the complicated process of law-making and will be discussed in the next section.

Instrumental, ideological and symbolic use of legislation

Laws, including tax laws, are seen by many as an appropriate instrument to engineer social and economic changes. Such an approach embeds the basic error that society and law are two separate entities, so that legal changes and laws can be used to influence society (Griffiths 1979). It opposes the view emphasised by non-instrumental approaches that laws are interrelated with social processes. Instead, it implicitly adopts a 'determinist', top-down command idea of law. Griffiths argues that it is no surprise that many laws seem to have little or no impact since the legislator so often proceeds on the basis of such an instrumentalistic approach. Although instrumentalism has proven to be an unsuccessful approach both in the sociology of law and in the practical art of establishing legislation (Griffiths 1979), many institutions are still wedded to it. Tax reform programs subsidised by international organisations like the World Bank and the Asian Development Bank strongly reflect this approach. Many even presume that laws are – or ought to be – solely instrumental. Frequently, however, laws are symbolic or ideological rather than instrumental. Often a law may contain all three elements or two of the three. Aside from these shortcomings, the main problem with this approach is that it does little to assist us in describing and analysing who and/or what influences tax reform.

The ideological approach to law is clearly visible in a country like Vietnam, where laws are supposed to reflect the socialist ideology of the government. Western societies, too, know the ideological use of law. One of the best-known studies is by Douglas Hay on eighteenth-century criminal law, placing this law in its political context of protecting the property-owning classes (Bottomley and Parker 1997). In the tax law area, one could argue that steeply progressive income tax laws are often a reflection of social-democratic values, while a flat income tax is often associated with neo-liberal ideology.

In contrast with instrumentalist laws, symbolic legislation has as its main function the satisfying of opposed social interests. One of the most important writers in the area of the symbolic use of law is Thurman Arnold. He argues that it is 'through the art of laws that abstract ideals are manipulated to disguise the impossibility of realising them in practice' (Cotterrell 1986: 108). Arnold sees law as a useful instrument to unite very different interests, ideals and opinions: 'It fulfils its functions best when it represents the maximum of competing symbols' (ibid.).

The symbolic use of law can be of great interest in the area of taxation, where instrumental and symbolic use of law may coincide.[3] Take, for example, tax incentives, which are used in a variety of ways to give relief to particular groups in society, or at least appear to do so.

In some countries in the Asian region, the practice of taxation by negotiation is still common. These countries may obtain much-needed international approval by reforming their tax systems according to the wishes of the International Monetary

Fund (IMF), World Bank or Asian Development Bank. Little may change for the average taxpayer regardless of the formal legal changes. As pointed out by Campbell (1996) in his study of fiscal reform in Eastern Europe, the desire to please foreign actors can play a crucial role in the tax legislative process, even if actual implementation is not really seriously contemplated. The desire to become members of the European Union (EU) and General Agreement on Tariffs and Trade (GATT) was, in this case, the motivating force. This illustrates that although most research on symbolic use of law refers to unifying competing interests on a national level, it can equally apply to an international setting.

These three approaches are not all that helpful for describing or explaining who and/or what influences tax reform. They have merit as all three approaches influence the political response that governments may take as part of tax reforms. Instrumentalism will not provide the answers to our question, 'Who and what truly influences the tax reform for our two case studies?'

Relevant theories

Theories in the area of policy-making and legal theory have their shortcomings, as explained in more detail below. They vary greatly among themselves, and one approach alone never seems entirely comprehensive. It is for this reason that combinations of different theories are often used in case studies.

Campbell, for example, used four theories in tandem, although they have very different premises. Analysing fiscal reform in Eastern Europe, he concluded that:

> Post-communist fiscal reform was constrained by concerns for reducing the monitoring and enforcement costs of tax collection, using tax policy to stimulate economic growth, cultivating ideological consent to taxation … developing memberships and associations with various international communities like the European Union, GATT, IMF and the World Bank … electoral considerations, interest group struggles, policy legacies, and political institutions.
>
> *(Campbell 1996: 74)*

In other words, each of the different forms of institutionalism had its merit in explaining the fiscal reforms. However, he does not answer these questions: What is the contribution of each approach? Is one more important than another and why? Campbell's work illustrates the basic problem of using various theories simultaneously. Comparing data from different case studies demands a certain consistency, but because of the different assumptions of the theories used, it becomes very difficult to describe different case studies in the same consistent way. Moreover, most theories pay little attention to the role of particular persons influencing policy-making. They may focus on the role that individuals play in a group or larger context, but they rarely go beyond that.

This is not to say that the characteristics of particular individuals are the most important factors in law-making. Individuals and groups undoubtedly have their own characteristics and agendas, but the way in which they pursue and translate their interests is shaped by institutions (Hall and Taylor 1996). Which leads us back to the institutional theories, including classical democratic theory, interest group or pluralistic theories, globalisation theory, the public policy model, the agenda-setting approach, the rational model, the incremental model and the garbage can model (for further discussion on these theories, see Heij (2007), and other chapters in this book).

Schumpeter (1954) and Goldscheid (1958) believed that fiscal sociology provides a macro-historical model that explains the dominant drivers of change in society, its politics and economics. Schumpeter, who wrote his famous 'The crisis of the tax state' in 1918, and Goldscheid were products of their time and they saw their approach as an alternative to Marxism and other theories in the social sciences in their time. Schumpeter's 1918 paper took an inter- and multi-disciplinary view of fiscal policies, budgets, fiscal history and the fiscal burden put upon citizens. The paper touches on many issues, but the various observations are not used to develop a coherent theory.[4] For a long time, few others built further on Schumpeter's work.

Campbell was inspired by Schumpeter's work and has been one of the leading fiscal sociologists in recent times. He views fiscal sociology as the sociological analysis of taxation and public finance (Campbell 1993: 163). Campbell developed a hybrid model for the policy-making processes with particular reference to the determination of tax policy (see Figure 23.1).

The model starts off with the possible causes of tax increases. Under the heading 'Crisis', Campbell identifies three causes: geopolitical conflict, macro-economic conditions, or fiscal crisis. It is true that in times of war taxes tend to increase.[5] If a domestic economy becomes more open, that is, dependent on imports and exports, taxes are also likely to increase. Finally, in the case of a fiscal crisis, government revenues tend to fall short and taxes increase. Campbell's reasons seem helpful in explaining changes in levels of tax; this part of the model may apply to many cases of tax reform and may be expanded to examine cases where the aim of tax reform is different from increasing taxes. In some Asian countries the aim of recent tax reform was to simplify and streamline the existing tax system, sometimes with the aim of higher tax revenue, but also with the aim of attracting foreign investors. The symbolic use of tax laws, especially when foreign investors are involved, should not be underestimated.

It is important to realise that when the political response is one of change, it does not mean that there is a real change taking place. It is not uncommon for tax law changes have a merely symbolic character, as when the formal tax burden is changed, but the real tax burden hardly changes at all.

Campbell sees three elements influencing the political response: the structure of the state, political representation and class, and interest group pressure. After Campbell developed this model, he added new features based on his work in Eastern Europe. He added that the response was not only to address possible fiscal reform but also to (Campbell 1996: 46):

- fulfil the requirements of foreign actors;
- alleviate domestic political demands;

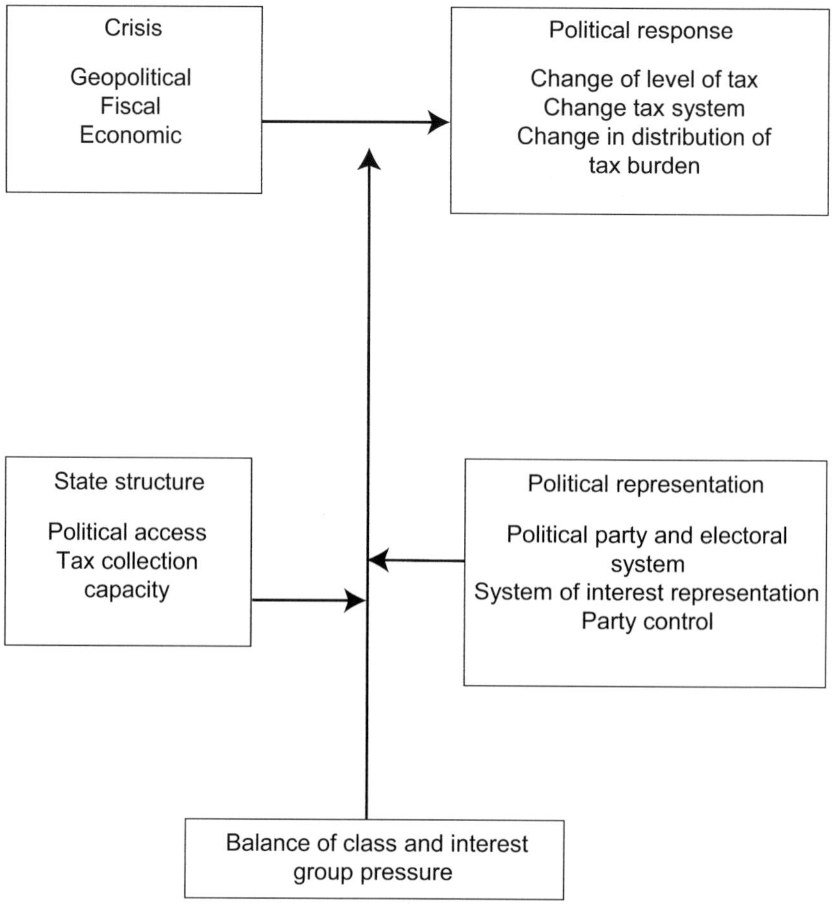

Figure 23.1 Conceptual model of the determination of taxes (Campbell 1993)

- conform to policy legacies inherited from former regimes; and
- facilitate the development of market economies.

The political response will be influenced by the characteristics of political representation including factors such as the political party and electoral system, and the system of interest representation.

Most work in this area focuses on democratic societies or the former communist countries in Eastern Europe. Very little work has been done in regard to non-democratic societies in, for example, Southeast Asia.

This part of the model refers to the state's institutions, as discussed earlier under sociological institutionalism, including the tax administration. Is there easy access to these institutions and how capable is the administration in securing tax compliance? According to Campbell, the fiscal problems of post-communist states are as much institutional problems of state-building, state-dismantling and policy-making as they are of poor macroeconomic performance. This is confirmed in the work of Steinmo (1993), who conducted a comparative study of tax-policy developments in Sweden, the USA and the UK. It is not only characteristic of post-communist states but also of Western democracies that the existing institutional structure plays a major role in the shaping of a country's tax system. Steinmo convincingly demonstrates that over a period of more than a century the institutional structure of Sweden, the USA and the UK influenced the design of tax laws and the political choices made in regard to tax policies.

The small amount of research in this area indicates that if interest groups have easy access to tax policy-making this will result in a lighter tax burden. The US tax system is a good example. If access is more difficult the tax burden is likely to be heavier, as is the case in Sweden (Steinmo 1993). Nevertheless, much more work needs to be done in this area to support any firm conclusions. With interest group theories in mind, this part of the model could also be expanded.

Campbell's work is the most interesting amongst the often general and broad descriptive theories. He has made a genuine attempt to combine the descriptive parts of tax reforms with explanatory factors. He has succeeded in identifying the relevant factors that influence tax reform. Unfortunately even his model has its shortcomings. It is tailored for democracies with open and transparent electoral systems. It heavily focuses on institutions rather than individuals as possible key actors in tax reform. Finally, his model seems to pay little attention to the cultures within institutions and how that relates to political representation and the role of government.

Refined model for research

I now come to the theoretical model that I used for my two case studies and subsequently revised as a result of the findings. I begin with the conclusion, based on the foregoing discussion, that no one of the existing approaches covers and explains the different aspects of the legislative process of tax reform. Organisational and sociological institutionalism and interest group theories attempt to give some explanation of the reasons why law-making processes have developed in a certain direction. None of them is adequate, but they all contribute insights into the myriad factors that influence the law-making process.

The theories of fiscal sociology are to some extent descriptive and have not developed into one comprehensive theoretical approach capable of a consistent explanation of fiscal development. Campbell's model is the most useful one, covering both the description and explanation of tax. It is the only model that identifies the relevant factors that influence tax reform. Therefore, the most attractive option is using Campbell's model combined with aspects of organisational and sociological institutionalism and an interest-group approach adjusted for a non-Western setting.

Overarching the model (see Figure 23.2) is the definition of tax. Having the definition of tax at the top of the model is crucial. What is included within this concept affects all parts of the model. An inclusive definition is the most important prerequisite to adequate analysis.

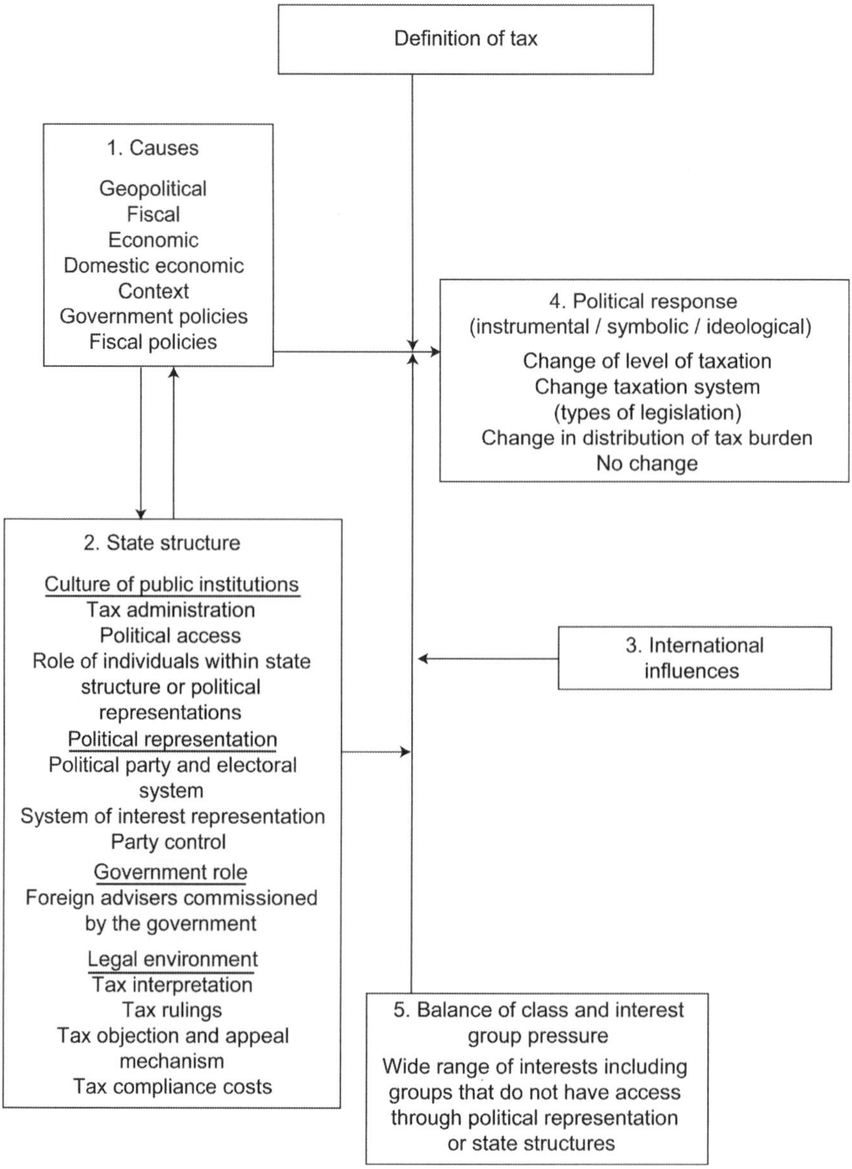

Figure 23.2 Revised model for research

International factors may influence domestic tax reform. International factors play a role, as demonstrated in the case of Vietnam. It is on the right side reflecting that it is of influence, but still subject to the constraints of particularly state structures.

The cause of fiscal reform should be modified as the word 'crisis' seems too strong. I propose to use the word 'causes' instead. The box containing the 'Context' should move to the box on Causes (previously labelled as 'Crisis'). The context is more important in the lead-up to the reform rather than influencing the reform itself. When we include the 'Context' under Causes, we allow the model to provide an in-depth context including an historical overview of the tax policies, economic policies and domestic features that all play a role in analysing the causes of reform.

Campbell's part of the model on state structures is refined and expanded. The model distinguishes between the legislative and the executive, and the institutions serving the executive. In non-democratic societies these boundaries are often blurred. For this reason, they are combined here in box 4. The 'Culture of public institutions' has been added, reflecting the importance of sociological institutionalism and emphasising the culture within an institution that shapes the actions of individual actors. Tax policy-makers and tax administrators are part of a bureaucracy and will pay detailed attention to their role within the institution. As trained bureaucrats they will follow acceptable practices and procedures established within their organisation. However, when used for the case studies, it starts to became clear that different elements are less easily separated. For example, the culture of public institutions, political representation, and the government role may be so intertwined with a party dominating bureaucracy as well as the parliament. This makes it impossible to discuss these different elements separately as may be logical for a case study in a democratic country. I have added a heading under State structure, 'Legal environment'. What has become evident is that taxpayers' faith in the tax legal system plays an important role in their inclination to invest in efforts to influence tax reform processes.

What has become clear is that state structures and a planned economy do influence one another. Thus, the 'Context' helps us to understand how the context and the state structures influence one another. For that reason, the box on 'Causes' (which includes 'Context') is linked to the box on state structures.

If we expand the state structure component and add the component of key individuals (champions of change, see Owens 2006: 131), the model becomes even more useful.[6] It would also address the concerns outlined by Kardell (2004: 36–7) that Campbell's model fails to take account of the fact that the state is not instrumentally responsive to a single class interest, but to a range of interests.

The role of the government has also been added as a separate category: the executive is often the driving force in reform. Then there is the role of foreign advisers, who will not provide their services without government permission.[7] A senior government member will carry the final responsibility for authorising a technical assistance project taking place within his or her country. So it is important that foreign advisers are included within the government role. Embedded here is the role of individuals.

Box 5 is new and represents the wider context and captures various aspects of this. Tax reforms are influenced by the domestic economic context and by government preferences in policies, particularly in fiscal policies. These contexts are not stand-alone parts and are influenced by the state structure and the system of political representation.

Box 5 refers to interest groups. As discussed earlier in this chapter, Risse-Kappen's (1996) work on interest groups is relevant to the theoretical framework, although his conception of interest groups is too limited for non-democratic societies. If people have no right to organise themselves, the term interest groups may have a different meaning. For example, it may cover influential local groups closely linked to the political ruling class. The power of multinational corporations (MNCs) can also influence tax reforms and can fit under the umbrella concept of interest groups. In 1989 Caltex Indonesia's CEO described the company's approach to expressing dissatisfaction with the government's tax policy:

> If the rate of return here becomes too low for us, or if the risks become too high, we will begin to disengage. This point must be clearly conveyed [to policy-makers]. We don't give ultimatums, we just file our regular budget reports and it's clear from the figures that we're cutting back. They call us up and ask why our figures are going down, and then we explain … But what is important for us is that the fiscal terms here in Indonesia be kept as good as possible … We have lots of choices in where to invest around the world, and we keep a close watch on all of them.
>
> *(Winters 1996: 24)*

As a part of the mass of interest groups, those groups in society that may be seen as threatening the status quo are also included. In non-democratic societies these groups may hold no electoral power and may have no access to interest representation so they do not belong in box 4. However, they may be a threat to the political stability of ruling governments and in that sense they actually may have influence.

In box 4 the aspect of symbolic use of law is made explicit and included is the possibility that the response is 'no change at all'. There are examples where there is an apparent political response, but very little actual change at all. For political or other reasons tax reform is introduced whilst the end result is no change whatsoever. So for each sort of political response it is possible that the response is in fact only symbolic. The box on political response is also expanded. We also need to expand the types of legislation and include not only instrumental and symbolic but also ideological legislation.

Such a revised model can be used for other tax reform case studies in both developing and developed countries. The model is adjusted to cater for some of the specifics of non-democratic countries, such as a limited role of interest groups, different electoral considerations, no independent press and no independent judicial system. A relatively high percentage of developing countries exhibit such features. It also addresses the issue of tax corruption: the payment of extra-legal fees in order to meet tax obligations (or to lower them). The issue of tax corruption is real in many countries, both developed and developing, but is often more prevalent in developing countries.

The model covers the key aspects of the reform and is detailed enough to cater for the specifics of individual cases. Ideally, I would like to see the model tested in a developed country with a well-established democratic system.

Notes

1 For example, Steinmo (1993); Campbell (1993, 1996); and Urrutia *et al.* (1989).

2 Comparisons between different tax systems in different countries are therefore almost impossible. Statistical analysis and international tax comparisons are rarely accurate due to the different classification of tax versus non-tax revenue.

3 Although that in itself is not enough to label tax laws as symbolic legislation. There is the danger to label laws as purely symbolic just because they fail in their implementation.

4 As pointed out by Moore (2003), this is understandable as Schumpeter's paper was written to answer the question of whether the Austrian tax state could survive the political and economic turmoil of contemporary central Europe, and not to develop an overall theory.

5 Those increases are not always reversed after the war, as pointed out by Peacock and Wiseman (1961).

6 I am aware, as pointed out by Kardell (2004), that Campbell's model may not explain the mechanisms of success.

7 If it concerns bilateral aid, often government-to-government aid agreements are in place, and there are similar agreements between multilateral donors and recipient countries. If the services are funded by the recipients themselves, government permission is still required.

References

Bottomley, S. and Parker, S. (1997) *Law in Context*, Sydney: The Federation Press.

Campbell, J.L. (1993) 'The state and fiscal sociology', *Annual Review of Sociology* 19: 163–85.

——(1996) 'An institutional analysis of fiscal reform in post communist Europe', *Theory and Society* 25: 45–84.

Cotterrell, R.B. (1986) *The Sociology of Law, An Introduction*, London: Butterworths.

Goldscheid, R. (1958) 'A sociological approach to problems of public finance', in R.A. Musgrave and A.T. Peacock (eds), *Classics in the Theory of Public Finance*, London: MacMillan.

Griffiths, J. (1979) 'Is law important?' *New York University Law Review* 54: 339–74.

Hall, P.A. and Taylor, R.C.R. (1996) 'Political science and the three new institutionalisms', *Political Studies* XLIV: 936–57.

Heij, G. (2007) *Who pulls the strings*, unpublished PhD thesis, University of Groningen, the Netherlands.

Kardell, A.L. (2004) 'Modelling the determinants of industry political power: Industry winners in the economic recovery Tax Act of 1981', *Sociology* 138.

Moore, M. (2003) *The New Fiscal Sociology in Developing Countries*, annual meeting of the American Political Science Association, American Political Science Association.

Owens, J. (2006) 'Fundamental tax reform: An international perspective', *National Tax Journal* LIX (March).

Peacock, A.T. and Wiseman, J. (1961) *The Growth of Public Expenditure in the United Kingdom*, Princeton, NJ: Princeton University Press.

Risse-Kappen, T. (1996) 'Exploring the nature of the beast: International relations theory and comparative analysis meets the European Union', *Journal of Common Market Studies* 34(1): 53–80.

Schumpeter, J. ([1918] 1954) 'The crisis of the tax state', *International Economic Papers* 4(34): 5–38.

Snyder, F.G. (1980) 'Law and development in the light of dependency theory', *Law and Society Review* 14(3): 723–804.

Steinmo, S. (1993) *Taxation and Democracy: Swedish, British, and American Approaches to Financing the Modern State*, New Haven, CT and London: Yale University Press.
Urrutia, M., Ichimura, S. and Yukawa, S. (eds) (1989) *The Political Economy of Fiscal Policy*, Tokyo: United Nations University.
Winters, J.A. (1996) *Power in Motion: Capital Mobility and the Indonesian State*, New York: Cornell University.

24

TAX PLANNING IN PRACTICE

A field study of US multinational corporations

Emer Mulligan

As part of the research undertaken for a PhD at the University of Warwick, UK, this study entailed 20 in-depth interview sessions, involving 26 interviewees from 15 companies, all extremely senior personnel in their respective organisations. The aim was to obtain insights into the practice of tax planning in large multinational companies. The companies were all in the same industry (information technology – IT) and geographical location (Silicon Valley, California, US), and the process of both theoretical development and obtaining interview data is described in this chapter.

Theoretical development

The theoretical development consisted of two separate but integrated stages. The first stage consisted of constructing a descriptive framework, which is a useful tool around/through which to describe and understand the make-up and dynamics of interaction in the broader tax arena and environment within which corporate tax executives must operate. The second stage brings together the core theoretical constructs as drawn from three strands of literature, namely tax planning, new institutional sociology (NIS) and endogeneity of law, through which an understanding of the findings of this study is enhanced, with a particular emphasis on their explanatory power at the organisational level of analysis. These core constructs were drawn upon when operationalising the interviews conducted at the organisational level.

Stage 1: a descriptive framework of the tax arena

This framework draws heavily on Dillard *et al.*'s (2004) framework of the context and processes associated with creating, adopting and discarding institutional practices, i.e. a general institutional model of organisational change. Their framework sets out a dynamic social context within which institutional change takes place. Applying the Dillard *et al.* framework in an international tax context provides a particularly rich tool for 'setting the scene', and identifies the players at each level of analysis, in itself a valid pursuit, particularly in a study of this nature where the application of NIS in a tax planning context is new.

This framework, as depicted in Figure 24.1, encapsulates three levels of social systems, namely the economic and political level, the organisational field level, and the organisational level, implicitly representing a hierarchy of institutional influence. Different 'actor sets' exist and are presented at each level in the tax arena, with some being more influential than others. Different roles are played out at each level, ranging from the implementation of tax plans and associated processes at the organisational level, to developing and setting standards of practice at the organisational field level, and developing and enacting tax laws at the economic and political level.

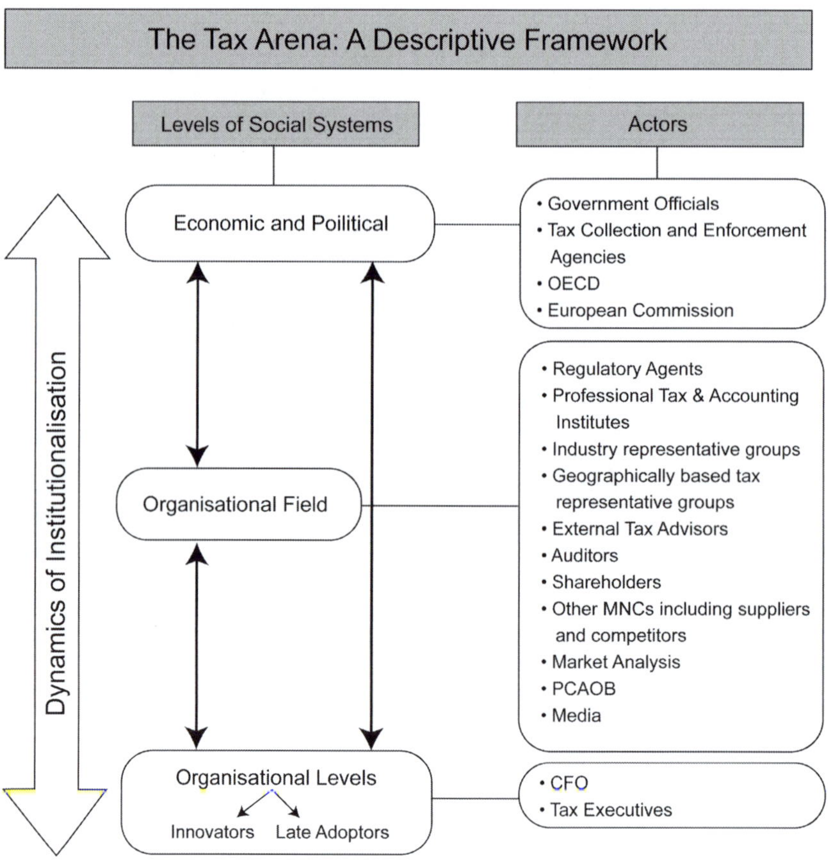

Figure 24.1 Theoretical framework: stage 1

Arguably, the various actors share a common interest in the jurisdiction and legitimacy of the taxation profession as a whole. However, it is important to recognise that actors and interest groups at each level are operating in different contexts, have different interests, different sources of power and different audiences to whom their claims for legitimacy must be articulated (Perrow 1985). There will accordingly be tension and controversy between the different levels around, for example, new tax planning practices and processes. This study provides some insight into the nature of such tension and controversy, how it arises in the tax arena and how resolutions are often found. The latter is reflected in the dynamic, dialectic and recursive relationship between the levels of analysis, as indicated by the directional arrows. These actor sets as depicted in Figure 24.1 are sourced in part from interview findings, secondary research, and the author's prior knowledge of the tax arena acquired through working in tax practice frequently dealing with MNCs' tax affairs. The three levels of analysis, their associated actors and agencies, and sources of legitimacy are described below, and the potential dynamics of this framework in a tax context are considered.

The economic and political level

The first level is the overall *economic and political level* within which norms and values of a society are established. They identify formal rationality, private property rights, wealth accumulation and free trade as the norms and values of Western market capitalist societies.

The MNCs in Silicon Valley that participated in this study, being members of such a Western market capitalist society, approach tax planning on the basis that for any company aspiring to and actively engaging in tax planning with a view to minimising its worldwide tax bill (and thereby maximise return to its investors), would be a 'norm' and very much accepted generally at the economic and political level.

The primary actors at the economic and political level include government officials, regulators and legislators. The State can act as mediator and be a source of change or stability. The various tax laws, i.e. the 'elements' of the political and economic system in a tax context, 'represent the properties of the prevailing systems of social integration' (Dillard *et al.* 2004: 513). The existence of these tax laws and the (rather simplistic) assumption that all tax planning is 'legal' contributes to this perception (at the economic and political level) of tax planning being legitimate.[1] The practice of tax planning therefore enjoys a strong level of support from this level; however, there is also a tension at this level between a government needing to enact tax laws that are 'good for business', which effectively renders it an 'investment partner' (Scholes and Wolfson 1992), yet satisfy the diverse range of social and economic objectives typically a part of any programme for government, many of which may not be perceived as 'good for business'. This results in compromise on the parts of government in terms of both tax legislation and the implementation thereof. While there are different political and tax governance structures in place throughout the world, generally, the primary actors identified at this level in a tax context would include government officials, tax collection and enforcement agencies, the European Commission and the Organisation for Economic Co-operation and Development (OECD).

The tax organisational field level

The organisational field is possibly the most important and influential level in the context of understanding the tax planning arena. Based on the findings of this research, the tax field consists of tax professional associations/institutes (such as the Tax Executives Institute in Silicon Valley), the tax division of industry-specific representative groups (such as the Semi-Conductor Industry Association), geographically based tax representative groups (such as the Silicon Valley Tax Directors Group), external tax advisers, auditors, other regulatory agents, tax academics, other MNCs including suppliers, distributors and competitors, financial analysts, the media, and others to whom the profession articulates its claims to legitimacy and status (for example shareholders).

While the primary empirical level of this study was at the organisational level, a small number of interviews were conducted at the organisation field level with tax advisers to MNCs, the findings from which provide another insightful perspective on the process and practice of tax planning.

The organisational level

This is the individual organisational level, i.e. the individual MNCs in this study. The primary actors here would include leaders of the tax function (typically a Vice-President of Tax, and CFO) and all tax executives within each company. These are the individuals charged with managing the tax function in their respective organisations, which incorporates both tax compliance and tax planning. This is the primary empirical level of investigation in this study as most of the interviewees are senior in-house tax executives. As the findings from this study demonstrate, the 'power' of the tax function varies from one organisation to the next for many reasons, but tends to be influenced hugely by the individuals in key roles who exercise their power through both 'formal and informal authority structures' (Fligstein 1991: 313). These individuals tend to be concerned with their legitimacy both internally vis-à-vis other functions and externally vis-à-vis other tax executives, auditors and tax regulators, etc., thereby providing a rich terrain of tension at this level.

Scott (2001) refers to three classes of variables, namely attributes, linkages and reference groups, which may help to identify organisational features associated with early adoption rates which appear potentially relevant in the tax domain, particularly in the context of MNCs adopting the latest tax plan/structure that has been adopted elsewhere in Silicon Valley. Company size is clearly identified as an important attribute, as is the impact of the characteristics of the CFO. The latter emphasises the potential power vested in certain individuals within an MNC. Adoption rates in the tax domain may also be examined through assessing the linkages that MNCs and their tax directors have with other actors in their environment, such as other tax executives, institutes. The third variable, which is reference groups, concerns the question of which organisation to copy/emulate? Tax executives arguably take comfort from the fact that they are interpreting the uncertain tax laws in the same way as certain other organisations, which ultimately might lead to the mentality that they all (the 'experts') cannot be wrong. The findings of this study provides evidence of leaders and adopters co-existing (often quite harmoniously) when it comes to tax planning practices and processes among MNCs in Silicon Valley.

Dynamics of the framework

The framework has significant explanatory power in terms of understanding the institutional relational dynamics between the three levels. This model represents the recursive nature of the institutionalisation process, resulting importantly in the context of the tax domain in 'a significant degree of structural stability enabling and constraining action' (Dillard *et al.* 2004: 513). Tax laws, while not always liked by business, are often 'negotiated' and well anticipated by tax executives, who are often allowed sufficient time (for example between announcement and enactment) to take account of/adjust for such new laws in their tax plans. The latter of course presupposes the necessary dynamic aspect of effective tax planning (Scholes and Wolfson 1992).

Actors at all levels engage with actors at both of the other levels. Individual tax executives engage with their representative groups at the organisational field level. They engage with actors at the political level either indirectly (for example through having its views on some tax law related through a representative lobby group), or directly when, for example, meeting with a Minister for Finance of a country into which the company is considering putting a new plant. The framework therefore represents a complex web of interaction between the three levels. This study provides insights into the dynamics of interaction between the different levels, highlighting various points of tension.

Stage 2: core theoretical constructs

Stages 1 and 2 of the theoretical framework are inextricably linked. Stage 1, as represented in Figure 24.1, provides a descriptive framework that sets the scene of the tax arena in terms of three levels of social systems, the various actors at play at each level and the dynamics of institutionalisation in the tax arena through a complex web of interaction between actors at the different levels of analysis. Stage 2 then brings together the core theoretical constructs from three strands of literature, namely tax planning, NIS and endogeneity of law, through which the practice and process of tax planning in MNCs and the dynamics of institutionalisation in the tax arena in Silicon Valley is analysed.

Stage 2 of the framework is diagrammatically represented in Figure 24.2.

Tax planning

The tax planning literature made two distinct contributions to the study. First, it was drawn upon when deciding on what aspects of the tax function to discuss with the

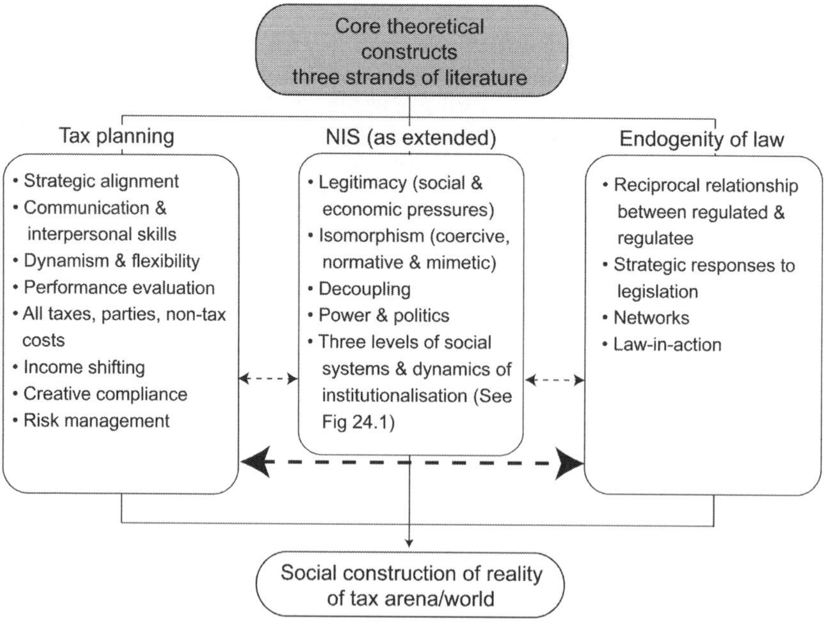

Figure 24.2 Theoretical framework: stage 2

interviewees. The second contribution is by way of some rich theoretical constructs which constitute an important part of this stage of the theoretical framework, as represented in Figure 24.2.

The key theoretical constructs drawn from the tax planning literature which principally address normative attributes of effective tax planning, and a sample of the relevant references, are as follows:

- The *strategic alignment* of tax was put forward as both normative and aspirational in the literature (for example, Valente 2002; Yancey and Cravens 1998; James 2005; Karayan and Swenson 2007).
- *Communication and interpersonal skills* were identified as critical to ensure inter alia that senior management and in-house tax personnel work towards optimisation of after-tax profits (Wilson 1995; Levine and Lerner 1993; Pricewaterhouse-Coopers 2001).
- *Dynamism and flexibility* were considered to be core attributes of effective tax planning (Hoffman 1961; Scholes and Wolfson 1992; James 2005).
- *Performance evaluation* of the tax function was broadly considered to be important and necessary, though little consensus exists on how best this can be carried out (Douglas and Ellingsworth 1996; Rego 2003; Phillips 2003).
- *All taxes, all parties and all non-tax costs* should be considered as part of any effective tax planning (Scholes and Wolfson 1992; Wilson 1993; Yancey and Cravens 1998).

- *Income shifting* is advocated by many as an effective form of tax planning (Scholes and Wolfson 1992; Samson 1998; Fallan *et al.* 1995).
- *Creative/innovative* approach to tax planning discussed in the literature, whereby adherence to the strict letter of the law is of more concern than adherence to the spirit of the law (McBarnet 2001a, 2001b: Fallan *et al.* 1995).
- The need to have and exercise a tax *risk management* policy, dealing with operational, planning and compliance risk is extremely important in the context of operating within what is sometimes an uncertain legal environment (Hoffman 1961; PricewaterhouseCoopers 2001).

New institutional sociology

The core theoretical constructs within NIS (as extended somewhat in this study) provide a particularly rich lens through which to analyse and discuss the findings of this study. These constructs and a sample of the relevant references are as follows (see Chapter 10):

- *Legitimacy* is a core concept within NIS and is rooted in the idea that in order for organisations to survive in their social environment they need to be socially acceptable and credible. Achieving legitimacy in the eyes of the world, the professions, etc., is extremely important and valued (Scott 2001; Powell and DiMaggio 1991; Carruthers 1995). An important theoretical progression recognises the co-existence or interaction between social and economic pressures, whereby efficiency concerns and institutional processes are not oppositional (Scott and Meyer 1991; Powell 1991; Hopper and Major 2007). This framework therefore takes account of both social and economic sources of legitimacy, with, however, a greater focus being given to the social sources when discussing the findings.
- Institutional *isomorphism* constitutes the adaptation of institutional practice by an organisation. Three classifications (although not mutually exclusive) are recognised in the literature, i.e. coercive, mimetic and normative (Meyer and Rowan 1991; DiMaggio and Powell 1991a; Covaleski and Dirsmith 1988; Scott 2001). The findings of this study provide evidence of all three sources of isomorphism in action in the tax arena in Silicon Valley.
- *Decoupling*, which refers to the situation in which the formal organisational structure or practice is separate and distinct from actual organisational practice. The resulting formal structures may well be in conflict with efficiency criteria (Meyer and Rowan 1991; Scott 2001; Carruthers 1995).
- *Power and politics* have been called for as an extension of the NIS perspective (Perrow 1985; Covaleski and Dirsmith 1988; Dillard *et al.* 2004; Hopper and Major 2007), and is incorporated in this framework and captures the role of powerful actors inside and outside of their organisations.
- Three levels of analysis or *levels of social systems* and the associated *dynamics of institutionalisation* are well recognised within the NIS literature (Dillard *et al.* 2004; Hopper and Major 2007). These levels, namely economic and political, organisational field and organisational level, are incorporated in Figure 24.1 and were described earlier.

Endogeneity of law

This perspective pays attention to active agency and the play of power and politics in the context of understanding the social construction of the meaning of tax laws, and helps to explain the transition from 'law-on-the-books' to 'law-in-action'. In their strategic responses to tax regulations (Oliver 1991), and through various networks of power, organisations frequently play a role in the construction of the law that regulates them (Suchman and Edelman 1996; Edelman and Suchman 1997; Covaleski and Dirsmith 1988; etc.). There is thereby a reciprocal relationship between the regulator and the regulatee reflecting a political process around the making and implementation of tax laws, which is an important aspect of this framework.[2]

There are conceptual alignments between some aspects of the tax planning literature (McBarnet 2001a; McBarnet and Whelan 1992), the dynamics of institutionalisation (Dillard *et al.* 2004), and the endogeneity of law literatures (Suchman and Edelman 1996; Edelman *et al.* 1999; Edelman and Suchman 1997; Covaleski *et al.* 2005), which is represented by the dotted line in Figure 24.2. This diagram depicts the social construction of the reality of the tax arena/world, which the findings of this study support, which are interpreted through the lens of NIS (as extended) and endogeneity of law perspectives and tax planning principles.

Selection of companies and interviewees

The study focused on the practice and process of tax planning in US MNCs in the IT sector. The headquarters of all of these companies are based in the Silicon Valley area in California. US MNCs were chosen in 2002 for a number of reasons and the interviews were conducted in 2005. There was (and still is) a significant number of US MNCs operating in Ireland.[3] US investment in Ireland continues to be extremely important to the Irish economy. In 2001, when the companies studied were selected, 1,240 overseas companies had a base in Ireland.

I chose to focus on US MNCs in the IT sector as based on initial conversations with contacts in the Irish Department of Finance this sector is perceived by them as being 'very significant'. Focusing on one industry facilitated more in-depth interviews. Having identified the relevant MNCs grouping, I then set about gaining access to and securing interview time with the heads of tax in some companies in this grouping. I successfully obtained interview time with such individuals largely through pursuing two primary sources of contact with these companies. Obtaining access in this way, I believe, resulted in a less time-consuming process than might normally be the case, particularly when seeking interviews with such tax 'elites' (Odendahl and Shaw 2001). First, I personally knew a couple of individuals working for such companies, based in Ireland, who worked in the finance function. Second, I 'luckily' introduced myself at a Tax Research Network Conference to a tax professor based at San Jose State University, who happened to know professionally (and personally in some cases) the head of tax in a number of Silicon Valley-based IT companies. Both of these 'contacts' were very happy to ask their 'contacts' within the companies to facilitate my research through giving interviews. Resulting from this process, I secured interview time with tax executives in 15 US MNCs in the IT sector, I interviewed 26 tax executives from these companies, many of whom were heading up the tax function in their organisations. The others were all in senior management positions reporting directly to the head of tax. It was very important to interview the 'right' people, i.e. in this case the ones who could answer the questions posed in the interview schedule. In addition to interviewing in-house tax executives, I interviewed three tax advisers to US MNCs. Two of these advisers are senior tax partners with two of the 'big four' accountancy practices based in Dublin, Ireland. Due to my own background as a tax manager with one of the 'big four' in Dublin, I was well positioned to secure these interviews myself. The third adviser is a Silicon Valley-based tax adviser to these companies and is a partner with a large US legal firm. He agreed to the interview once asked by one of my personal contacts (who knew him professionally), as referred to above. I chose to interview these tax advisers as I believed, again, that they were well positioned to give the type of information being sought in this study as they specialise in providing tax advice to US MNCs, many of which are in the IT sector. The interviews with the advisers were carried out at an earlier stage of the research process.

The primary data collection method employed was face-to-face, semi-structured interviews in two phases. First, I conducted six 'preliminary' interviews to, inter alia, establish links with players in the US MNC tax planning arena, help give focus to the research questions, give me an idea of what kinds of information such interviewees are willing to divulge, establish what such individuals consider to be critical/ of interest to the tax planning business community, to help me decide on what types of questions are most likely to provide answers that will ultimately explain and help understand the practice and process of tax planning and to assist me in considering possible conceptual frameworks for interpretation of findings from subsequent interviews to be conducted in phase 2. The interviewees were told in advance in broad terms what the interview was going to be about.

The process of constructing an interview schedule for the phase 2 interviews consisted of: analysis and consideration of the findings from phase 1 interviews; revisiting the tax planning literature; and in-depth consideration and development of the potential theoretical underpinnings of this research. The second phase interviews, all with in-house tax executives in US MNCs, took place in 2005. The final interview schedule was sent via email to all of the interviewees in advance of the interviews. This schedule was informed by many aspects of the tax planning literature, the draft theoretical framework, findings of exploratory interviews and by secondary research conducted on the MNCs participating in the study and on some topical international tax planning areas.

Interviewees were careful not to disclose any specifics of tax plans, nor did I ask for them. TE 26 (one of the preliminary interviewees) had informed me that tax Vice-Presidents would happily discuss generalities of tax but not specifics. I respected that and understood the sensitivities around potentially commercially sensitive tax details. Notably, in a small number of cases I interviewed different tax executives from the one organisation (for example a Vice-President and the international tax director). Their responses were very similar.

My professional tax background was a real advantage when conducting the interviews. It meant that I was familiar with many of the tax technical terms which invariably came into the conversations, such as permanent establishment, transfer pricing, etc. It also gave me a certain credibility in the eyes of the interviewees. In my current and prior work experiences I have conducted many different types of interviews and this, combined with my tax technical background, enabled me to quickly develop a friendly and professional rapport with the interviewees, and employ the necessary investigative skills 'to draw people out and ... ward off premature closure' (Miles and Huberman 1994: 38). I was also mindful not to be 'passive' (by nodding, smiling where appropriate, etc.), which can be unsettling for interviewees (Silverman 1993: 96).

The interview transcripts, post-interview notes and email correspondence received from interviewees before and after the interviews constituted a large amount of qualitative data requiring detailed analysis. Qualitative data analysis involves processes of reduction, classification and interpretation (Lillis 1999) and the challenge lies in making sense of large volumes of data (Patton 2002).

Following the coding process, I created NVivo Coding Reports (for principal and subcodes), and saved these as Microsoft Word documents. I then read and re-read these documents and started the process of extracting the richest and most appropriate quotations. This was followed by further analysis of those quotations, drawing theoretical inferences, resulting in predominant themes that became the platform from which the structure and presentation of the empirical chapters evolved.

The companies that were studied are all operating in a rapidly changing business environment. An analysis of the findings in relation to risk-management practices, in particular, can be found in a recently published article in the *British Tax Review* (Mulligan and Oats 2009). The interpretive methodology used in this study allowed for unique insights into the actual practices of the interviewees, which arguably could not be obtained through other methods such as questionnaires. The unique theoretical framework developed in this study by combining the three strands of literature of tax planning, NIS and endogeneity of law provided a very powerful lens through which to interpret and analyse the findings.

Notes

1 Of course the attitude of some tax executives to dealing with such uncertainties vary, which in itself may be problematic in terms of this working assumption at the economic and political level.

2 See Suchman and Edelman (1996) for their views on what NIS has to offer the Law and Society tradition, providing new insights on understanding compliance with the law, specifically 'Depicting legal compliance as institutional isomorphism recasts law as a broad cultural framework that influences organizations both mimetically and normatively, not merely through coercive material incentives' (ibid.: 920).

3 I am a lecturer at the National University of Ireland in Galway and have therefore a natural interest in all companies operating in Ireland.

References

Carruthers, B.G. (1995) 'Accounting, ambiguity, and the new institutionalism', *Accounting, Organizations and Society* 20: 313–28.

Covaleski, M.A. and Dirsmith, M.W. (1988) 'An institutional perspective on the rise, social transformation and fall of a university budget category', *Administrative Science Quarterly* 33: 562–87.

Covaleski, M.A. Dirsmith, M.W. and Mantzke, K. (2005) 'Institutional destabilization and the new public management: The case of tax incremental financing', *International Journal of Public Policy* 1: 122–46.

Dillard, J.F, Rigsby, J.T. and Goodman, C. (2004) 'The making and remaking of organization context', *Accounting, Auditing and Accountability Journal* 17: 506–42.

DiMaggio, P.J. and Powell, W.W. (1991a) 'Introduction', in W.W. Powell and P.J. DiMaggio (eds), *The New Institutionalism in Organizational Analysis*, Chicago, IL: University of Chicago Press, pp.1–38.

Douglas, R.F. and Ellingsworth, P.J. (1996) 'What management expects: Evaluation of the tax department and its executives', *Tax Executive* 48(1): 29.

Edelman, L. and Suchman, M.C. (1997) 'The legal environment of organizations', *Annual Review of Sociology* 23: 479–515.

Edelman, L.B., Uggen, C. and Erlanger, H.S. (1999) 'The endogeneity of legal regulation: grievance procedures as rational myth', *The American Journal of Sociology* 105(2): 406–54.

Fallan, L., Hammervold, R. and Gronhaug, K. (1995) 'Adoption of tax planning instruments in business organizations: A structural equation modelling approach', *Scandinavian Journal of Management* 11(2): 177–90.

Fligstein, N. (1991) 'The structural transformation of American industry: An institutional account of the causes of diversification in the largest firms 1919–79', in W.W. Powell and P.J. DiMaggio, Chicago, IL: University of Chicago Press.

Hoffman, W.H. (1961) 'The theory of tax planning', *The Accounting Review* 36(2): 274–81.

Hopper, T. and Major, M. (2007) 'Extending new institutional analysis through theoretical triangulation: Regulation and activity-based costing in Portuguese telecommunications', *European Accounting Review* 16: 59–97.

James, S. (2005) 'Taxation research as economic research', *Taxation: An Interdisciplinary Approach to Research*, Oxford: Oxford University Press.

Karayan, J.E. and Swenson, C.W. (2007) *Strategic Business Tax Planning*, Hoboken, NJ: John Wiley & Sons.

Levine, M.A. and Lerner, H.J. (1993) 'Outsourcing: Opportunities and challenges for the corporate tax executive', *Tax Executive* 45(5): 375–81.

Lillis, A.M. (1999) 'A Framework for the analysis of interview data from multiple field sites', *Accounting and Finance* 39(1): 79–105.

McBarnet, D. (2001a) *Can Tax Policy Survive the Avoidance Industry? Analysing Strategies in Tax and Accounting, in the UK and Australia*, 11th ICAEW Tax Research Network Conference, Nottingham University Business School, 17–18 September.

——(2001b) 'When compliance is not the solution but the problem: from changes in law to changes in attitude', *The Australian National University Australian Taxation Office Centre for Tax System Integrity* Working Paper (18).

McBarnet, D. and Whelan, C. (1992) 'Regulating accounting: Limits in the law', in M. Bromwich and A. Hopwood (eds), *Accounting and the Law*, Hertfordshire: Prentice Hall.

Meyer, J.W. and Rowan, B. (1991) 'Institutionalized organization: Formal structure as myth and ceremony', *The New Institutionalism in Organizational Analysis*, Chicago, IL: Chicago University Press, pp.41–62.

Miles, M.B. and Huberman, A.M. (1994) *Qualitative Data Analysis*, Thousand Oaks, CA: Sage Publications.

Mulligan, E. and Oats, L. (2009) 'Tax risk management: Evidence from the US,' *British Tax Review* 6: 680–703.

Odendahl, T. and Shaw, A. (2001) 'Interviewing elites', *Handbook of Interview Research: Context and Method*, Thousand Oaks, CA: Sage Publications.
Oliver, C. (1991) 'Strategic responses to institutional processes', *Academy of Management Review* 16: 145–79.
Patton, M.Q. (2002) *Qualitative Research and Evaluation Methods*, Thousand Oaks, CA: Sage Publications.
Perrow, C. (1985) 'Review: Overboard with Myth and Symbols', *American Journal of Sociology* 91: 151–55.
Phillips, J.D. (2003) 'Corporate tax-planning effectiveness: The role of compensation-based incentives', *Accounting Review* 78(3): 847–74.
Powell, W.W. (1991) 'Expanding the scope of institutional analysis', in W.W. Powell and P.J. DiMaggio (eds), *The New Institutionalism in Organizational Analysis*, Chicago, IL: University of Chicago Press.
Powell, W.W. and DiMaggio, P.J. (eds) (1991) *The New Institutionalism in Organizational Analysis*, Chicago, IL: University of Chicago Press.
PriceWaterhouseCoopers (2001) 'Tax Function 2001'.
Rego, S.O. (2003) 'Tax avoidance activities of US multinational companies', *Contemporary Accounting Research* 20: 805–33.
Samson, W.D. (1998) 'Instructional resource: Using tax history to teach the concepts of tax planning', *Issues in Accounting Education* 13(3): 655–92.
Scholes, M.S. and Wolfson, M.A. (1992) *Taxes and Business Strategy: A Planning Approach*, Englewood Cliffs, NJ: Prentice Hall.
Scott, W.R. (2001) *Institutions and Organizations*, Thousand Oaks, CA: Sage.
Scott, W.R. and Meyer, J.W. (1991) 'The organization of societal sectors: Propositions and early evidence', *The New Institutionalism in Organizational Analysis*, Chicago, IL: Chicago University Press, pp. 108–40.
Silverman, D. (1993) *Interpreting Qualitative Data*, London: Sage.
Suchman, M.C. and Edelman, L.B. (1996) 'Legal rational myths: The new institutionalism and the law and society tradition', *Law and Social Inquiry* 21: 903–41.
Valente, P. (2002) 'Tax Planning in the global village', *International Tax Review* 13(6): 47–50.
Wilson, G.P. (1993) 'The role of taxes in location and sourcing decisions', in A. Giovannini, R.G. Hubbard and J. Slemrod (eds), *Studies in International Taxation*, Chicago, IL: University of Chicago Press.
——(1995) *Corporate Tax Effectiveness: Adding Value Through the Tax Function*, Cambridge, MA: Harvard University.
Yancey, W.F. and Cravens, K.S. (1998) 'A framework for international tax planning for managers', *Journal of International Accounting, Auditing & Taxation* 7(2): 251–72.

25

POLICY MAKING IN ACTION

Tax and retirement

Lisa Marriott

Introduction

This chapter discusses a mixed methodological approach to a comparative, historical, tax policy case study. The case study is the taxation of retirement savings in New Zealand and Australia.

A variety of approaches to retirement savings taxation have been adopted throughout the Organisation for Economic Co-operation and Development (OECD) countries: this research compares the approaches of Australia and New Zealand. These countries are of particular interest as they have adopted different approaches to retirement saving and its associated taxation.[1]

The chapter commences with an outline of the methodology adopted in the research. In particular, it highlights and discusses the specific components of the research, and the advantages and disadvantages of each of the components. Topics covered include historical and comparative research, data collection and analysis and research design. The benefits of undertaking theoretically informed research are also briefly discussed, prior to the concluding comments.

Methodology

The research is qualitative in nature, adopting a comparative, historical approach and using an institutional-based theoretical framework for analytical purposes. The methodology is augmented and strengthened by reference to a range of disciplines, such as public policy, history and political science, where required. Reference to a broad range of disciplines is intended to provide greater insight into the topic and increase the validity of the approach used. The inter-disciplinary approach adopted is necessitated both from the multi-disciplinary nature of the topic under investigation and from the intended contribution to the policy debate, which is the aim of the research.

Historical research

The research contains elements of political, economic and social history: political history in relation to the tax policies introduced by the New Zealand and Australian governments, economic history to investigate the background from within which policies are structured, and social history to contextualise the issue of retirement savings.

In order to fully understand the current issues, and how these may be addressed, it is important to explore the historical events that have merged to form the present environment. The historical approach is used to highlight previous influences on current policy. Eccleston suggests that almost every aspect of the policy process is influenced by past policy decisions:

> The power and interests of key actors are shaped by political, cultural and economic legacies, while the institutions and practices that influence political decision making are themselves the product of historical events. This has led many policy analysts to argue that one must look to the past in order to understand the future.
>
> *(Eccleston 2004: 26)*

Accordingly, it is necessary to consider economic and social factors, historical events, and political influence during the time period investigated, in order to fully explore the institutional environment that has formed the current tax policy for retirement savings.

A number of perspectives and definitions of historical research exist. These include Jenkins' (1991: 6) suggestion that history is a series of discourses about the world, which do not create the world, but instead they give meaning to it; and Carr's (1961: 81) position that 'the study of history is a study of causes'. Regardless of the definition adopted, it is generally agreed that past and present events are inexorably linked (e.g. Fleischman and Tyson 1997: 93). Typically the study of history is credited with the ability to help us to understand the past, provide an appreciation of how current practices are developed and help to put the practices into perspective (Fleischman and Radcliffe 2003: 19; Goldberg 1974: 410). Thus, the primary objective of the historical component of this research topic is to develop a perspective on the current issue (Previts and Bricker 1994: 626) and provide information to assist in explaining the present-day situation (Avi-Yonah 2003: 4).

Adopting an historical focus allows attention to focus on events that may be significant, but are slow-moving. This may be particularly relevant when investigating policy development, which can evolve in an incremental manner. In the absence of an historical perspective, the potential arises for significant elements to be omitted from the analysis.

It is also important to recognise the limitations associated with undertaking research with an historical perspective, including the view that 'claims of objectivity are dysfunctional' (Merino 1998: 604) and that historical study inevitably involves 'relatives rather than absolutes; broad rather than narrow views; generalisations rather than specifics; and partial rather than total truths' (Lee 1990: 4). A further weakness, but one that is not specific to historical research, is that any perspective is 'always filtered through the lenses of language, gender, social class, race and ethnicity' (Denzin and Lincoln 2005: 21). Most researchers agree that there are no objective observations; rather, observations are socially situated in the world of the observer and the observed. The most objective history will inevitably remain a selection undertaken by the researcher and interpreted with the particular beliefs of that researcher. Most historians acknowledge that researcher awareness of the limitations of historical research may assist in ameliorating their influence on the research output. This limitation can also be addressed through triangulation, which is discussed later in this chapter.

One of the primary benefits from adopting an historical approach in this research was the ability to provide a detailed context from which current day events could be analysed. As a number of influences (political, social and economic) were influencing the policy direction, it was important that these were explained and interpreted within the context of the time. In the absence of this background, the current day events are isolated and lack an appropriate depth of analysis.

An advantage with undertaking 'current historical' research is the potential to augment the document source data with interview data. Interviews are discussed in greater detail later in this chapter and are valuable for historical analysis. As this research investigated a recent 35-year period, individuals involved in the policy decisions in New Zealand and Australia were available to discuss the roles they played in the process. An additional benefit also existed from the sufficient remoteness of the time period, resulting in dilation of the potential political sensitivity around the topic and, accordingly, individuals were willing to discuss their involvement.

Comparative research

The key concept of comparative research is the selection and analysis of similarities and differences of two or more phenomena, with the aim of providing an explanation of the similarities or differences found. In this research, a comparative approach is adopted to assess the validity of interpretations of specific or unique political phenomena (Hopkin 2002: 252). In addition, a comparative case study approach provides a richness of detail that is unlikely to be gained through a single case study.

One of the key issues with comparative studies is in establishing the credibility of the two subjects for comparative purposes. In the case of Australia and New Zealand, this is not difficult. They are both southern-hemisphere Commonwealth countries with similar demographic profiles, social policy objectives and British colonial heritage. Furthermore, the countries have similar economic, social and legal systems, small populations, and relative ethnic homogeneity. In addition, the two countries have close trade relationships and considerable trans-Tasman exchanges of populations, both of which are assisted by geographical proximity.

New Zealand and Australia are believed to be as suitable as any other possible pairing for comparative purposes. McLean (2003: 14) claims that 'these two have more in common with one another than either has with any other country on the planet ... they are probably simply more alike than any other two separate nations'.

A number of the benefits attributed to comparative research are similar to those associated with historical research, for example both comparative research and historical research are credited with allowing traditionally accepted explanations for events to be questioned and tested. In addition, comparative research and historical research both claim to highlight differences in national systems. Nonetheless, a number of unique benefits are also apparent.

French historian Bloch (1967: 52) claims that the most obvious benefit that may be gained from a comparison between facts drawn from different societies is to discern the mutual influences exercised by these groups. Many researchers argue that countries learn from one another, and accordingly one of the benefits of undertaking comparative research at a national level stems from societal learning from comparing different behaviours in similar or diverse contexts (e.g. Grew 1980; Zeff 1971). Hence, undertaking in-depth international comparative research provides some insights into the extent to which learning has transferred between New Zealand and Australia.

As with historical research, limitations exist in relation to comparative research. Comparative analysis between countries significantly increases the variance to be explained (Teune 1978: 47). Furthermore, it is difficult to test arguments rigorously across a complete population, given the significant information requirements of comparative historical research (Amenta 2003: 103). While extending the research parameters to a cross-country approach undoubtedly increases the complexity of the topic, the perceived benefits from the approach are believed to outweigh the limitations. The potential for learning increases significantly through the inclusion of both New Zealand and Australia in the research. In addition, the topic is sufficiently narrow in scope to allow for meaningful comparison.

Comparison is necessarily limited by the differences in political, economic and social structures in New Zealand and Australia. It is not possible to hold everything else constant while only the tax treatment of retirement savings is tested. As Skocpol (1979: 39) stresses, comparative historical analysis is no substitute for theory. Comparative historical analysis may be greatly assisted with the aid of theoretical concepts. Consequently, the research adopts a theoretically informed approach.

Comparisons are used in this research to identify and clarify patterns that are unique, as well as common, in New Zealand and Australia. In addition, the comparative exercise using New Zealand and Australia highlights the reasons behind why New Zealand did not follow the direction of Australia and why Australia did not follow the path of New Zealand. Perhaps the greatest utility gained from the comparative approach in this research is the ability to highlight how the same situation may be interpreted in different ways in different countries, in order to support the particular political perspective of the time. To illustrate this point by way of example, New Zealand and Australia had almost identical demographic projections of ageing populations, but the countries utilised this information to support different policy arguments. The following quotes provide an indication of the different interpretations in the two countries:

- New Zealand: 'Contrary to scaremongering by politicians and superannuation companies, New Zealand's population is not ageing faster than most nor is there any immediate age-dependency crisis' (*National Business Review* 1992: 11).

- Australia: 'The Government is convinced that it would be reckless and irresponsible not to respond now to the demographic imperative of an ageing Australia' (Kerin 1991: 15).

Thus, the comparative exercise highlights the different interpretations of the same information to achieve the desired outcomes: in New Zealand, this was reduced state involvement in private saving, and in Australia, it was increased state involvement.

Data and data analysis

Data were collected from primary and secondary sources. Primary sources included archival records, submissions to government committees, government documents and media reports. Secondary sources included academic and practitioner commentary on the policy changes over the time period investigated and interest group publications. An important primary data source came from the use of semi-structured interviews. Forty-seven interviews were undertaken in Australia and New Zealand with individuals who played influential roles in the policy formation process. Not all interviews are used in the written analysis, but they have all been useful in providing insights into the environment and clarifying historical details provided in documents.

The qualitative data computer program NVivo was used for analytical purposes. All interviews and primary and secondary source documents were coded in NVivo to assist with increasing the validity of the research output through the use of an accepted research tool for categorisation.

Archival research

Documents from Australia were predominantly located in the Australian National Library. Due to the recent time period under investigation it was not possible to access some archival material in Australia. This is not considered problematic as the primary documents that were not sighted were government documents, such as Cabinet Papers, briefings and internal government discussion documents. In Australia, significant commentary occurred in the public domain on the various changes to the policy in relation to retirement savings taxation, which provides an alternative source of information. Documents such as submissions to Select Committees in Australia were made available and these formed an important part of the analysis.

Newspapers and journals in both New Zealand and Australia were used to supplement the analysis, as were articles and commentary on the debates of the time. In New Zealand, archival documents were also used for analytical purposes. These included submissions to Consultative Committees, Cabinet Committee papers, budget reports, internal New Zealand Treasury correspondence and papers, and ministerial statements. Additional papers were provided by the New Zealand Treasury and retrieved through the Official Information Act 1982.

The primary advantages of undertaking archival research and document analysis are derived from the broad range of possible documents from which to gauge different perspectives. Documents such as the submissions to committees, government reports and consultation documents provided a wide range of perspectives on the topic. In some cases, such as where access to individuals was not possible, the documents provided a replacement for other information sources. In addition, document and archival analysis provided a broad information base from which to start the detailed research.

Interviews

The research uses documents combined with interviews to triangulate the information found in primary source documents. The use of interviews provides the opportunity to investigate aspects of historical experience that may not be documented elsewhere. Accordingly, through the insights of eyewitness accounts, interviews provided rich evidence about past events. The interview process included semi-structured questions on individuals' involvement in the policy process, their perceptions of this process and their perspectives on the key dominant influences or constraints.

As well as creating a record where none exists, interviews can supplement existing records. Furthermore, interviews have the potential to reveal disagreements or disputes that may not be recorded in documents. This critical perspective acknowledges that by focusing on individual experiences and interpretations, interviews can provide an alternate viewpoint on the traditionally accepted explanation of history. Thus, interviews have the potential to clarify other forms of history or to challenge conventional views.

A number of criticisms and drawbacks have been connected to interviews. These include the potential for distortion of memory over time and the personal bias of participants. Furthermore, interviews have the potential to privilege some viewpoints above others. However, as acknowledged by Thomson and Gauld (2001: 194), this problem is shared by many research methods, both quantitative and qualitative. The broader contextual environment and the utilisation of a wide range of data sources is intended to mitigate, to the extent possible, any potential privileging of perspectives.

Interviews were undertaken with individuals in New Zealand and Australia who were involved in policy decision-making during the 35-year period under investigation. Participants included:

- commentators of the time (academic and non-academic);
- senior trade union officials;
- senior public-sector officials;
- members of the Consultative Committees, Task Forces and Senate Select Committees;
- members of parliament, including cabinet ministers;
- employer group representatives; and
- industry group representatives.

Participants were chosen because of their involvement in the policy development process in the time period investigated. It is believed that the participants are sufficiently diverse in their positions and perspectives to alleviate particular individual biases and increase the likelihood of a balanced view.

The interview data provides unique insights into this case study, which would not have been possible through the use of primary- or secondary-source documents alone. A primary benefit achieved was the level of detail that was provided by individual actors, which did not exist in the written documents. Interviews emphasised details of complex interactions and debates that facilitated analysis. Furthermore, the use of interviews facilitated investigation of links that were not apparent in the documents, such as the influence of globalisation on the policy approaches adopted.

Perhaps the most significant benefit gained from the interviews was the ability to outline and explain some of the events that were unknown prior to the research publication. In addition, interviews provided greater validation of the document interpretation as there were no contradictory findings between the interviews and the documents. This resulted in enhanced credibility of the output. In addition, interviews provide greater detail on environmental factors, such as personality dynamics, which are not readily apparent from documents.

Interviews minimise the subjectivity that is inherent in historical research and also mitigate for belief transference. The ability for the voices of the actors of the time to be heard creates a unique record within research such as this. Interview quotes can be effectively used to demonstrate different viewpoints, and ultimately provide the opportunity for information to be gained that is not otherwise available.

Theoretical framework

An institutional theoretical framework is used for analytical purposes in the research. The institutional framework is used to study political and social institutions in New Zealand and Australia, and to assess the influence of institutional factors on policy formation in relation to the taxation of retirement savings. The adoption of institutional frameworks facilitates analysis of how the state, interest groups and individuals impact on the tax policy area, and the degree to which policy outputs reflect the preferences and influence of such groups. Historical institutionalism, a branch of institutional theory, was used for analytical purposes. For a detailed discussion on historical institutionalism, please refer to Chapter 11 of this book.

The primary benefits of undertaking theoretically informed research are the provision of a framework for analysis. The theoretical framework provides a starting point for discussion, together with guidelines for possible expectations. It is of interest both where the findings agree and disagree with the theoretical framework, and any empirically based challenges to the theoretical framework can make a significant contribution to the literature.

Conclusion

There is benefit to be gained from research that adopts a broad perspective, investigating social, political and economic variables across national boundaries. Different methodological approaches provide us with new ways of interpreting policy decisions. While generalisation is limited from the methodological approach of this research, replication of such studies raises much potential for debate on the topic of institutional influence within policy formation.

The methodology utilised in the research has the potential to enhance understanding of social policy development by providing a temporal aspect to a topic that is typically approached solely from a current perspective. This, in turn, provides insights into the predictability of the impact of particular policies. While the research does not claim predictive capability, the development of more appropriate theory for policy predictions may be assisted by historical comparative research.

Note

1 Two primary differences exist: New Zealand offers only a small tax incentive for retirement saving and no mandatory saving schemes exist, while Australia offers generous tax incentives and a compulsory occupational retirement saving scheme exists, which requires an employer contribution of 9 per cent.

References

Amenta, E. (2003) 'What we know about the development of social policy: Comparative historical analysis in the social sciences', in J. Mahoney and D. Rueschemeyer (eds), *Comparative Studies in Comparative Policies*, Cambridge: Cambridge University Press.

Avi-Yonah, R.S. (2003) 'Tax stories and tax histories: Is there a role for history in shaping tax law?' *Michigan Law Review* 101(6): 2227.

Bloch, M. (1967) *Land and Work in Mediaeval Europe: Selected papers by Marc Bloch*, London: Routledge and Kegan Paul.

Carr, E.H. (1961) *What is History?* London: MacMillan.

Denzin, N.K. and Lincoln, Y.S. (2005) 'The discipline and practice of qualitative research', in N.K. Denzin and Y. Lincoln (eds), *Handbook of Qualitative Research*, 3rd edn, Thousand Oaks, CA: Sage Publications.

Eccleston, R. (2004) *The Thirty Year Problem: The Politics of Australian Tax Reform*, Australian Tax Research Foundation Study No. 42.

Evans, R.J. (1997) *In Defence of History*, London: Granta Books.

Fleischman, R.K. and Radcliffe, V.S. (2003) 'Divergent streams of accounting history: A review and call for confluence', in R. Fleischman, V. Radcliffe and P. Shoemaker (eds), *Doing Accounting History: Contributions to the Development of Accounting Thought*, Amsterdam: JAI Elsevier Science.

Fleischman, R.K. and Tyson, T.N. (1997) 'Archival researchers: An endangered species?' *The Accounting Historians Journal* 24(2): 91.

Goldberg, L. (1974) 'The future of the past in accounting', *The Accountant's Magazine* 73(820): 405.

Grew, R. (1980) 'The case for comparing histories', *The American Historical Review* 85(4): 763.

Hopkin, J. (2002) *Comparative Methods*, Basingstoke: Palgrave MacMillan.

Jenkins, K. (1991) *Re-thinking History*, London: Routledge.

Kerin, J. (1991) *Superannuation Guarantee Levy: An information Paper*, information paper released by the Hon. John Kerin, Treasurer of the Commonwealth of Australia, December.

Lee, T.A. (1990) *Accounting History and Thought*, New York: Garland Publishing.

McLean, D. (2003) *The Prickly Pair: Making Nationalism in Australia and New Zealand*, Dunedin: University of Otago Press.

Merino, B.D. (1998) 'Critical theory and accounting history: Challenges and opportunities', *Critical Perspectives on Accounting* 9: 603.

National Business Review (1992) 'Super taskforce puts off evil day for government', 21 August: 11.

Previts, G.J. and Bricker, R. (1994) 'Fact and theory in accounting history: Presentmindedness and capital market research', *Contemporary Accounting Research* 10(2): 625.

Skocpol, T. (1979) *States and Social Revolutions: A Comparative Analysis of France, Russia and China*, Cambridge: Cambridge University Press.

Teune, H. (1978) *A Logic of Comparative Policy Analysis*, London: Sage Publications.

Thomson, G. and Gauld, R. (2001) 'Finding the unseen, listening to the unheard: Using primary sources for research in the New Zealand health sector', *Social Policy Journal of New Zealand* 17: 183.

Zeff, S.A. (1971) *Forging Accounting Principles in Five Countries: A history and an analysis of trends*, Champaign, IL: Stipes Publishing Co.

26
THE DELPHI TECHNIQUE

Chris Evans and Kate Collier

1 Conceptual issues

This chapter explores the Delphi technique, which is 'a qualitative method for obtaining consensus among a group of experts' (Lewis-Beck *et al.* 2010).[1] It usually seeks to obtain this consensus through 'repeated iterations (usually by email) of anonymised opinions and of proposed compromise statements from the group moderator' (Bloor and Wood 2006). The problems to which the method is applied are generally complex and lacking simple definition or obvious solutions, which makes it a very useful tool in the taxation context.

It has not been used significantly in the area of taxation to date, although its use is beginning to grow. Early examples of its use and usefulness in this field include Birkett (1989) and Evans and Walpole (1999). More recently it has been used by Evans *et al.* (2007) in the context of personal tax reform in Australia; Collier *et al.* (2009) in a modified form in a project for the Indonesian Directorate General of Taxation; Chen and Cheng (2009) in relation to the development of a model for a vehicle licence tax in Taiwan; and Guglyuvatyy (2010) in relation to environmental taxation. The first two of these recent applications of the Delphi technique are explored in greater detail in Sections 2 and 3 of this chapter.

The word Delphi refers to the hallowed site of the most revered oracle in ancient Greece, where forecasts and advice were sought (Fowles 1978). The Delphi methodology as commonly understood in modern usage 'operates on the principle that several heads are better than one in making subjective conjectures … and that experts will make conjectures based upon rational judgement rather than merely guessing' (Weaver 1971: 268). It is a dialectical process designed to foster the exploration and distillation of expert opinion (Helmer 1983).

In essence, therefore, it is 'a systematic, iterative method of forecasting based on the collection of opinions from a group of experts. Its objective is to obtain a consensus of opinion from these individuals about future trends, events or changes in a field of practice; or alternatively, to clarify and perhaps explain the nature of revealed dissent or divergence of opinion' (Carley 1980, quoted in Birkett 1989: 4). Birkett goes on to note that it 'replaces open debate by a carefully designed program of anonymous testing ... [utilising] a nominal group technique; members of the group are confronted by the opinions of other members, but face to face interaction does not occur' (ibid.). Anonymity ensures that the biasing effect of group pressures, dominant individuals and the like is reduced.

The methodology was originally developed in the 1950s by Norman Dalkey and Olaf Helmer, and combines quantitative and qualitative techniques to explore future possibilities.[2] It was initially utilised by the RAND[3] Corporation as a tool for forecasting aspects of future warfare, but has subsequently been used in a variety of ways, well beyond technological forecasting, in industry, government and academia.

One major variation is the 'Policy Delphi', the main goal of which is to expose different options and opinions regarding an issue and the principal pro and con arguments for these positions (Slocum 2005). For example, the Policy Delphi methodology has been used to examine public health issues such as drug use (Rainhorn *et al.* 1994); military policies (Linstone and Turoff 2002); library practices (Howze and Dalrymple 2004; Hsieh *et al.* 2006); and educational policy issues (Adler and Ziglio 1996; Clayton 1997), as well as the tax-related issues discussed in this chapter.

Delphi activities are fundamentally exploratory tools, where individuals plumb their knowledge, share it with others, and use what is shared with them to refine their own thinking. Delphi activities, particularly in the policy context, are not necessarily intended to generate consensus, although it is possible for consensus to emerge. Delphi activities are also not intended to quantify beliefs, although quantification can help focus participation. The goal of Delphi activities is simply to reveal (not create) patterns of thought, areas of consensus or disagreement, or questions to pursue (HERO 2001).

Most applications of the method use written questionnaires, either mailed or emailed,[4] but face-to-face individual and group interviews have also been used, as well as computer conferencing procedures (Dunn 1994).

The number of participants in a Policy Delphi are typically selected to represent a wide range of opinions, and may comprise anything between 10 and 30 (Dunn 1994), although successful Delphis have been conducted with as few as four (Slocum 2005). Research generally indicates that 12–15 constitutes a sufficient number of experts to ensure reliable outcomes. The size of the panel is ultimately determined by the nature of the topic under review and the budget of those administering the technique. Unlike traditional statistical surveying, the goal is not to select a representative sample of the population. The whole premise behind the Delphi theory is that the panel members are in fact experts in their field and because of this expertise can provide more accurate results (Bourgeois *et al.* 2006). It is also important to ensure that the experts chosen to participate are capable of representing the many facets of the issues under examination – the intention is not to select a panel of experts who would typically have a consensual or homogenous view from the outset (Slocum 2005: 115).

Rayens and Hahn (2000) outline the major characteristics of the Policy Delphi. It is a multistage process involving the initial measurement of opinions (first stage), followed by data analysis, the design of a new questionnaire based on a group response to the previous questions, and a second measurement of opinions. Feedback – information about the beliefs of other participants during the first stage survey – is used during the second stage to facilitate consensus on policy beliefs. This process allows participants to reconsider their opinions in the light of the views of other participants and can be repeated until consensus is reached or saturation of opinion occurs.

The number of stages typically ranges between two and five (Critcher and Gladstone 1998). Rayens and Hahn (2000: 309) note that first-stage Policy Delphi questions may include four categories of items:

- forecast items, which provide the panel members with a statistic or estimate of a future event. Participants are asked to judge the reliability of the information presented, and typically use response choices which range from 'certainly reliable' to 'unreliable';
- issue items, where panel members rank issues in terms of their importance relative to others, generally using a scale that ranges from 'very important' to 'unimportant';
- goal items, which elicit opinions about the desirability of certain policy goals, eliciting responses from 'very desirable' to 'very undesirable'; and
- option items, where respondents identify the likelihood that specific options might be feasible policy goals. For option items the range of responses is usually from 'definitely feasible' to 'definitely unfeasible'.

Following this first stage, the data are analysed to determine participants' positions on each interview item. Based on these measurements, some items are omitted from subsequent stages due to a lack of variability in responses. Items for which consensus has been achieved are not included in subsequent stages (ibid.: 310).

Three principles typically underpin the Delphi methodology. These are anonymity (although this may be sacrificed where face-to-face interview processes are utilised), asynchronicity and controlled feedback.

Anonymity, it is argued, ensures that panellists' personalities do not influence group behaviour. The status of the respondent does not come into play, and panellists may be more willing to offer opinions that might otherwise be seen to be unpopular or risky. In similar vein, panellists may be more willing to change their opinions rather than having to defend a locked-in position that has their name attached to it (Delbecq *et al.* 1975, cited in HERO 2001).

One of the most important aspects of a Delphi is the ability – within broad parameters – for the panellists to respond when and how they want to. They are not constrained to discuss the same topic at the same time, as would be the case in, for example, a focus group or other face-to-face interaction. Asynchronous communication allows the members of the panel to respond at their own convenience.

The third underlying principle – controlled feedback – emphasises the iterative nature of the Delphi. The results of one activity or question are used to inform the development of the next. It is obviously critical to the success of the Delphi to ensure that results are fed back to panellists in as unbiased a manner as possible.

Studies comparing the Delphi's results with other methods have confirmed the effectiveness of the methodology on the basis of both its capacity to generate ideas and its effective use of participants' time (Ulschak 1983), as well as its capacity for accuracy when forecasting is involved (HERO 2001).

However, the methodology is not without its critics. Makridakis and Wheelwright (1978, cited in Gunaydin 2006) summarise the general complaints against the Delphi method in terms of first, a low-level reliability of judgements among experts and therefore dependency of outcomes on the particular judges selected; second, the sensitivity of results to ambiguity in the questionnaire that is used for data collection in each round; and third, the difficulty in assessing the degree of expertise incorporated into the forecast.

Among the major concerns listed by Martino (1978, cited in Gunaydin 2006) are:

- the simplification urge: experts tend to judge the future of events in isolation from other developments. A holistic view of future events where change has had a pervasive influence cannot be visualised easily. At this point cross-impact analysis is often of some help;
- sloppy execution, both by the research team and the panel of experts: there are many ways to do a poor job. Execution of the Delphi process may lose the required attention easily;
- format bias: it should be recognised that the format of the questionnaire may be unsuitable to some participants, particularly in an international context; and
- manipulation of Delphi: the responses can be altered by the research team in the hope of moving the next-round responses in a desired direction.

These concerns could, however, be levelled at many other qualitative research techniques.

The remainder of this chapter explores the Delphi in action, initially in the context of a project related to personal tax reform in Australia and subsequently in relation to an Indonesian project designed to develop a Learning and Development strategy for the Indonesian Tax Office.

2 The Delphi in action: Australian personal tax reform

Background

Evans *et al.* (2007) used the Delphi as one part of a broader research project which was funded by the Australian Research Council in the period from 2005 to 2007. The aim of the project was to develop an improved model of the Australian personal income tax (PIT) system that was capable of commanding widespread expert and community support. The project combined various research techniques in an innovative way to:

- construct and test, using micro-simulation techniques, a series of hypothetical models of the PIT system in order to establish which models could best deliver

the required policy outcomes of assured revenue collection with the optimal blend of equity, efficiency and simplicity;
- subject some of the central issues and concepts underpinning those models to scrutiny and analysis by a panel of international tax experts (using the Delphi methodology) in order to establish strengths and potential weaknesses in the models and seek to establish a consensus around one single model;
- survey tax community attitudes to this expert-derived model in order to establish levels of potential resistance/acceptance by key stakeholders including taxpayers, tax practitioners, tax professional bodies and tax administrators; and
- fine-tune or revise the model to reflect community feedback.

Selection of panel

The literature is very clear about the critical importance of the selection of the panel of individuals to be involved in the conduct of a Delphi. The panel must obviously comprise experts in the field under review, and the panel must also be capable of adequately and accurately representing a range of possible opinions about the problems or issues being investigated. As noted above, the literature also suggests that the panel should comprise somewhere between 12 and 30 tax experts.

Given that other parts of the broader research project were exploring (by means of surveys and focus groups) the views of 'experts' who were tax professionals and representatives of tax professional bodies (as well as non-expert taxpayers more generally), the research team decided that it would exclusively use the Delphi to explore the views of senior tax academics. It was particularly interested in identifying tax academics with a specific interest (evidenced through research and writing) in the field of personal taxation. The research team also wanted to ensure that the panel it chose was capable of reflecting a variety of disciplinary perspectives, and therefore looked for personal tax academics from a mixture of legal, accounting and public finance backgrounds. Finally, the research team was interested in recruiting tax academics from both Australia and overseas, and particularly from broadly comparable tax jurisdictions such as the UK, USA, Canada and New Zealand.

An initial list of some 35 eminent personal tax academics was compiled by the research team, subsequently shortlisted (on the basis of the research team's own knowledge of, and contacts with, the persons on the list) to 18. All 18 academics were contacted in late 2005 or early 2006 to establish their willingness to participate; 13 agreed to participate.[5] The panel of 13 experts comprised six academics from Australia, three from the UK, two from the USA and one each from New Zealand and Canada. In terms of broad disciplinary background, six would be considered as primarily having a legal background, five come from an economics/public finance perspective and two would be categorised as being from an accounting background – although all 13 would be seen principally as tax experts and many had overlapping expertise.

In line with the key principle of anonymity already noted, the identity of each of the participants was kept separate from other members of the panel, so that only the research team knew the composition of the panel. This anonymity was preserved throughout the process, although in the relatively closed community of tax academia it is quite possible that some of the panel members may have been aware of the identity of some other members of the panel – though none of them would have been aware of the composition of the entire panel.

The research team was therefore satisfied, overall, that the panel that it had assembled had the appropriate expertise, breadth of opinion and internal integrity to be able to provide the sort of feedback and information about personal tax issues that was required in the Delphi phase of the project.

Design and process issues

The research team held a number of meetings in early 2006 to establish the specific areas upon which it was looking for input, in the first round of the Delphi, from the panel of experts. Ultimately four broad areas were identified, relating to the general principles underpinning tax policy and tax mix; the personal tax base; tax rates; and tax administration. The debate about which aspects and issues to include under these four broad headings was further shaped by some of the outcomes that emerged from the first phase of the research project (micro-simulation of potential personal tax models) and by the realisation that panel members would only be prepared to devote a certain amount of time to completion of the first round – none had unlimited time to devote to the Delphi. The survey could therefore not be as long or detailed as might otherwise have been desirable.

The survey instrument used in the first round of the Delphi was issued on 17 March 2006. It comprised 21 questions categorised under the four headings identified above. Panel members were also given clear instructions about what they were required to do, and some details about the Delphi methodology itself and about personal tax reform in Australia (considered to be vital for international experts). It was decided to administer the survey instrument using email technology – largely on the basis of timeliness, ease of access and general acceptance of that medium within the academic community. At that stage it was anticipated that there would be up to three rounds of questioning involved in the Delphi.

In line with the literature relating to the Delphi process, the 21 questions comprised a mixture of 'forecast', 'issue', 'goal' and 'option' questions, with an emphasis on the latter two categories. In fact, only one question would readily be classified as a 'forecast' question, and only two questions were specific 'issue' questions. The 18 remaining questions fitted broadly equally in either the 'goal' or the 'option' categories.

Panel members were asked to complete and return the first-round surveys within two weeks – by 31 March 2006. Responses were received from nine of the 13 panel members within that timeframe and from the other four within five days of 31 March. This was a somewhat unexpected and exceptionally positive rate of response, perhaps accounted for in part by the novelty of the methodology within the taxation discipline, but perhaps also attributable to the careful priming of the panel by the research team over preceding months. The covering information had suggested that panel members would need about 30 minutes to complete the instrument. This proved to be a significant understatement, with some panel members indicating that they had spent over an hour on the first-round responses.

The information contained in the Round One responses was then collated and analysed in the period through to mid-June 2006, at which point (18 June 2006) Round Two of the Delphi was issued to the panel. The number of questions in Round Two was reduced significantly, from 21 to just six, compared to Round One. This was because the research team found that there was a high level of agreement (or sometimes indifference or expected disagreement) for 15 of the 21 questions asked in Round One. There was therefore no reason to probe those 15 areas any further. Instead Round Two aimed to explore the strength of opinion related to six key areas[6] upon which consensus had not clearly emerged.

In Round Two panel members were initially reminded of the question or issue that was being raised in each of the six questions and of the response that they had volunteered in Round One. They were also given a customised anonymous summary of the responses of the other 12 panel members combined with their own response (often tabulated), together with a more detailed document that provided, verbatim, the responses to each of the six questions of all 13 panel members. The 13 experts were then separately asked to reconsider their own Round One responses to each of the six questions, with the opportunity to revise or confirm those responses after having considered the anonymous feedback from other experts.

The panel members were again given a two-week time period in which to respond. The timeliness of responses in Round Two was nowhere near as good as that in Round One – only seven members were able to submit their responses within the specified period, with two others responding up to five days late, another two responding up to one month after the initial required response date, and one responding seven weeks after the initial deadline. A response from the final panel member was never received, despite the issue of a number of reminders.

There was little evidence of changes in opinion as a result of the second round of the Delphi, and little evidence of the likelihood of a consensus emerging on the six questions that were under review. On that basis it was decided not to continue with a third round of the Delphi.

Outcomes

It is relatively simple to offer conclusions about the process of the Delphi methodology, but more difficult to provide definitive conclusions about the value of the data derived from that process. So far as methodology is concerned, the Delphi used in this particular project was remarkably easy to operate, and from that perspective it compares very favourably with other methodologies designed to elicit opinions and attitudes. It also proved to be cheap to administer, and the choice of an electronic (email) platform proved to be very effective. Response rates and times were good, and the cooperation of the experts was generally exceptional.

The most problematic area was in the design of the Delphi, and particularly in framing questions in such a way as to measure the strength or value of changes in responses that can occur over successive rounds. The questioning technique adopted in this particular Delphi was to leave questions open-ended, in order to give the experts as much opportunity as possible to express opinions. This was a perfectly justifiable approach, but in hindsight it made the measurement of change of opinion a very difficult task. A Policy Delphi is, in essence, a qualitative rather than a quantitative methodology, and does not lend itself easily to statistical analysis. If the process were to be repeated, however, it is quite likely that there would be a greater reliance on Likert scales, which can produce measurable outcomes, for many of the questions, rather than the heavy reliance on open-ended questions.

The Delphi provided the research team with clear insights into a number of areas where there was broad international consensus on certain aspects relating to the design and development of the PIT in an open, developed economy, and also highlighted other areas where there was no consensus. It established, inter alia, that:

- there was broad support from the experts for the generally accepted criteria of equity, efficiency, simplicity and revenue adequacy as appropriate criteria for evaluating a PIT, with general agreement that equity ranked as the single most important criterion;
- there was no general agreement, however, about the appropriate role of the PIT in the overall tax mix;
- there was general agreement that the Australian PIT should be characterised, so far as possible, by as broad a base as possible combined with rates that are as low as can be sustained;
- the experts considered, on the whole, that the individual was a more appropriate tax unit than the family;
- there was a strong view expressed by the experts that the superannuation concessions and the 50 percent capital gains tax (CGT) discount were the tax expenditures that caused the greatest level of distortion within the Australian PIT. Moreover, the experts generally agreed that the CGT discount would be the first choice of tax expenditure that could be removed to broaden the tax base, that 'ideally' capital gains should be taxed on the same basis as other forms of income, and that there were strong grounds for introducing a de minimus annual exemption to remove relatively insignificant capital gains from the tax base;
- there was strong endorsement for the view that all income tax brackets or thresholds should be indexed annually for inflation, though less agreement on precisely how this elimination of bracket creep should be implemented;
- the experts generally agreed that alignment of the corporate rate and top personal rate (or at least a reduction in the gap) was desirable, but there was no general agreement on the optimal number of tax rates or scales that should be contained in a PIT;
- the experts identified significant advantages that were likely to ensue with less comprehensive annual filing (primarily relating to simplicity and compliance costs) but also identified some disadvantages (primarily related to the capacity for non-compliance that less filing might permit); and
- there was little agreement – even after experts were given the opportunity to reconsider their positions in the light of the views of their peers – on key design

issues such as the deductibility of work-related expenses, rules relating to negative gearing, the level of the tax-free threshold, or on the potential for alternatives such as a negative income tax or a hybrid flat tax to counter some of the problems associated with Australia's PIT.

The product of the Delphi was therefore useful in a confirmatory, developmental and clarifying role. It reinforced outcomes that had emerged from other parts of the broader project. This use of the Delphi for triangulation purposes alone was sufficient justification for its adoption. Moreover, the Delphi provided the research team with clarification on a number of issues, and provided a rich seam of information that repaid detailed mining. The outcomes also assisted, in a developmental fashion, in shaping the future direction of the research.[7]

3 The modified Delphi in action: an Indonesian case study

Background

A modified Delphi was used in 2009 as part of a comprehensive review of the Learning and Development infrastructure of the Indonesian Tax Office (DGT), an organisation of more than 33,000 personnel. The project was undertaken by Learning by Design (LBD), a Sydney-based firm using consultants from the University of Technology Sydney and The University of New South Wales. The project included the conduct of a 'needs assessment' as a basis for the development of learning content, delivery mechanisms, and monitoring and evaluation strategies for the organisation. The aim of the project was to assist the DGT to finalise its Learning and Development strategy, taking into consideration the findings and recommendations of the needs assessment.

A needs assessment can be viewed as a type of research project as it involves the systematic in-depth investigation of an issue and achieves this through the use of research methods such as surveys, interviews and focus groups. A modified Delphi methodology was included as an integral part of the research approach chosen. The next section of the chapter describes why the Delphi approach was chosen, how it was designed and modified to suit the cultural and organisational requirements of the DGT and analyses its effectiveness as a research strategy in this context.

Rationale for the use of Delphi in a modified form

A previous needs assessment had been carried out for the DGT by LBD in 2007, and whilst the needs assessment and its findings were positively received, its recommendations were not adopted. This appeared to be because the DGT senior management (Echelon 2 – see below) had not been interested or fully engaged in the needs assessment process. A Policy Delphi was selected as a research approach in the 2009 needs assessment because of its potential to provide a highly motivating experience for participants (Hahn and Rayens 1999). It was viewed as a strategy that had the potential to engage senior management not only in the needs assessment process from the beginning but also to allow management to reach consensus on issues that emerged from the research. The Delphi also enabled senior management to suggest whether proposals were viable and should be included in the final recommendations to be presented to the Board of Directors at the end of the project.

There were also cultural reasons for the choice of a Delphi approach. The DGT has a strong top-down hierarchical structure with different levels or 'echelons' reporting up to the top level, Echelon 1 (the Director-General of the DGT). One of the characteristics of this paternalistic Indonesian community type (Warnecke and DeRuyter 2009; Rajab 2009; Rokhman and Collier 2011) is that any organisational change commonly starts from a superior or leader at the top of the hierarchy. The radical changes involved in the implementation of a Learning and Development plan meant that it was important to choose a research strategy that would involve senior management. The 'expert' element of Delphi particularly appealed to the hierarchical, paternalistic culture of senior management and was a persuasive factor in encouraging their engagement in the development process.

Other cultural influences also affected the decision to use of a modified version of Delphi. A face-to-face model of Delphi was chosen because this is the preferred channel of communication within the DGT. Electronic communication is still in the developmental stage within the organisation and is used less frequently by senior management who tend to be older and less comfortable with new technology, though mobile phone communication is very popular and used by all personnel. The use of paper surveys with senior management had proved to be ineffective in the earlier 2007 LBD project as they are often given to lower echelons or 'subordinates' to fill in as they are not seen as a management priority.

Face-to-face modifications of Delphi have proved effective (Hahn and Rayens 1999) and have incorporated interviews with participants rather than just circulating electronic or paper surveys. They have the advantage of greatly increasing the participation and engagement in the Delphi process, which was a priority in this project.

In addition, the modified face-to-face Delphi approach adopted in this project used group meetings rather than individual interviews. This was because the researchers wanted to incorporate the local cultural value of *musyawarah* as a means of encouraging participation in the Delphi process. *Musyawarah* is, in simple terms, a group discussion that aims to achieve consensus.[8] *Musyawarah* requires the involvement of a group of people and their participation in the successful implementation of an agreement; *musyawarah* is not an isolated activity. This is not surprising as Indonesian culture is generally communal (Geertz 1973; Tsing 1993; Beatty 2009).

Another underlying value of *musyawarah* is equality. Participants are considered to be equal and their contribution to the activity is seen as equally valuable. In *musyawarah* an appointed person may chair the discussion, yet every member of the discussion group is granted an equal say in the process of decision-making (Collier *et al.* 2009; Collier and Rokhman 2011).

The essential Delphi characteristics were otherwise retained, but a group face-to-face format that leveraged off the *musyawarah mufakat* tradition was trialled in this cross-cultural context. Group, face-to-face meetings also ensured that all panellists were carefully inducted into the Delphi approach and that they filled in the surveys and received immediate feedback, which could then be discussed. Surveys were still completed anonymously.

The design and implementation of the Delphi for the Indonesian context

The Delphi panel consisted of representatives from Echelon 2 managers and a range of other key stakeholders such as donors (the World Bank, the Australian Technical Assistance Management Fund and the International Monetary Fund), together with those in the DGT responsible for Human Resources and Learning and Development. This made up a panel of 12. Two panel meetings were conducted, which were referred to as Round 1 and Round 2 of the Delphi.

Information on the Learning and Development needs of the DGT were initially collected through a variety of means including interviews, document analysis and a survey. The data from these were analysed and grouped into issues of importance that emerged from the responses of a range of personnel from Echelons 3 to 6 in the area of Learning and Development. The issues raised in the needs assessment were translated into statements by the researchers, and these became the basis for the Round 1 Delphi survey. The survey used a five-point Likert scale to measure the level of agreement of the Delphi panellists to 20 statements which were arranged into two equal sections: 'challenges and opportunities', and 'achievements'. The survey was a means of reinforcing whether issues that were seen as key to personnel working in lower echelons of the organisation were viewed in the same way by senior management. For example, in the first round of the Delphi the panellists were asked if 'Monitoring and evaluation of Learning and Development need to be strengthened and linked to behaviour at work and to the DGT strategic plan'. The use of a Likert scale produced quantitative data that were easy to process and analyse.

In Round 1 of the Delphi process panel members attended a meeting together and were presented with an overview of the aims of the Learning and Development review, the place of the Delphi and their role as panellists within this project. Each member of the panel was then asked to complete the survey independently and anonymously and hand the surveys back to a research assistant. The results were then quickly summarised and the areas that emerged as having the least level of agreement were used as a basis for a general discussion as to why this may have been the case. The facilitator of the discussion ensured that the discussion focused on the issues and that no individual opinions were identified.

In Delphi Round 2 all panellists were asked to respond before the meeting to a survey on the findings that emerged from a workshop held for regional personnel involved in Learning and Development, and to three case studies that were developed to illustrate existing good practice in key areas of Learning and Development in the DGT. Once again a five-point Likert scale was used to discover the level of agreement of panellists to the issues raised in the pre-meeting survey. The results from the Delphi Round 1, the workshop and case studies, and the survey provided a basis for a series of principles and proposals that were designed to form the basis of a future Learning and Development strategy for the DGT.

The aim of the Round 2 Delphi meeting was to move panellists towards a consensus on the relevance and feasibility of the principles and proposals put forward by the research team. Panellists were asked one more time to respond using a five-point Likert scale to the principles and proposals. As in the Round 1 Delphi meeting, the results of the survey were quickly summarised and, where there was disagreement, were used as a basis for a discussion of the feasibility of the principles and proposals and their chances of implementation.

An analysis of the effectiveness of the Delphi approach in the DGT

The Delphi approach was successful in engaging senior management and key stakeholders in the needs assessment and recommendation process of the project, which had been one of the main aims of the researchers. The panellists attended meetings, filled in the surveys and participated in a discussion of the issues that emerged. The level of agreement of the panellists in the surveys was strong – this could be because the statements presented to them were the distillation of the detailed research conducted as part of the needs assessment. Where there were differences, however, the Delphi process encouraged focused discussion on the areas of dissent and helped to clarify whether the principles and proposals to be submitted to the Board of Directors would be accepted and implemented. The face-to-face group approach based on the cultural practice of *musyawarah mufakat* certainly appeared to suit the panel and helped their engagement.

The problems that were encountered during the Delphi process were mainly administrative. Organising the Delphi panel to attend the meetings was often difficult to co-ordinate, as was allowing enough time at the meetings for briefing and engagement in the Delphi process. The discussions after the survey results had been presented were frequently shortened because of a lack of time.

Most importantly, the members of the Board of Directors of the DGT, many of whom were part of the Delphi panel, were fully engaged in the final presentation of findings and proposals of the Leaning and Development project and strongly endorsed its findings. The part played by the Delphi approach in educating and involving senior management in this project appeared to be a significant factor in promoting this engagement and the positive outcomes of the project.

4 Conclusion

The Delphi methodology draws upon 'the collective opinion and expertise of a panel of experts' (Gupta and Clarke 1996) and is one of the less-utilised strategies in tax research but one well suited to the complex issues raised in the context of taxation. It is unique because it allows researchers to collect data and describe agreement about specific issues or policy options among key players in a decision-making situation (Hahn and Rayens 1999).

This chapter has outlined the theoretical framework that underpins the Delphi approach, including the Policy Delphi method. Through the examination of two contrasting case studies it has demonstrated how the Delphi can operate in practice in a tax environment. The case studies give an indication of the range and flexibility of the Delphi approach and how it can be modified to suit different research needs and cultural contexts. The ability of Delphi to motivate and engage participants in solving problems or predicting future events (Howze and Dalrymple 2004) is one of its key strengths as a research strategy, but the level of involvement required and the choice of appropriate panellists can be its most challenging aspects.

Notes

1 This section of the chapter is based upon an article written by Evans (2007).
2 Dalkey, however, has claimed that he and Helmer were never entirely happy with the use of the term Delphi, arguing that the term implied 'something oracular, something smacking a little of the occult', rather than a methodology designed to identify the best possible outcomes from less than perfect information (Dalkey 1968, cited in Gunaydin 2006).
3 An acronym for Research and Development.
4 Dedicated software packages for computer-based surveys are also available (HERO 2001).
5 Those who declined the opportunity of participating generally cited a lack of time or lack of current interest in the personal tax area as the reasons for not taking part.
6 Work-related expenses; revenue-loss offsets; tax expenditures; tax-free thresholds; flat taxes; and negative income taxes.
7 Full details of the outcomes of the project are available in Evans *et al.* (2007).
8 Indonesians believe the best decision is one arrived at by consensus amongst the people involved. A literal translation of consensus in the language of Bahasa Indonesia is *mufakat*. Hence the more complete term of *musyawarah* is *musyawarah mufakat*. However, when the word *musyawarah* is used it usually means that the participants of a discussion will try to reach a consensus – a *mufakat*.

References

Adler, M. and Ziglio, E. (1996) *Gazing into the Oracle: The Delphi Method and its Application to Social Policy and Public Health*, Philadelphia, PA: Taylor and Francis.

Beatty, A. (2009) *A Shadow Falls: In the Heart of Java*, London: Faber and Faber.

Birkett, W. (1989) *The Demand For, and Supply of, Taxation Education: A Delphi Study*, Sydney: Task Force for Accounting Education in Australia.

Bloor, M. and Wood, F. (2006) *Keywords in Qualitative Methods*, Thousand Oaks, CA: Sage Publications.

Bourgeois, J., Pugmire, L., Stevenson, K., Swanson, N. and Swanson, B. (2006) *The Delphi Method: A Qualitative Means to a Better Future*, www.freequality.org/sites/www_freequality_org/Documents/knowledge/Delphimethod.pdf#search=%22Laura%20Pugmire%20Delphi%22 (accessed 16 August 2006).

Chen, Y.-S. and Cheng, C.-H. (2009) 'A Delphi-Based rough sets fusion model for extracting payment rules of vehicle license tax in the government sector', *Expert Systems with Applications*, London: Elsevier.

Clayton, M. (1997) 'Delphi: A technique to harness expert opinion for critical decision-making tasks in education', *Educational Psychology*, Vol. 17, No. 4: 373–86.

Collier, K. and Rokhman, A. (2011) *Leadership and Learning in the Indonesian Tax Office (DGT): Using Workplace Learning Groups to Provide Local Leadership in a Globalized Workplace*, paper presented at the ELLTA Conference, Penang, Malaysia (February).

Collier, K., Ayuandini, S. and Rokhman, A. (2009) *The Challenge of Change in the Indonesian Tax Office: Sustaining Local Culture through Workplace Learning Groups in a Globalized Workplace*, paper presented at The International Conference on Indonesia-Japan Cultural Diplomacy, Jenderal Soedirman University, Indonesia.

Critcher, C. and Gladstone, B. (1998) 'Utilizing the Delphi Technique in policy discussion: A Case study of a privatized utility in Britain', *Public Administration* 76: 431–49.

Dunn, W. (1994) *Public Policy Analysis: An Introduction*, 2nd edn, New Jersey: Prentice Hall.

Evans, C. (2007) 'Unravelling the mysteries of the oracle: Using the Delphi methodology to inform the personal tax reform debate in Australia', *eJournal of Tax Research* Vol. 5, No. 1: 105–34.

Evans, C., Tran-Nam, B. and Andrew, B. (2007) 'Towards systemic reform of the Australian personal income tax: Developing a sustainable model for the future', *Australian Tax Forum* Vol. 22, No. 2: 13–45.

Evans, C. and Walpole, M. (1999) *Compliance Cost Control: A Review of Tax Impact Statements in the OECD*, Sydney: Australian Tax Research Foundation (Research Study No. 27).

Fowles, J. (1978) *Handbook of Futures Research*, Connecticut: Greenwood Press.

Geertz, C. (1973) *Ritual and Social Change: A Javanese Example in the Interpretation of Cultures: Selected Essays*, New York: Basic Books.

Guglyuvatyy, E. (2010) *Identifying Criteria for Climate Change Policy Evaluation in Australia*, University of NSW Faculty of Law Research Series, Working Paper 25.

Gunaydin, H. (2006) *The Delphi Method*, Optimization Group, www.iyte.edu.tr/~muratgunaydin/delphi.htm (accessed 16 August 2006).

Gupta, U. and Clarke, R. (1996) 'Theory and applications of the Delphi technique: a bibliography (1975–94)', *Technological Forecasting and Social Change*, Vol.53, No.2: 185–211.

Hahn, E. and Rayens, M. (1999) 'Consensus for tobacco policy among former state legislators using the policy Delphi method', *American Journal of Preventive Medicine* Vol. 16, No. 2 (February): 81–88.

Helmer, O. (1983) *Looking Forward: A Guide to Futures Research*, Beverley Hill: Sage Publications.

HERO (2001) *The HERO e-Delphi System: Overview and Implementation*, Human-Environment Regional Observatory, Pennsylvania State University, hero.geog.psu.edu/index.jsp (accessed 16 August 2006).

Howze, P. and Dalrymple, C. (2004) 'Consensus without all the meetings: Using the Delphi method to determine course content for library instruction', *Reference Services Review* Vol.32, No.2: 174–84.

Hsieh, L.-F., Chin, J.-B. and Wu, M.-C. (2006) 'Performance evaluation for university electronic libraries in Taiwan', *The Electronic Library*, Vol.24, No.2: 212–24.

Lewis-Beck, M., Bryman, A. and Futing Liao, T. (2010) *Encyclopedia of Social Science Research Methods*, Thousand Oaks, CA: Sage Publications.

Linstone, H. and Turoff, M. (eds) (2002) *The Delphi Method: Techniques and Application*, Reading, MA: Addison-Wesley.

Rainhorn, J., Brudon-Jakobowicz, P. and Reich, M. (1994) 'Priorities for pharmaceutical policies in developing countries: Results of a Delphi survey', *Bulletin of World Health Organisation* 72: 257–64.

Rajab, B. (2009) *Ketika Budaya Ikut Bersalah*, www.forumbudaya.org/index.php?option=com_content& task = view& id = 654& Itemid = 34 (accessed 23 November 2010).

Rayens, M. and Hahn, E. (2000) 'Building consensus using the policy Delphi method', *Policy, Politics and Nursing Practice*, Vol. 1, No. 4: 308–15.

Rokhman, A. and Collier, K. (2011) 'The Importance of e-leadership and workplace learning for e-government implementation in Indonesia', paper delivered at ELLTA Conference, Penang.

Slocum, N. (2005) *Participatory Methods Toolkit: A Practitioner's Manual: Delphi*, Belgium: King Baudouin Foundation and Flemish Institute for Science and Technology.

Tsing, A. (1993) *In the Realm of the Diamond Queen*, Chichester: Princeton University Press.

Ulschak, F. (1983) *Human Resource Development: The Theory and Practice of Needs Assessment*, Virginia: Reston.

Warnecke, T. and DeRuyter, A. (2009) *Expanding the Analysis of Welfare Regimes in Southern Europe and Asia*, www.welfareacademy.org/pubs/international/policy_exchanges/asp_papers/1761.pdf (accessed 23 November 2010).

Weaver, W. (1971) *The Delphi Forecasting Method*, Bloomington, *Phi Delta Kappa*, Vol. 52, No. 5: 267–73.

27

TAX RESEARCH GOING FORWARD

Lynne Oats

In Chapter 1, whilst acknowledging the current vibrancy of the field, I observed that tax research is nonetheless paradoxical. Its inherent interdisciplinarity allows us to think about tax from a variety of disciplinary perspectives, yet within the 'mainstream' of these disciplines, tax research remains marginalised and generally mired in positivist modes of enquiry, frequently not acknowledged as such. This is not, of course, true across all disciplines or in all places, but is sufficiently worrying to lead to calls for more expansive work. It is in this spirit that this volume was conceived. While much valuable insight is produced under the banner of rational choice or black letter approaches, there is room for more interpretivist work that considers how tax rules and policies play out in practice. The contributors to this book demonstrate the value of such work in their individual studies, which draw out aspects of the way tax operates in society that may otherwise be overlooked if approached from a positivist perspective.

Take, for example, the case of tax research within the discipline of accounting. In 2010 Hanlon and Heitzman published a paper that purports to present a review of tax research in accounting, as well as economics and finance to the extent that they overlap with accounting. In many ways this paper exemplifies the 'methodological imperialism' (Kvale and Brinkmann 2009) that permeates tax scholarship within this field. While acknowledging that tax research emerges in different disciplines with different perspectives, the authors nonetheless proceed to describe tax research in accounting as being exclusively within the positivist domain, without any recognition that alternatives are available. This is curious, because within accounting research generally, while the positivist mainstream maintains its hegemony, most particularly in North America, there is nonetheless a clearly defined and well respected alternative strand of scholarship that embraces interpretivism in all its various guises.

In accounting, more so than in law and politics, publication of journal articles is central to prestige and promotion. The recent history of accounting research is one of shifting approaches, from largely normative prior to the 1970s, to being largely positivist in the subsequent decades. Notwithstanding this shift, accounting scholarship has a long history of dissension from positivism. Chua (1986: 601) dates what she describes as 'signs of unease … about the state and development of accounting research' from the late 1970s. Roslender and Dillard (2003: 327) analyse the Interdisciplinary Perspectives on Accounting (IPA) project, which they describe as 'a reaction to the positivist and functionalist orientations and their attendant motivations'. Undoubtedly it has led, as Laughlin (2007) notes, to opening up new spaces for accounting research. Williams (2004: 575) has been a particularly vocal critic of 'positive economic missionaries', who he argues have colonised academia and distorted accounting research. McIntosh (2004) endorses Williams' (2004) sentiments and suggests the control over academic accountants in North America by an elite group of researchers acts to, in effect, police accounting knowledge. A more recent example of discomfort in mainstream accounting (as distinct from tax accounting) is the polyphonic debate in which a number of (young) accounting researchers discuss the achievements and future prospects of interpretive accounting research (Ahrens *et al.* 2008).

In finance, even more so than in accounting, scholarship has for a considerable time been dominated by quantitative, positivist approaches. A number of scholars are now starting to question the rigidity and limitations of such research. Bettner *et al.* (1994) go so far as to suggest that capital markets research so dominant that it now actually defines finance research. This is not to say that capital markets research is not valuable. In the area of finance, for example, it has led to the emergence of new financial instruments as well as a better understanding of how regulatory developments affect behaviour in the market. Bettner *et al.* (ibid.) ask us to remember, however, that those researchers engaged in quantitative/capital markets research have reaped enormous rewards from perpetuating their activities in terms of enhancing their own social capital.[1] The myopia of finance scholarship is also examined in Frankfurter and McGoun (1999, 2002); Frankfurter (2006); and Keasey and Hudson (2007).

Dillard (2008: 895–6) notes that 'in the US, one must come to grips with the pervasive and suffocating grip of financial economics on the prestige hierarchies within academic accounting and the institutional context within which it resides … and mainstream accounting research has institutionalized financial economics as the only rigorous and thus acceptable, source discipline'. Even more pessimistically, he says 'there is a trend towards worldwide domination of the accounting research agenda relegating accounting research to a sub area of financial economics … we ignore the political power controlling our discourse at our peril' (ibid.: 896).

By ignoring the wider context within which tax policy is developed and put into operation, tax accounting scholars risk falling into the trap described by Keasey and Hudson (2007). In their explanation of how 'finance theory maintains both its momentum and hegemony' (ibid.: 933), the authors suggest that the community of finance scholars reside within a house with no windows, into which they take data from the outside world but without the rich complexities of its context, and 'create puzzles to generate renewed research activity to reconcile the new data with existing [positivist] finance theory' (ibid.), never questioning the efficacy of the underlying theories. A more expansive vision tax research, not only within the discipline of accounting but also law and other disciplines, that is concerned with social and institutional practices, will go some way towards challenging entrenched ways of thinking

In focusing on interpretive *fieldwork* in this book, other forms of interpretive work have been left out, not because they are not considered to be valuable, but rather because of space considerations that led to the circumscribed scope of this book. Obvious omissions include the recent work on narratives (for example Jones 1999) and culture (for example Likhovski 2010), linguistics (for example Pasternak and Rico 2008), as well as the tax legal scholarship that draws on legal philosophy more broadly.

The aim of this book is to inspire new directions in tax research, inviting scholars to escape from what is often perceived as the 'right' way to do tax research and consider alternative ways of approaching tax as a field of enquiry. Young scholars, as well as some not so young, frequently find themselves shepherded into particular ways of thinking and may not even be aware of alternatives.

We need to continue to question the dominant modes of enquiry, not only within accounting and finance, but within other disciplines also. There is a pressing need for reflexivity among tax scholars, for an acknowledgement of the philosophical underpinnings of the work we do, so that its limitations (and all forms of research have limitations) can be properly evaluated.

Notes

1 Indeed, they describe capital markets research as akin to *Flatland*, a reference to the 1952 novel by E.A. Abbott in which the main character is 'jolted from the two dimensional world of Flatland into a world of three dimensions … [in which] soon he discovers a multitude of unpleasant, hidden truths concerning the values, norms and ideologies of his repressive world' (p. 2). Baker and Bettner (1997) draw on this analogy in their commentary on the absence of interpretive and critical research in the mainstream accounting literature.

References

Ahrens, T., Becker, A., Burns, J., Chapman, C., Granlund, M., Habersam, M., Hansen, A., Khalifa, R., Malmi, T., Mennicken, A., Mikes, A., Panozzo, F., Piber, M., Quattrone, P. and Scheytt, T. (2008) 'The future of interpretive accounting research: A polyphonic debate', *Critical Perspectives on Accounting*.

Baker, C.R. and Bettner, M. (1997) 'Interpretive and critical research in accounting: A commentary on its absence from mainstream accounting research', *Critical Perspectives on Accounting* 18: 293–310.

Bettner, M.S., Robinson, C. and McGoun, E. (1994) 'The case for qualitative research in finance', *International Review of Financial Analysis* 3(1): 1–18.

Chua, W.F. (1986) 'Radical developments in accounting thought', *Accounting Review* 61(4): 601–32.

Dillard, J. (2008) 'A political base of a polyphonic debate', *Critical Perspectives on Accounting* 19(6).

Frankfurter, G. (1994) 'The nature of man: II', *International Review of Financial Analysis* 3: 225–34.

——(2006) 'The Theory of Fair Markets (TFM) toward a new finance paradigm', *International Review of Financial Analysis* 15: 130–44.

Frankfurter, G. and McGoun, E. (2002) 'Resistance is futile: the assimilation of behavioural finance', *Journal of Economic Behaviour and Organisation* 48: 375–89.

——(1999) 'Ideology and theory in financial economics', *Journal of Economic Behaviour and Organisation* 39: 159–77.

Hanlon, M. and Heitzman, S. (2010) 'A review of tax research', *Journal of Accounting and Economics* 50: 127–78.

Jones, C. (1999) 'Mapping tax narratives', *Tulane Law Review* 73: 653–97.

Keasey, K. and Hudson, R. (2007) 'Finance theory: A house without windows', *Critical Perspectives on Accounting* 18: 32–951.

Kvale, S. and Brinkmann, S. (2009) *InterViews: Learning the Craft of Qualitative Research Interviewing*, 2nd edn, Thousand Oaks, CA: Sage.

Laughlin, R. (2007) 'Critical reflections on research approaches, accounting regulation and the regulation of accounting', *British Accounting Review* 39(4): 271–89.

Likhovski, A. (2010) '"Is tax law culturally specific" Lessons from the history of income tax law in mandatory palestine', *Theoretical Inquiries in Law* 11, 725.

Locke, J. and Lowe, A. (2008) 'Evidence and implications of multiple paradigms in accounting knowledge production', *European Accounting Review* 17(1): 161–91.

McIntosh, N. (2004) 'A comment on "recovering accounting"', *Critical Perspectives on Accounting* 15: 529–41.

Pasternak, M. and Rico, C. (2008) 'Tax interpretation, planning and avoidance: Some linguistic analysis', *Ackron Tax Journal* 23: 33–80.

Roslender, R. and Dillard, J. (2003) 'Reflections on the interdisciplinary perspectives on accounting project', *Critical Perspectives on Accounting* Vol. 14, No. 3: 325–51.

Williams, P. (2004) 'Recovering accounting as a worthwhile endeavour', *Critical Perspectives on Accounting* 15: 513–17.

INDEX